From Fear to Hope
Alternative Australian Narratives on War and Peacemaking

Pamela Leach

Contents

Acknowledgements

We are grateful to the Department of Veterans Affairs for the grant that enabled this study and the public meetings that generated much of the material contained in this book.

We are also most appreciative of the contributions of the speakers who gave their energies to prepare stimulating and engaging papers and who presented these at the public meetings. Appendix B provides more detail about each of the four conversations and their contributors. Alphabetically, contributors include:

Diana Abdel-Rahman

Margaret Bearlin

Tessa Bremner

Ronis Chapman

Chris Clark

Glenda Cloughley

Jonathan Curtis

Anthea Gunn

Guy Hanson

Ryan Johnston

Dean Sahu Khan

Chloe Mason

Karl-Eric Paasonen

Peter Stanley

David Stephens

Graham Walker

Sue Wareham

Further, the Quaker Peace and Legislation Committee thanks the organisations and institutions which have contributed further materials for the book. These include the National Library of Australia, the Women's International League for Peace and Freedom (WILPF), and the Australian War Memorial.

We are grateful to Ninh Ho for her cover design.

Disclaimer: This volume, commissioned by the Quaker Peace and Legislation Committee, provides an opportunity to take the Anzac Conversations, and their fruits, a step further. It affords a platform for further investigation into some of the themes that were raised in the initial face-to-face sessions.

It does not in any way claim to be comprehensive in its research or engagement with the profound questions it raises. Rather, it too is a conversation, now with a wider body of readers, in the hope that many more who are concerned with these or related themes may take up the questions and arguments put forward. The intent is not to generate unanimity but to foster respectful and fruitful dialogue in the Australian community. It is hoped that readers will find some of the material presented challenging enough to respond with their own reflections. The author and editor, Pamela Leach, assumes full responsibility for any errors.

Chapter I
Introduction

War is not just an event that happens; it is a relationship that continues.
–Di Bretherton[1]

Peace is not an absence of war. Peace is an absence of fear.
‾Ursula Franklin[2]

The world continues on a perpetual war footing not because we prefer it to peace but because we have failed to understand the real nature of both peace and war. This is an astonishing claim as arguably no life has been untouched by global militarism since the late 19th century. Yet unless we penetrate the heart of these dynamics, our hopes for a fearless generation will be in vain. Di Bretherton and Ursula Franklin point to key pieces of the puzzle. Although virtually countless elements enter the mix that can lead to violence, human relationships, particularly those of loving respect, lie at the core of peace. If we regard lives as sacred, see each person as encapsulating the potential of our species, we soon find it impossible to destroy that nugget of essential goodness, no matter how it is clothed. 'No one is an island' it is said. Indeed, a person can only come to exist by belonging to a web of being: as sister, daughter, nephew, mother, uncle, grandfather, great-grandparent. By this logic a West African traditional belief came about, that there can be no such thing as an orphan: everyone belongs somehow in the human fabric. Sadly, in an age of 'terrorism' and genocide on an industrial scale, we have too many orphans and refugees who have effectively lost all belonging. Their 'web' has been destroyed and their familiar home has been appropriated or bombed flat.

This book seeks to scrutinise peace and war, to wring greater understanding from these concepts, or perhaps the reverse: to inject deeper meaning into terms that have been so widely used that they have come to mean anything and nothing. In particular the initiative to write has come from the desire to bring to light narratives alternative to those that have held the limelight and provided the backdrop against which most Australian conceptions of war and peacemaking have been built. The domination of certain stories has discredited others that might add importantly to a rich and nuanced comprehen-

---

[1] Di Bretherton, *As the Mirror Burns: Making a Film about Vietnam.* The Thirtieth Backhouse Lecture. The Religious Society of Friends (Quakers) in Australia, 1994.
[2] Ursula Franklin, personal communication with Pamela Leach, August 2015.

sion of Australia's history. This undertaking requires fortitude because it is rarely popular to go behind given accounts, accentuating their limitations, in order to bring forward other ideas and facts. So the reader of this volume must be prepared for some confronting material that could vary importantly from previously accepted narratives. At a minimum, openness is required, to consider a plurality of voices and the 'truths' they purport.

Why have Quakers specifically undertaken this project? The struggle to understand the impulses, indeed apparent imperatives for violence and war has been ongoing for Quakers, or The Religious Society of Friends, since their inception in the 17th century. Born into the era of the English civil war, with chaos, turmoil and human tragedy raging, it seemed self-evident to early Friends that the spiritual message of gospel love was the political solution to all bloodshed. It would have been impossible for them to imagine the carnage that the 20th century would hold. Through a 21st century lens, the scope of destruction, brutality and loss, human, environmental and cultural, lies beyond what our hearts and minds can hold or fully comprehend.

After Federation, Australian Quakers felt it important to outline their position with respect to violent conflict in order to ensure that this avenue would be alive in their nascent land. 'We think it right, at this our first annual general meeting, to renew our protest against all war . . . Preparations for war, instead of contributing to peace, produce suspicion, jealousy, and mistrust between the nations. It is better to sow steadily and consistently the seeds of goodwill and concord.'[3]

This written work comes as a companion piece to a series of 'Anzac Conversations', colloquia led by a committee of the Quaker national body, Australian Yearly Meeting. In 2015 this Canberra-based Quaker Peace and Legislation Committee (QPLC)[4] convened four public events intended to interrogate and expand upon accepted understandings of what it means to memorialise war and peacemaking, and how these engagements have contributed to or impacted on the knitting of the Australian historical, social, cultural and public policy fabric. The papers and conversations document many engaging initiatives and generated a number of potent threads for further action. The topics and contributors are listed in Appendix B. The papers presented are touched upon or explored further in this volume.

The committee was responding to the tide of memorialising energy and expenditure that was sweeping Australia on the hundredth anniversary of the Gallipoli campaign in World War I. It was noted that Australia was busy out-remembering nations such as Britain, which suffered a much higher casualty level, and France, where some of the worst fighting and losses of World War I were incurred. It is well known that part of the importance of this 1915 'Anzac' event entailed the first military action of Australia in its own capacity, through the Australia and New Zealand Army Corps (ANZACs), following the founding of the Commonwealth of Australia in 1901. A century later, commemoration of the many events that together constituted World War I has brought back what has long been understood as the particular significance of the Gallipoli battle for Australia. 2015 heralded a host of sober events, education initiatives and celebrations of the heroism, sacrifice, and consolidation of the nation that 'resulted'. However, as will be discussed, some aspects of the commemoration have been less than sober or well-considered.

To begin the process of Anzac centennial commemoration, of recalling, refreshing and reexamining this trail and its many meanings we must engage in several levels of analysis. These seek to discover not only new facts about events that have taken on the scale of national founding narratives, but to cause us to look deeper within ourselves. It is here, first, that we recognise our own capacity for violence

---

[3] General Meeting for Australia, 1902. http://c.ymcdn.com/sites/
www.quakers.org.au/resource/resmgr/WW1_poster/WW1_Exhibition_banners_Part2.pdf accessed
    26 October, 2016.
[4] All abbreviations are listed in Appendix A.

and the ways in which we respond to this power. Confronting this reality honestly gives us a common bond with all people on every side of every conflict. It is also essential if we are to accomplish one of the greatest leadings of Quakers and pacifists, among others: to remove the causes of war, as contributor Tessa Bremner underscores.

We do experience intractable injustice, to which anyone might respond violently, unless we have always in view that we have choices about how we respond. As communities and nations, keeping a multitude of options open in peacetime, and honing them, is essential, so that we do not fall blindly into the trap of warfare as our 'only' option when a situation heats up. Rather, we can build on our capacities and well-seasoned relationships to work creatively with difference, with plurality, in the context of local, regional or global problems. The question arises: has Australia's choice of identifying the virtue of its nationhood through its military prowess ultimately been wise and beneficial?

What are the mechanisms that prevent us from seeing and understanding the whole of war, with all its winners and losers, its earliest preparations and its irreversible impacts on lives and societies even generations on? Why are we so blind to the militarism that even now seems to be accelerating? How are we socialised, through civil and formal education, family loyalties, the media, and our class and gender backgrounds to harden particular narratives as truths? If we are not mindful, these risk becoming our singular and permanent sources of the 'real', impermeable to later revelations and new associations.

Yet when given voice, our stories are often revealed not to match even those of our siblings, our families, our neighbours, our colleagues, our parents or children. Memory is fickle, twisted by chemistry, emotion and maturity as well as outside influences. Flashes of insight can return after decades of suppression. These can offer new light or cast dark shadows. The secrets of war, of warfare, and of the upside down worlds that result are all too often locked away. Yet they fester, and if brought into the open can leave us no choice but to reexamine the very foundations of our lives. David Malouf describes the permanent disorientation of war that besets us all, and the universal hunger for peaceful life in a simple, poignant scene.

> One day when his company was back in support he was sent out with a dozen others to look for firewood in what remained of a shattered forest … They were astonished, coming into a clearing at the centre of it, to see an old man in baggy pants and braces digging . . .When the man plunged his spade in for the last time and left it there it had the aspect of some weird, unhallowed cross. But it wasn't a grave. The bit of earth he had dug was larger than a body would require. The old man, who did not acknowledge their presence, had taken up a hoe and was preparing the earth in rows. It was the time for winter sowing, as any farmer among them would know, but it was the measure of the strangeness of all things here, of the inversion of all that was normal, that they saw immediately from what he was doing that the man was crazy. [5]

It is one of the great mysteries of Australian history that the Anzac experience at Gallipoli has been interpreted in both popular writing and official statements as a good thing for the nation at a formative time. Hailed as a glorious victory, behind it lies not only a colossal military defeat but a travesty of leadership and loyalty to those who put their trust in their superior officers. There has been a widespread failure to question this 'nation-building' rhetoric that has made of it a victory no matter what, or to inquire further why it remains, in the words of one playwright, Allen Seymour, *the one day of the year*. In the past, Australia's military history has been presented largely through an exclusively military perspective, which has often taken a decidedly bellicose and conservative angle and excluded other discourses. Peter Stanley, a contributor to this project, has underscored the narrowness of this predominant view in his scholarship.

---

[5] David Malouf, *Fly Away Peter*, Penguin, 1983, pps. 105-6.

During the centenary, many lenses were focused once again on the events of 1915 and multiple, often new, interpretations have been offered. The aftermath of the war has gained depth and significance. With the passage of time, new artifacts have come to light, and lives and organisations have evolved that enrich and perhaps complicate our understanding in engaging and challenging ways. As we look back on this and other Australian wars, 'full cost accounting' is coming to bear, often for the first time. What are the narratives that embrace this complexity, however confronting to our sacred and founding stories? These are tremendously important if we are to know ourselves as a country, a society, and also if individual and familial stories are to be brought more in line with their true complexities and hidden subplots. The Quaker testimony to truth demands no less, at least for those who initiated the project, and it is hoped will result in an offering to the wider public who may wish to interrogate their own histories, beliefs and truths.

It was hoped through the Anzac Conversations initiative that a more complete and balanced or plural picture might emerge. More importantly, there is a conviction that every interrogation of violence may expose opportunities for the present and future in which peace can be built. The ways and means for making and keeping peace may thus be refined. QPLC's impulse was in line with the Report of the National Commission on the Commemoration of the ANZAC Centenary (www.anzaccentenary.gov.au). It stated: "The most bitter disappointment for the original Anzacs was that their war was not, in fact, the 'war to end all wars'. The best way we can honour their memory is to focus our thoughts on how we might reduce the risk that future Australians will have to endure what they endured". This hardly sounds like an exhortation to make war into Australia's national pastime.

As the history of the violence of WWI is traced, it can be seen that violence bred more violence and brokenness, while nonviolent options remained open. The stories of how groups and individuals took up these torches of peacemaking, and witnessed to the immorality of war, paves a path to our own doorsteps and contemporary responses to war and its victims. What are we doing about militarism and current conflicts around the world, and the responses of our own population and government? And so the project, and this volume, grew to embrace other Australian conflicts and initiatives to challenge violence through peacemaking.

The reader will find that this publication interweaves multiple narratives: those of wars and destructiveness, those of nonviolence and its challenges. It shines a light on the power of artistic expressions as alternatives to the formal historical record: poetry, fiction and music, photography and film, painting and drawing. Living as we do in a world that is organised according to the balance of (fire)power between nations, it does take courage and creativity to attempt to work, speak or even dance outside these parameters. And yet, there are many who are convinced, through experience, study, deep grief and belief, that the grain of the universe lies in the direction of peace, not willful destruction. We hope this book will give cause for reflection, study, discussion, and perhaps actions that make our fragile planet-home more livable and safe for all living beings.

Chapter II
World War One: Shadows, Gaps and Forgotten Voices

They might have entered a different day, and he wondered if there really had been a change of weather or he only saw the change now because that girl had planted some seed of excitement in him whose sudden blooming here in the open air cast its own reflection on things. He felt panicky. It was as if the ground before him, that only minutes ago stretched away to a clear future, had suddenly tilted in the direction of Europe, in the direction of events, and they were all now on a dangerous slope.6

The way in which events are narrated plays a powerful role at the time and in course of subsequent understanding, decision-making and the shaping of policy and action. For example, there is no doubt that World War I, with its authentic and ideological legacy, played a role in the eventual unfolding of World War II. Although the commemoration of World War I generated, in addition to monuments, a flood of media material, books and commentaries, there remain many shadowy areas. Some have been kept quiet, while others have been accidentally overlooked and still others erased. This is partly because history is most frequently painted with a broad brush, focusing on covering the actions of leaders, campaigns, battles and statistics.

The living, breathing hearts and minds of people are not so well documented. History as a discipline has not seen personal experience as the best reflection of events, but rather a biased source. Yet what does bias signify if it is not the lens of someone who has in some way become emotionally invested, touched by circumstance. To validate the experience of those who have been, however unwittingly or intentionally, silenced by History is to fill out the record and to enrich our understandings.

The National Library of Australia has explored the experience of World War I as represented through letters, diaries, mementos and photos. These 'keepsakes', after which their exhibition is named, give us lasting and detailed insights, many of which have been lost or sealed for many years. According to the Director of Exhibitions, Guy Hansen, these keepsakes show how the experiences of soldiers and nurses, as well as politicians, artists, writers and families at home, created the fine texture of our collective memory. The keepsakes also include personal papers of leaders such as General John Monash and politicians, as well as media and propaganda posters. But they also expose the gaps in the public record. As they stare out from their photos, including many last minute portraits taken on the occasion of weddings shortly before setting sail, these people do not know as we do what was to lie ahead: that

---

6 Malouf, *op. cit.*, p. 36.

of the 400,000 who would enlist, 60,000 Australians would be killed and how many more would have their lives ruined. [7]

Oral histories have the special poignancy of capturing intimate first person experiences, as it is now no longer possible to speak with a soldier or nurse who served in that war. A young pilot in the latter part of the conflict speaks of being sent into the air alone with only a few hours training. One task he recalled was to fly along German lines and count how many dead there were on the enemy side. This must have been terrifying work. He said "I think today and shudder at what I could do in those days." He also shared the warnings of mates who had often-accurate premonitions that they would not come home from certain missions. [8]

Alec Campbell (1899-2002) was the last surviving member of the Gallipoli campaign as an Australian on the British side. During an oral history interview in 2001, he reflected that at age 16 or 17 one does not look for reasons to go to war, it was what everyone was doing. With our much more advanced knowledge of brain development, we know how very true this is. With grim irony he reflected "In fact we did not realize what war was until afterward". And perhaps we have yet to know. By way of training they learned rifle shooting, some running in the morning, but "nothing strenuous". He recalled however that "Gallipoli was not a good place to serve at all. In our company half of them were hit. On the boat over a man was hit – you had never seen a man killed. The trenches were just ditches, you didn't like to get out, but we had a path down to the beach. You were aware of stray rifle fire . . ." but they obviously took the risk with some frequency for a bathe and good clean up. He recalled spending five months in hospital afterward, so the quality of life in the trenches cannot have been good for Alec's health, or that of his mates. However, he went on, "Egypt was exciting, for a sixteen year old who had never been out of Tasmania . . ." and it is generally understood that travel was one of the big enticements for many who enlisted, especially with unemployment at home as the main alternative. [9]

Peter Stanley, a military historian from the University of New South Wales in Canberra, underscored that the focus of literature and interest in World War I has always remained on those who fought overseas. Yet not only those who died, but all who lived through the conflict were changed by it. This is not memorialised but lives on in the fabric on Australian society. In no way was a sparsely populated country in the Antipodes passed over. All those at home, including women, trade unionists, children, German internees and pacifists were deeply affected by a society divided by war. Robert Bollard's work *In the Shadow of Gallipoli: The Hidden History of Australia in World War 1* challenges the notion that Australians were overwhelmingly enthused by the advent of war. On the contrary, he contends there is much evidence that reflects a sense of pessimism and resignation. [10] Others suggest that conflicted emotions captured the moment.

> It was a time immediately after the news had come of the landings at Gallipoli and the slaughter of the following weeks. People's attitude to the war was changing. Even [Jim's] father, who hadn't been concerned at first, was suddenly fiercely patriotic and keen for battle. A new seriousness had entered their lives, which was measured by the numbers of dead they suddenly knew, the fact that history was being made and that the names it threw up at the time were their own . . . And his father felt, Jim thought, that his son ought

---

[7] National Library of Australia, 'Keepsakes: Australia and the Great War'
http://www.nla.gov.au/exhibitions/keepsakes accessed 12/3/2016.

[8] National Library of Australia, *op. cit.*

[9] National Library of Australia, *op. cit.*

[10] Alex Salmon, 'Australia's hidden opposition to WWI revealed' a review of *In the Shadow of Gallipoli: The Hidden History of Australia in WWI,* by Robert Bollard, New South Publishing, 6 August 2013. *Green Left Weekly,* Issue 976.

to be lost as well.[11]

Women were at both ends of the war: representing it and characterising it for the public through the letters home they received and circulated or reported about within their communities. In truth these letters most often tended to conceal the horrifying conditions and trauma of the Australians at war.[12] Women were still considered to be fragile creatures needing protection. It was also a matter of simple compassion, knowing they would already be worrying a great deal about their beloved family members and friends at the front. The often-brutal truth of the conditions are better recorded in personal diaries, but even then, they were often carefully edited with the expectation they might be shared eventually or fall into enemy hands. In particular, direct contact with the adversary rather than his weaponry is almost never mentioned. It is more often life at sea, in the trenches, in the air, that is described. The Keepsakes exhibition includes many such tomes, and other vital records that do reflect experiences at the front.

While the grand narrative of Australian history leads us to believe that the majority of Australian men sprang to the first call of the bugle to enlist, this is far from the reality. Marilyn Lake corrects the record thus:

> . . . only a minority of those eligible to enlist in Australia actually chose to do so, as Joan Beaumont has reminded us in her recent book, *Broken Nation*. Among eligible men in Australia, nearly 70 per cent chose not to enlist, a fact often forgotten in popular commemoration of the war that assumes the recruits were representative of their generation. The failure of attempts to introduce conscription meant that, in Australia, men could not be forced to the front to kill other men. Those who chose not to enlist were stigmatized as shirkers, cowards, stay-at-homes, but many were conscientious objectors on religious grounds, many had other family responsibilities and many, perhaps persuaded by the Sisterhood of International Peace and the Women's Peace Army, considered that mass violence was wrong and futile. In Australia, WILPF's (Women's [International] League for Peace and Freedom) affiliated groups, the Sisterhood of International Peace and the Women's Peace Army were among those organisations whose efforts contributed to the defeat of conscription in 1916 and 1917 and the gathering pressure to secure a negotiated peace settlement, which became ALP policy by mid-1918.[13]

The legacy of the work of women remains, of both those who served the forces and those who worked directly for peace, but connecting the dots is more difficult. The letters of Sister Anne Donnell, who worked in hospitals in England, France and Lemnos, Greece near Gallipoli were published in 1920 as *Letters of an Australian Army Sister*. Such works describe the ugly conditions the nurses, stretcher bearers and doctors faced attempting to treat the wounded of Gallipoli and the stamina and courage of women at the front. Donnell's book is more graphic for the inclusion of some photos. It also includes glimpses of off-duty mischief in which many young soldiers engaged to let off steam. Another sister, Bertha Mary Williams, kept autograph albums that record the thanks of those in her care. These little books are filled with her own drawings and poems that describe, by another form of expression, life at the front.[14]

Nurses were the women most publicly involved, but all felt their lives impacted. It is known that two Indigenous women served as nurses, but one, Marion Leane Smith, served in a British unit in

---

[11] Malouf, *op. cit.,* p. 54.

[12] Tessa Bremner, presentation to 'Anzac Conversations' colloquium, 21/6/2015.

[13] Marilyn Lake, WILPF Centenary Exhibition Launch Speech, Canberra Museum and Art Gallery, 27/02/15, pps. 2-3.

[14] National Library of Australia, *op. cit.*

England after enlisting in Canada, and the background of the other remains unclear.[15] Women had a significant role as a labour force in supporting the war through work in factories, including munitions factories, which could be very dangerous. They also filled a very wide range of positions that had been held by men who had enlisted. This included keeping large outposts, stations and farms in operation, and overseeing significant workforces.

Women were very active in the anti-war and anti-conscription movements. Working with trade unionists to maintain living standards also made an impact on life at home. It is probably fair to say that all Australian women at the time were stretched to fill gaps. The cost of living was high and they had to cope with scarcity of some household goods. In the workplace, on farms, in the fisheries, as well as in their roles as mothers, daughters, and friends, women were pressed and torn. They tightened the fabric of civil society that had progressively larger holes ripped through it.

> 'I lost my boy,' he told her accusingly. He had never addressed her before. 'I know,' she said. 'I'm very sorry.' He regarded her fiercely. She had wanted to say more, to say that she understood a little of what he might feel, that for two whole days after she heard she had been unable to move; but that would have been to boast of her grief and claim for herself something she had no right to and which was too personal to be shared, though she felt, obscurely, that to share it with this man who was glaring at her so balefully and with such a deep hatred for everything he saw, might be to offer him some release from himself and to let Jim, now that he was dead, back into his life.[16]

As the war developed, the conscription campaign exacerbated strong divisions in the Australian population. While 20,000 men enlisted in the first month of the war (13,603 of whom had pre-war cadet experience), two-thirds of the eligible men did not go to war, and even some with physical or other disabilities suffered accusations of disloyalty. Of those who did enlist, many were primarily enticed or forced by a salary to offset the hardship their families were enduring at a time of economic recession, while some just became enthused by imagining a paid trip overseas. Although the relatively small initial response indicates that the politicians were working at odds with a hungry majority, this did not deter official and political agendas. Those who spoke out against the war often found themselves and their families in danger of physical abuse and ostracism.

The two efforts at conscription, referenda in 1916 and 1917, both rejected by the Australian population, underscore that the resistance to the war was widely and deeply felt. Yet the repeated effort to implement forced service suggests that the political tone continued to be strongly in favour of the war. What was the source of the determination to feed the war machine when it was clearly so divisive? The answer to this lies in part with the same energy that has so consistently celebrated the Australian contribution to Gallipoli, although it was in fact a horrendous defeat for Britain and its allies. Rather than bringing on shame, the campaign afforded Australia the opportunity to accomplish two paradoxical objectives.

On the one hand, the youthful Australia was able to demonstrate, through its army corps (although allied with that of New Zealand), its status as an independent state, having gained that status on 1 January, 1901. On the anniversary of the landing at Gallipoli, in 1916, Prime Minister Billy Hughes said that it was there that 'Australia had put on the toga of manhood'.[17] Apart from the surprising

---

[15] Chris Clark, 'Indigenous service in Australia's armed forces in peace and war –
overview', Australian War Memorial, https://www.awm.gov.au/indigenous- service/report-
executive-summary accessed 9/2/2016.

[16] Malouf, *op. cit.,* pps. 130-1.

[17] Billy Hughes as cited in *Australians at War Secondary Curriculum,*
http://www.australiansatwar.gov.au/pdf/aaw_secondary_p1.pdf accessed 9/11/16.

notion that Australia reached 'manhood' wearing a dress, it is evident that Hughes was making a reference to a classical and distinctly European era of Greek or Roman heroism and glory based on military might. It is questionable what resonance this image would have had for the 'Diggers' or the Australian public, many of whom would not have had an education that embraced the fashion statements of the ancients.

On the other hand, probably the majority of Australian citizens wanted very much as a newly formed nation-state to prove continued loyalty to the monarchy and claim their proud place within the British Empire. Labor leader Andrew Fisher pledged, after his success in the polls, that Australia would support the Empire to 'The last man and the last shilling'. Deceptively, the initial success in overcoming a German force in New Guinea led to assumptions that the war would be over quickly.[18] This misconception, which repeated itself in most subsequent wars, offers another reason why some men enlisted. A short and painless sacrifice was all that was being asked, they imagined.

The two horns of the dilemma of belonging are not uniquely Australian, but continue to rear their sharp points to this day in all the remaining member nations of the Commonwealth: Canada, New Zealand, et cetera. Sixteen members remain for whom the British monarch is also theirs, at present Queen Elizabeth II, and the total membership of the Commonwealth includes 53 states. Even now, questioning whether Gallipoli was a good thing for Australia can bring outrage in many quarters. However, the sore point is more likely to be the seat of patriotism than any defense of the monarchy. While Anzac Day may be more popular than ever, there seems to be a divergence between personal affection for the Queen and a sense that Australia is a mature state and ought to have a political structure that reflects this. A 1999 referendum rejected the republican option by 55 per cent, although for some the devil was in the details, not the principle. Today it is uncertain, with a new popularity of the right, but broad support by the Greens, Labor and many independent MPs and senators for republicanism. However a change to the constitution would normally require at least a two-thirds majority and the agreement of all states. This is a high bar over which to pass, a fact which lends Australia its stability.

Military historian Peter Stanley underscored the little-mentioned discrimination many people experienced during the war, though they often could trace decades, centuries, or in the case of First Nations peoples, possibly eighty millennia of belonging to this land. Those of German origin experienced internment during the war, a pattern which followed them like a dark shadow after armistice. Afghan cameleers were denied the opportunity to serve because of their race.

> They stood about on the doorsteps of shattered houses, defending their property – a few chickens, a cow, a cellar full of dusty bottles – against the defenders, who were always on the lookout for something to eat or steal, or for a woman who could be induced into one of the dirty barns, or for any sort of mischief that would kill boredom and take their minds off what lay ahead. There were several wars going on here, and different areas of hostility, not all of them official.[19]

Indigenous people have served in the Armed Forces at least since Federation, according to scholar Chris Clark. Pictorial evidence suggests that some served considerably earlier for the forces of Victoria and New South Wales. At the same time, paradoxically, White Australia and its previous component colonies were fighting the 'Black' or 'Frontier Wars' against the same First Nations. This was Australia's unnamed, unspoken civil war that hid in many instances a genocidal impulse. The Aboriginal peoples were massacred, marginalised, disadvantaged, and disenfranchised from their own lands and culture, as Clark describes.[20]

---

[18] Salmon, *op. cit.*
[19] Malouf, *op. cit.*, pps. 70-1.
[20] Clark, *op. cit.*

However, it is not surprising, especially with the strong efforts made to assimilate the Aborigines, that some may have sought a path of recognition and respect by supporting the cause of the newly emerging or founded state. Most Aboriginal Australians who did enlist were those able to claim that they were 'substantially of European origin' as was required, if they were of pale complexion, while others were refused because they were visibly of Aboriginal background. Some 'full blooded' Diggers, such as Douglas Grant and Frederick Prentice, were admitted because they were raised in white households.

One might imagine that there was a determination to serve among most of the Indigenous people who did so. However, this could be to misinterpret the actions of these individuals. They may have been motivated by a perceived promise of equality, or like many of their cobbers were simply looking for a decent wage to support their families. There is no question that First Nations people were suffering hardship, and a stable income would have been seen as pure grace by many families. Others may not have wished to see their children enlist, but many young people of all backgrounds were known to register quietly and inform their families after the fact, appearing at home in uniform as an unspoken sign.

Most often, however, the contribution to the services by First Nations peoples has been invisible. The lack of official records conspired with the likelihood of fairer Indigenous people being admitted. The contribution of First Nations peoples is even now gradually emerging.[21] In the early 1930s, the journal *Reveille* began the appeal for information on Indigenous servicemen from World War I. Photos tended to fail to identify individuals by race, but occasionally lists and photographic records are revealing when identifiable family names are found. More often in recent times family members have come forward to assist in completing the record, while in some cases photos have provided surprises for historians and relatives alike. The contributions of First Nations servicemen and women are further being recognised with the help of family genealogies and other evidence. It is an unfortunate byproduct of their displacement and loss of cultural and familial ties that many have no such family archives to consult.

The rules varied, from initial admission of anyone, to a prohibition on Aboriginal soldiers, to a further shift. The hunger for volunteers was such that over the course of the war some recruiters became lax in this matter. This perceived need is supported by the eventual change of the rule in 1917 to admit those who could prove to a medical officer that they had one white parent, no matter their skin tone. Current figures suggest approximately 823 enlisted and about 675 embarked for overseas. Other estimates argue that the number of Indigenous people enlisted in WWI was closer to 1200. Research continues.[22] After all, it would be a long time before members of First Nations were to count as 'people' for the Australian census.

Aboriginal people served in almost every branch of the AIF, according to Clark, including the flying corps, though not as airmen. Their casualty rate was proportional to that of other Australians. Indigenous men were decorated for courage in the field, including four Distinguished Conduct medals and many others. A small number reached commissioned rank, and Alfred John Hearps from Tasmania served as second lieutenant until he was killed in 1916. It is not known whether First Nations men served in the navy, because it did not require the same expansion of personnel as other branches of the forces.[23]

Certainly Aboriginal families suffered as much if not more when they lost their family members in

---

[21] Australian War Memorial, *Too Dark for the Light Horse Aboriginal and Torres Strait Islander People in the Defence Forces*, Memorial Box 3, Introduction, p. 3.

[22] Clark, *op. cit.*

[23] Clark, *op. cit.*

the war. In cultures of long duration, people are close, highly interdependent, and matter more than anything else. These Australians suffered the further agony that they and their children were not recognised or honoured in the way that other Diggers and their families were. This added indignity fanned the flames of resentment, understandably. Fighting, even in the most courageous of ways, did not subsequently raise the status of First Nations peoples back in Australia one *iota*. Those who survived the war to return home found themselves struggling with the same marginality and racism they imagined they had left behind.

Furthermore, while all service people had trouble falling back into step with civilian life, First Nations members of the forces were betwixt and between. Drawn into white life and having had no choice but to follow its order and values, they could not erase their acculturation to return to a life before this. The fact would not have been lost on other members of their communities that these individuals had lived 'as whites', yet most had no input whatsoever into how the forces were run, either formally or in terms of their more informal social cultures. They were required to fit the mold, although there is some evidence that their Aboriginal skills, such as bush craft and horsemanship, and other lore was used to good advantage when needed at the front.

> When the tiny town of Goombungee on the Darling Downs unveiled its memorial to the war dead of the district there were the usual ritual proceedings, with prayers, hymns, and a bugler who played the Last Post. When the names of all the fallen soldiers were read out, many people became emotional. At the back of the crowd stood a solitary dark woman. Her son had also been killed and she stood weeping throughout the whole ceremony. However, not one person sought to comfort her or bring her forward into the throng. She was, according to Eileen Parlour who witnessed the proceedings as a child, ostracised. The Aboriginal mother's name was Rose Martyn and her son, Charles, had been killed during an assault, led by two Australian Divisions, east of Ypres on 20 September 1917. The battle became known in British military history as the Battle of Menin Road and was the first time that two Australian Divisions had attacked side by side, employing a rolling barrage of artillery fire to cover their advance.[24]

Private Charlie Martyn's name does appear on the Goombungee War Memorial, but as First Nations people were not meant to be fighting, families had a low profile and little support from the RSL or community. Typical of the First World War, Martyn was buried in Zillebeke, Belgium, terribly far from home, and with the impossibility of according him a traditional burial. For many in his community it would have been as if he were still 'missing in action'. If Charlie Martyn had survived, he might have been granted an 'exemption certificate' from the trust account system by the Queensland government. Although not automatically issued to all ex-servicemen, it would have entitled him to white wages, instead of two-thirds as was paid to other Aboriginal workers. It would have been a sign of being deemed 'civilised' and able to assimilate into white society (but could be repealed at any moment). The system was hated by First Nations people but not repealed until 1985.[25]

In the western Queensland community of Mitchell, the Indigenous returned servicemen secured a promise from the Premier Theodore to make them eligible to vote. The Chifley Labor government finally made this dream come true, many Aboriginal deaths later, after World War II in 1949. The federal vote was given to ex-servicemen, but Charlie Martyn, like so many of his mates, did not live to cast that first historic ballot. They had sacrificed themselves for an Australia that offered them no rights.

---

[24] C. E. W. Bean, *Anzac to Amiens*, 1961, Ch. 21 as cited in The Australian War Memorial, *Too Dark for the Light Horse, op. cit.*, p. 9.
[25] The Australian War Memorial, *Too Dark for the Light Horse, op. cit.*, p. 10.

A recent exhibition at the Tasmanian Museum and Art Gallery (TMAG) has revealed interesting details about the community context of First Nations men who enlisted from the Furneaux Group, over seventy islands off north-east Tasmania. Among these Flinders Island and Cape Barren Island are the largest and best known. These Islanders have been fighting their own battle for survival since the late 18th century, when European sealers began arranging for, or buying, or abducting Aboriginal wives, mainly from Tasmania, and installing them on the Furneaux Islands. As Van Diemen's Land was being 'cleared' through the 'Black Wars', from 1824-31, despite fierce resistance, many Indigenous people died.

The captured 135, from various Tasmanian Indigenous ethnic groups, were moved to Wybalenna, a settlement on Cape Barren Island, where their 'Protector' George Augustus Robinson had promised to 'civilise and Christianise' them. Forbidden from practising their own culture, in unfamiliar territory, they died rapidly of respiratory and other disease, poor food and despair. In 1847 less than 50 survivors were moved back to the mainland, close to Hobart. Ten women stayed with the sealers, possibly evading the settlement all along.

In 1878 First Nations people from these islands petitioned the Governor to reserve Flinders Island for them. Instead, 4000 acres on Cape Barren Island were set aside, and the rest of the land assigned to white settlers. In 1890 a school opened. Most Indigenous families survived by catching 'mutton birds' or short- tailed shearwaters, which live in burrows on the islands, and by fishing. In 1891 the census showed 139 people of Aboriginal descent in Tasmania, most living on Cape Barren Island. Advocating for themselves, an Islander Association formed. Sealing continued, but soon the market failed as the demand for fur declined and other sources of oil were found. The Cape Barren Reserve Act of 1912 protected a small designated area for the Indigenous community.

The TMAG Exhibition is entitled 'The Suspense is Awful: Tasmania and the Great War'. It records, through an easily-overlooked presentation on a small tablet screen, how the Furneaux Islands were hard-hit by the enlisting of 28 men. This represented a great proportion of the workforce of the little communities. One might well wonder why such a high number signed up, especially considering their recent treatment by the British. It was only two years before the outbreak of war that the Reserve Act had deprived them of what little land seemed to remain, in a place hallowed by the memory of the death of so many ancestors. For a few, the motivation was no different from other Diggers, to make some money and see the world when times were tough at home.

But there is a further twist to the tale for most. As has been noted, only men who could prove that they were 'substantially of European origin' could enlist, and many of these men certainly had some Aboriginal features, as the exhibition shows. Like most rural and remote communities, Cape Barren was exempt from cadet corps conscription scheme because resources were scarce and critical mass was missing. However, when schoolteachers Mary and James Bladon arrived in 1911, they thought a cadet corps would 'whip these boys into order'.

The Bladons beseeched the Premier for money to set up a cadet program, which was granted. When recruiting Lieutenant Charles Littler arrived in 1914, he found receptive young men with ability in shooting, riding and fighting. A sampling of their profiles will give some idea of who they were. It is interesting to note that the Aboriginal ancestry of the Cape Barren men is much better known than that of the Flinders Island ones. Also important is the strong indication that these men were closely related, brothers and cousins with common ancestors.

Claude Brown was descended from two of the full-blooded Indigenous women who lived on Cape Barren: Plinparinna and Pulawutiltiltarana. While training in England he was found to have a hearing loss and was discharged in December, 1917. He returned to Cape Barren Island and worked as a labourer. However life was hard due to rheumatism and other ailments, but he did not succeed in having any disability accepted by the Repatriation Department. Eventually he was given a pension based on age. He was married twice and had at least two children, but eventually died alone and is buried in an unmarked grave in Launceston.

George Ernest Brown could be said to have fared even less well. His mother was a Maynard of the well-known islander family. Although he was declared unfit in 1915 due to curvature of the spine, a year later he volunteered again and was accepted (reflecting the greater hunger of the recruiters for soldiers). He was in training camp in Claremont, north of Hobart when he was infected by an epidemic of cerebral spinal meningitis and died. He is buried at the Cornelian Bay Cemetery in Hobart. Marcus Brown, his brother, volunteered, like a number of the boys, after the mutton bird season was over in 1916. He soon found himself at the Western front where at Messines, Belgium he was seriously wounded in one thigh during battle. He was transferred to Rouen hospital in Normandy, died in June 1917 and is buried there.

Like his brother George, John Albert Fisher was a single seaman from Cape Barren. Both were descendants of Richard Maynard and Elizabeth 'Granny Betty' who was an Indigenous Port Phillip woman and ancestor to several of the combatants. While George suffered ill health and disability, and was discharged without pension in 1918, John was seriously wounded at Passchendaele. The stretcher-bearers were unable to reach him. He died while waiting on the battlefield for aid to come in September 1917. He was buried in Belgium. George returned home to find his mother had died in the interval, unsure of which son was deceased, and he lived a hermit-like life in a house that still exists in ruins. He made a bare living 'scratching for tin' and lost part of his leg in 1930 from disease. George persisted in claiming a government pension, which was eventually awarded on the basis of emphysema and arteriosclerosis contracted during the war. His illness gradually overcame him and he was transferred to a care home in Launceston where he died in 1964, aged 72.

Morgan Mansell was descended from the Maynards on his mother's side and Pulawutiltiltarana and Wathikawitja on his father's. He departed Australia on HMAT Hororata in June 1917. He experienced several admissions to hospital and possibly caught bronchial pneumonia while in close quarters on board ship. He died of the condition in the Abbeville Australian General Hospital, France.

Thomas Edward Mansell was descended from Pularilpana and Tukultami, as well as Mansells on his father's side, and Plinparina, Pulawutiltiltarana, and Richard Maynard in his mother's family. He enlisted in January 1916 and travelled on RMS Orontes from Melbourne. He caught influenza, was hospitalised in Le Havre, where he soon died and was buried. His father read of his passing in the newspaper before receiving any official notification.

Edward Stafford Lewis Maynard volunteered as a single farmer from Flinders Island. He embarked on HMAT Ajana on 4 June 1915 and was killed at Lone Pine in Gallipoli on the 8 of August of that year. His service had been short and his remains were never recovered.

(Frank) Francis Thomas Maynard, aka Cohen, was a farmer from Flinders Island who volunteered in April 1915. He stated he had previous military experience guarding the wireless station on Flinders. He left Queensland on *HMAT Aeneas*. On 29 June, 1915 he landed at Gallipoli and was evacuated in December. On the 26 August 1916 his 26th Battalion was in the reserve trenches as Pozieres. Frank may have been caught by sniper fire. He is buried near Contalmaison.[26]

Not surprisingly, since many of the men never returned to the islands, the community at Cape Barren declined during the 1930s. The Depression hit hard and many families moved in desperation to the mainland to find employment. A remarkably large number followed the older generation into World

---

[26] Tasmanian Museum and Art Gallery, 'The Suspense is Awful: Tasmania and the Great War' (17/4/2015-28/2/2016) http://ww1exhibition.tmag. tas.gov.au/the- islanders.net/ (Roar

War II. It is noteworthy that this struggling little community made such a large commitment despite the desperate need for workers and men within their disadvantaged families. Quite likely, for the Islanders as for many other marginalised groups, enlisting was a way out of an economic corner and there were few options to support their families. Particularly in Aboriginal culture, extended family obligations remained strong.

After World War II the Cape Barren Reserves Act phased out reserves. Instead, challenging conditions were imposed to acquire 99-year land leases. One was granted. Between 1951 and 1958 the Islanders were forced to move as they no longer had land rights, and so they looked for work and shelter on the 'mother island' of Tasmania. In 1971 the Cape Barren community again asked for title to a reserve, and two years later the Flinders Island Community Association was formed. In 1977 Tasmanian First Nations petitioned the Government for land rights, and within two years an Aboriginal housing project began on Cape Barren. It was granted 0.6 hectares or 0.006 of a square kilometre of land, not much when one considers the size of many private stations even today around Australia. The largest is Anna Station in South Australia, at 23,677 square kilometres which was established in 1863.

In a significant moment that completes the circle for Tasmanian Aboriginal people, the unmarked graves of 100 Aboriginal people were found at Wybalenna. In 1995, the Tasmanian Government returned twelve sites of cultural significance to the Aboriginal people of the Furneaux Islands, including some land on Mount Chappell, Babel, Badger, Greta (Big Dog) and Cape Barren Islands. In 1999 Wybalenna was officially returned to the Indigenous people, and in 2005 Cape Barren and Clarke Islands, the other two largest islands were also returned. In 2006, Cape Barren Secondary School opened. In the same year the Flinders Island Aboriginal Association was given a land grant beyond the housing allotments.

For those who have populated Australia for possibly up to eighty millenia, having survived an ice age but suffered epidemics, extermination, massacres and every manner of abuse at the hands of Europeans, it is striking what loyal Australians they are. In the Furneaux Group, where First Nations peoples came at least 35,000 years ago, the men still chose to support the Government and Queen. For good reasons, such as acquiring rights, they wanted to 'qualify' as Australians, although those who came home would find themselves as ostracised as ever. Yet for many, their 'grooming' as boys, through the mandatory cadet corps (until 1929), could now be understood as an abusive indoctrination and assimilation process.[27]

> Packed again into a cattletruck, pushed in hard against the wall, in the smell of what he now understood, Jim had a fearful vision. It would go on forever. The war, or something like it with a different name, would go on growing out of here until the whole earth was involved; the immense and murderous machine that was in operation would require more and more men to work it, more and more blood to keep it running; it was no longer in control. The cattletrucks would keep on right across the century, and when there were no more young men to fill them they would be filled with the old, and with women and children. They had fallen, he and his contemporaries, into a dark pocket of time from which there was no escape.[28]

Jim's reflection echoes that of many who feel they are governed by a mad and superhuman machine. Yet it remains acutely important to maintain sight of the human control and decision-making pro-

Film), accessed 15/2/2016.

[27] Flinders Council, http://www.flinders.tas.gov.au/aboriginal-history, accessed 14/2/2016.

[28] Malouf, *op. cit.*, pps. 102-3.

cesses behind events, however large-scale. The Indigenous Furneaux men of Tasmania fought their way through both wars and have continued to struggle for the existence of their community and culture, against what must have often seemed a faceless bureaucratised enemy. It must not be forgotten that as fragmented as the records are for the Indigenous Diggers, there is little if any documentation about First Nations people who could have served but explicitly chose not to do so. They had no shortage of political and moral reasons to oppose the war, but specific details have now been shrouded by time. Perhaps we will yet find out more about the Aboriginal resisters to Australia's early wars, just as the puzzle is coming together about those who joined the forces.

Sadly, as the Australian War Memorial records, despite the very significant contribution of Indigenous Diggers, the conditions for their people by the end of the 1920s had deteriorated from the time of Federation in 1901. This reflected very poorly on the government and the populace of the day, who did not demand improvements. Curiously, the pattern of treatment was not offset by the vehement expressions of admiration for Indigenous servicemen and impassioned outpourings of mateship that were common during the war. It gave many white men and some women a first opportunity to relate to Australia's first peoples on an equal and notably admiring footing. Since First Nations people had been purged and were no longer seen as a threat, they were viewed as a dying race, more subject to ridicule than rights. The record suggests that overall Indigenous people had to struggle against the mainstream trajectory to win the status as people and citizens, with few allies.

> The public outrage in the capital cities over the police atrocities in the Kimberley district in 1927 and in Central Australia in 1928 were the only hopeful signs for the Aboriginal people that the white voters of Australia were becoming more sympathetic to their plight. However, it was not until 1967 that a referendum on the question of giving the Commonwealth Government power to legislate on Aboriginal matters was successfully put to the people. Agitation by the political successors to Maynard and Harris was largely responsible for forcing the Commonwealth Government to put the referendum question rather than any sense of obligation resulting from the gallant war service by a significant number of Aboriginal men in two world wars.[29]

Another missing story in the Australian popular account of World War I is the final chapter: just how dissatisfied so many people were with the outcome. Of course most were happy to have 'won' the war, if any winning were possible in such carnage. However, as Marilyn Lake describes,

> As with most progressives at the time, WILPF [Women's International League for Peace and Freedom] members were bitterly disappointed with the conditions of armistice and the subsequent Treaty of Versailles, whose punitive, vengeful, terms against Germany they condemned as 'revenge sowing the seeds of another world war' and how right they were. [WILPF's] timely and important exhibition at CMAG documents WILPF's continuing activism in support of peace education and disarmament in the 1920s and 1930s, when they managed to secure 117,000 Australian signatures for the world-wide disarmament petition, the highest per capita number of signatures collected anywhere. It suggests a determinedly anti-war Australian sentiment prevailed in Australia.[30]

How very tragic that the Great Powers, including Australia, did not take careful note of this movement, which foresaw another human catastrophe of unspeakable proportions if its warning were not heeded.

---

[29] The Australian War Memorial, *Too Dark for the Light Horse, op. cit.*, p. 15.
[30] Lake, *op. cit.*, p. 3.

Chapter III
After the 'War to End all Wars': Subsequent Wars

I belong to the generation sandwiched between two world wars. I was born two years before the outbreak of World War I. In my university years I reflected the hopes of the 'in-between' generation, believing that the promise of 'never again' would be honoured. I was one of the thousands who collected signatures in the early nineteen-thirties for a world-wide grand petition to the League of Nations when it was debating measures to halt the arms traffic and free the world from the fear of a further world war. I shared my generation's despair . . .[31]

1 October 1938 - between faith and fear: This has been a week of momentous happenings. It was 1914 with a difference. And the difference was the attitude of the people. There was no flag-waving and glory of war idea this time in Europe, only a deep horror of war, a realisation of what it would mean and a sort of fatalism . . . It seemed that the world would be plunged into war for no other reason than that Hitler was impatient . . . It was a tense evening – there must have been millions listening to that voice, millions of lives who were in Hitler's hands and he gave us no cause for hope. The speech sounded like that of a madman, certainly not like that of a man who had power of life and death over millions of people. His voice was full of hate and the echoes were caught up by the crowd, crying out in unison, Sieg Heil! Sieg Heil! After hearing this I was quite prepared for anything – the gods of War and Hate seem to have been let slip.[32]

As it did for all nations, World War II (1939-1945) had a very different kind of impact on Australia. For many there was a sense of confusion: a betrayal for both the Axis and the Allies following the full impact of agreements made or conditions imposed at the end of World War I. The Germans had more than enough of the grinding poverty of repayment of the war debt combined with the depression. The Allies felt they could not stomach the horrors of war but were given at least the impression that they had no choice. The lead-up to the war fueled their propaganda machine: Hitler had to be stopped by

[31] William Nicolle Oats, *Choose your dilemma: an Australian Pacifist in Hitler's Europe*, Hobart: Montpelier Press (1999), p. 1. In this volume, Oats, an Australian Quaker and pacifist from his early adult years, shares the letters he sent home to his mother.
[32] Oats, *op cit.*, p. 22.

force. Even an ardent pacifist like Quaker Bill Oats felt backed into a corner.

> 13 November 1938 – Somehow I wonder just how my ideas have changed over the last few weeks. Europe is no place for an idealist. It is torn by hatreds, scarred by suffering. I know I mustn't let myself be drawn into these hatreds, and yet when I see what is going on in Germany, in Spain, in China, when I realise the thousands of refugees who have simply nowhere to go, I begin to wonder where it will all end. The refugee problem is tragic in its enormity. We hear of thousands turned out in Germany this week, wakened at 5 a.m., taken to a police station, given an expulsion order, not allowed to go back home, even to say goodbye, but packed off in a train, locked in a carriage and dumped off at the border. Then when you find organised gangs destroying anything and everything Jewish and looting with the open consent of the regular police, one has to ask for grace and hate the offence and not the offender. We are reaping now the legacy of hatred which the last war sowed and I wonder when the legacy of hatred which Germany is now sowing will be revealed.[33]

In this passage we hear the young Quaker, Bill Oats, taking stock of the winding of the springs of war, and how the resulting pressures seem to lead to an inevitability. However he notes some of the earliest winding was done by the Allies, in imposing such harsh penalties on the Germans following World War I. Yet not so far down the track they come to feel dragged into war as if into a rip over which they have no control, and Australia is drawn helter-skelter with the rest of the British Empire. While the war began in the Mediterranean and North Africa, it spread to South East Asia and briefly onto mainland Australia: it was indeed a world war. One of the most significant aspects was a very expanded Pacific front, to the point that Prime Minister John Curtin disobeyed the British by bringing the troops home to defend Australia. There could be no question of 'merely helping out' in 'someone else's war,' although had Australia remained neutral rather than being so tied in with the Allies, perhaps it would not have been a direct target.[34] The war had come home, for which despite all indications that this could occur, most were unready.

> One night, for several hours, there was a bombardment that had them all huddled together with their arms about their heads, not just trying to stop the noise but pretending, as children might, to be invisible.[35]

By the time the Germans were defeated and the Japanese surrendered, 39,000 Australians had died in World War II, while over 30,000 had been taken prisoner, many of these by the Japanese. While prisoners of the Germans had a good chance of returning home, about 36% of those who were captured by the Japanese died. Roughly a million Australians served, men and women, a vast proportion of its small population of less than 7 million. The large numbers in service can be traced in significant part to the reestablishment of compulsory militia training in 1940, and the extension of 'training' so that militias could be sent into active service not only domestically but anywhere in the south-west Pacific. By 1942 there were at least 265,000 serving in the militia, of which roughly 200,000 transferred to the regular army.

It was a wearying, maturing war for the citizenry. As the Allied global power base had shifted so decisively from Britain to America, Australian politics and diplomacy refocused its allegiance. It would goose-step in a tight relationship with the US for the foreseeable future. One Australian administra-

---

[33] Oats, *op cit.,* p. 22.

[34] Government of Australia, 'Australians at War' http://www.australiansatwar. gov.au/ throughmyeyes/w2_main.asp accessed 9/2/2016.

[35] Malouf, *op. cit.,* p. 80.

tion after another has seemed happy with this new and stronger prospect for a military alliance with a state which had reason to be significantly more concerned and in tune with the fate of the Pacific than Britain had ever been. But a great many sacrifices would be demanded in the course of this relationship, and for many Australians, the cost was too high. World War II was a dramatic game changer for Australia.

> He had begun to feel immeasurably old. Almost everyone he had known well in the company was gone now and had been twice replaced. The replacements came up in new uniforms, very sweet, very clean, and looked like play soldiers, utterly unreal, till they too took on the colour of the earth or sank below it. It was like living through whole generations.[36]

Technology had changed substantially by the time of World War II, and the militarisation in the years leading up to the war accounted in large part for the scale of devastation for service people and civilians in all the countries that the war touched. No longer was this a case of well-plotted trenches, where pilots could fly over after a battle to count the dead, and apart from at sea, everyone had a fairly good idea of where the war was, geographically speaking.

> Nothing after this would ever be the same. War was being developed as a branch of industry. Later, what had been learnt on the battlefield would travel back, and industry from now on, maybe all life, would be organised like war. The coming battle would not be the end, even if it was decisive; it was another stage in the process.[37]

World War II was experienced as a free-for-all. The Allies and the Axis both targeted civilians and large population centres, in an effort to terrify the enemy and bring it to its knees. This was a new use of fear, whose logic is now labeled 'terrorism'. In the end, this tactic surpassed any human understanding with the dropping of not one, but two atom bombs on Hiroshima and Nagasaki respectively. Not only fear, but suffering of an inconceivable kind was imposed by Australia's ally. Never before or since has there been such an imposition of merciless killing, crimes against humanity, out of proportion with any act that could be conceived necessary to trigger capitulation. WWII was a psychological war in a new way, not only through the post-traumatic stress it caused. It must not be forgotten when fear itself became the weapon of choice.

The force of the weaponry, combined with its level of cruelty, seemed a far cry from the troops from opposing sides at the end of 1914 singing Christmas carols and playing soccer together. Again technology was in large part responsible, because with much larger range weaponry, it was very much easier to 'protect' and distance the fighters from their targets. In many cases it was only if one were captured that one came face to face with the 'other'. Exactly the same technology led to destruction that was vast and inhumane in ways inconceivable in WWI.

> I don't believe I shall ever cease to *feel* that war is the worst crime against humanity, and it is unalterably and irretrievably wrong. I see all our present problems as a judgment upon our fundamentally wrong ways of thinking and living. We have just refused to pay homage to the laws of life and we find we can't break these laws – they simply break us. But few people look at suffering in this way, because in most cases it is the innocent who are the sufferers.[38]

Oats points to the same conclusion that Di Bretherton and Ursula Franklin reached in the opening quotations of this volume. War shapes our ongoing relationships both among our fellow citizens and with those who are dubbed 'enemies' for a long time to come. Lack of respect lays down a particular kind of relationship and makes possible particular strategic policies. It may be observed, quite justi-

---

[36] Malouf, *op. cit.,* p. 100.
[37] Malouf, *op. cit.,* p. 112.
[38] Oats, *op. cit.,* p. 28.

fiably, that the Japanese used very cruel strategies in warfare. However the notion that this provides license to engage in yet more barbaric actions is false. The imposition of fear is at the core of war, and modern warfare has simply become more and more effective in working this strategy. Yet as Franklin remarks, this fear has caught us in a cycle that spins us round and round so that Australia seems to be on a perpetually militarised footing, and has been almost constantly at war or engaged in warfare since WWII. Differently stated, the actions of its ally, the US, have drawn it very deeply into the dark logic of unending violence, from which it seems not to know how to step away. The prospect of this bellicose ally leading Australia further up this path is very real and provocative, especially to our neighbours in the Asia-Pacific region.

WWI broke new ground, establishing that women had the physical and psychological strength to work, both in replacing men, keeping farms and businesses running, keeping the wheels turning in factories such as munitions, and also as nurses who served very ably at the front. Their double-edged 'reward' for this remarkable demonstration of capability was that women were even more central to WWII. Those at the front worked primarily as nurses, because of the much larger scale of Australia's war.

Sylvia Duke was one of 3477 Australian nurses who served. She was posted in the 6th Australian General Hospital in Greece. In extracts from Sylvia's letters to her friend, Sophie Healy, she wrote,

> I thanked God many times for the privilege of being born an Australian. They had such guts – they could always see another lad who was worse than they themselves – and then my dear the awful sensation of helplessness, that awful hopelessness when evacuation was imminent – we nurses were put on trucks and sent off down to the waterfront – matron and about 25 other sisters were on a truck ahead of us. They were boarded on a hospital ship but we arrived in the midst of an air raid, and as the planes were dive bombing the harbour they cut the ship's ropes and away she went leaving the remainder of us on shore. We returned to our former hospital and attempted to carry on – the casualties still pouring in every hour of every day ... We were on movement orders, we did our nursing in our outdoor uniforms expecting our orders to walk out at any minute – our nights were passed in empty houses – no beds or any such luxuries and believe me those tiled floors can be jolly hard to sleep on. And then my dear, when our next orders came to go once more – the boys saying 'Cheerio Sister, thanks so much. Hurry up – Go.'[39]

Private Jack Clarris was in the care of the Australian nurses and Voluntary Aid Detachments. In a letter home to his cousin Edward he describes a snapshot from his war.

> ... I am now in a Convalescent Depot in Egypt. I was wounded at El Alamein and have spent about eight weeks in hospital ... I would like to tell you something of the battle but fancy that the censor may object to that ... but I can say that Rommel and his Africa Corp got the biggest hammering they ever got. It was not by any means a walk-over and to see the way that our boys waded into him shall be something that I shall never forget. The lads have had such a belly-full of this place and they went in determined to do the job, which they did very efficiently, the only thing I am crooked on is the good lads that we left behind up there. We had more casualties in 10 days fighting at Alamein than they have had throughout the New Guinea campaign ... Our Australian girls ... are simply wonderful. When in hospital they do anything and everything for you bar eat your meals. No matter where you see our boys or girls over here it sends a surge of pride through you and makes you feel proud to be an Australian.[40]

[39] Government of Australia, 'Australians at War', *op. cit.*
[40] Government of Australia, 'Australians at War', *op. cit.*

These passages give insights into the pride that Australians felt in seeing the bravery, stamina and sacrifice of their mates. However it would be a misinterpretation to understand these voices as giving unequivocal support for war itself. Both record the horrific scale of destruction. So many died in action. Their pain was tragic but brief. For those who lived out a natural lifespan, many were plagued by memories too ghastly to live down but too traumatic to be shared, or perhaps even too incredible, to those who did not fight. Divisions that arose between those in uniform and others who for many good reasons did not join up were and remain often salted with this sting: a kind of mutual envy, born of misunderstanding or sheer ignorance of what the other had experienced and continued to endure.

It is noteworthy that the Australian Government, on its websites designed for schoolchildren about 'Australia at War' has chosen quite emphatically to reflect the patriotism that is experienced by those who enlist, and the sense of exhilaration that seems to accompany this. There are no records on the website of servicemen or women who have regretted taking any part in the war. As we know, the dead are mostly silent, except when they leave diaries or letters that reflect their feelings, and when these are made public as some have been in the National Library's 'Keepsakes' exhibition. Records of those who felt more disgusted than patriotic may have been destroyed by family members or never even returned to them. But the supporters and those who, once at the front, would have wished that Australia had never involved itself in World War II died in equal measure. Recent experience, for example, among American soldiers who voluntarily signed up for the Iraq war, is that quite a number felt a change of heart once they got to the front and experienced the treatment of the opposing forces and civilians alike. However, conscientious objection is only a possibility for those who refuse to serve on the basis of being pacifist, not for those who experience a crisis of conscience once at the front. A number of American personnel have sought refugee status in Canada to avoid being court martialed.[41]

The contribution of women in World War II was reinforced by the acceptance of more First Nations women in service. However their numbers have been even less well documented than those of men. Often it was those who later became renown as elders and leaders whose service retroactively was recorded. These women became part of a wider expansion of women's auxiliaries in each branch of the Armed Forces. At least nine Indigenous women joined the Women's Australian Auxiliary Air Force, several more the Australian Women's Land Army, and others the Australian Women's Army Service (AWAS).[42]

Among these was Kath Walker, later famous as the poet and rights activist Oodgeroo Noonuccal (1920-1993). She enlisted in the Australian Women's Army Service in 1941 or 1942 (records vary) after her two brothers were captured by the Japanese. She was promoted to Lance Corporal. As a signaler in Brisbane, she had contact with many people of different backgrounds, including European and Black Americans, who were beginning to lay the grounds for their civil rights movement. These contacts helped sow the seeds for her later advocacy of rights for First Nations Australians.[43] Noonuccal was discharged from the AWAS in 1943, after a serious ear infection left her with partial hearing loss, leaving her unable to serve in her former capacities. Ever determined, she went on to train in secretarial and bookkeeping skills at Brisbane Commercial College under the army's rehabilitation scheme.[44]

The Second World War brought a significant contribution by many dedicated Aboriginal and Torres Strait Islander recruits to auxiliaries that worked within Australia. A special platoon was raised in

[41] Canadian Quakers have provided support to some of these military personnel as they have sought asylum in Canada.

[42] Clark, *op. cit.*

[43] The Australian War Museum, *Too Dark for the Light Horse, op. cit.*, p. 17.

[44] Australian Poetry Library, Oodgeroo Noonuccal (1920 – 1993) http://www.poetrylibrary. edu.au/poets/noonuccal-oodgeroo, accessed 9/2/2016.

Wangaratta, Victoria, in 1940 and shortly after the Northern Territory Special Reconnaissance Unit (NTSRU) in Arnhem Land, which served for three years, until its role was reassigned (in an overtly racist manner) to the North Australia Observer Unit, staffed by white members who relied heavily on First Nations people as guides and to assist with survival. In 1942, an Indigenous garrison unit was established in the Torres Strait, which grew to the 830-strong Torres Strait Light Infantry Battalion. Although it was intended as defensive, it became involved in offensive patroling into Dutch New Guinea.

The choice of whether to serve was not entirely up to the First Nations peoples. Early in World War II they were permitted to enlist, and many joined up with alacrity, for the reasons mentioned above, as well as the opportunity to make an income for their families and to travel. Some were given assurances of citizenship if they did serve. However, in an about-face, the Defence Committee abruptly slammed the door on this practice in 1940. Whether it had received objections is doubtful but the Committee declared the service of Aborigines 'neither necessary nor desirable' because it might put off the enlistment of whites. However, the tone changed significantly when Japan entered the war. From the earliest days of Federation there had been discussion about whether First Nations peoples might not serve the country well by providing a northern defence force. No events precipitated this in World War I, but of course circumstances changed dramatically with the opening of the south-west Pacific front.[45]

Indigenous people, Torres Strait Islanders in particular, were recruited in significant numbers and overall the number of First Nations people was radically ramped up through both enlistment and conscription. For this reason it was self-evident that they would find themselves in the front line against the Japanese when they arrived in 1942. But suddenly it occurred to the Defence Committee that this might not be such a good situation for Australia after all. Far from softening up the enemy, First Nations people might take advantage politically of the situation.[46]

There were fears that Aboriginal contact with Japanese pearlers before the war might lead to their giving assistance to the enemy. Like the peoples of Southeast Asia under colonial regimes, First Nations people might easily have seen the Japanese as liberators from white rule. The pearlers depended on their luggers for their living. However these were confiscated with the excuse that they might fall into enemy hands. However the fear that the First Nations people might join the enemy using these boats or infiltrate Australia may well have swilled just under the surface. Few options remained but to enlist.[47]

Many did express bitterness at their treatment but Aborigines and Islanders supported Australia's defence effort in significant numbers, though as we have seen this may have been a matter of survival rather than choice. Apart from the many formally enlisted First Nations people, the Royal Australian Navy (RAN) also deployed 'informal' units. From Melville Island, off the Northern Territory, the unique skills of thirty-six mainland and islander First Nations people were used by Jack Gribble to patrol the coast and islands. But despite repeated promises, these coastwatchers were never formally enlisted and so never received any pay for their services.[48] They were to be content, even grateful, for the food they received as sufficient recompense. Even then, the rations had to be supplemented through their own efforts.

Another First Nations unit was set up, also at Melville Island, and known as the Snake Bay Patrol. This unit had a dual mission: to rescue any downed airmen and to protect the island from Japanese

---

[45] Australian War Memorial, *Too Dark for the Light Horse, op. cit.*, p. 18.

[46] Australian War Memorial, *Too Dark for the Light Horse, op. cit.*, p. 16.

[47] Australian War Memorial, *Too Dark for the Light Horse, op. cit.*, p. 17.

[48] Australian War Memorial, *Too Dark for the Light Horse, op. cit.*, p. 16.

infiltration. Many other First Nations people from the Northern Territory were involved in support roles, as labourers and in many other capacities. Because the auxiliaries were issued clothing, paid, accommodated and given rations by the army many felt they had joined up and were shocked to find they were only civilians with no entitlements at the end of the war.[49]

A Melbourne anthropologist, David Thomson, who had spent two years in East Arnhem Land in the 1930s, established a similar irregular unit consisting of fifty-one mainland Aborigines, five whites and a number of Pacific and Torres Strait Islanders. Three of these men had been previously jailed for killing Japanese lugger crews. It was now ironically their duty to fight off any Japanese they might encounter. Using their traditional bushcraft skills alone, they were to patrol and defend the coastal waters. They had no supply line to protect, feeding themselves as they went. Similar to others, they were not paid. Finally in 1992 they did receive back pay and medals, some 50 years after they commenced work. It goes without saying that their wages would have been worth much by this time, and many of the family members they would have wished to support were deceased. These are the injustices that cannot put right, indeed sour more with the passing of time and delay tactics.[50]

It is easy to see why many who had the opportunity joined the Torres Strait Light Infantry, and official forces. Even there, pay was so petty that what they could send home to their families was completely inadequate. Farms, army butcheries and construction sites were other employment options where First Nations people were put to work but held under surveillance by the whites. Some provided general labour, or hauled and shifted cargo. There can be no argument that the ill-treatment of First Nations people by the Armed Forces was merely an account of isolated or accidental incidents: that structural racism occurred is confirmed by such facts as the pattern that the Royal Australian Air Force (RAAF) demonstrated. It took full advantage of the cheap labour supply First Nations could be forced to provide by siting their bases and radar stations near missions.[51]

Even for those who were paid, remuneration remained pathetic. This was a matter of collusion between the Australian people and the political powers of the time, who were thinking beyond the horizon of war. While for a period the army attempted to increase wages above five shillings a week, the standard for First Nations, and the RAAF was for a brief time paying that much per day, pressures worked against these improvements. The civilian administration and station owners forced wages back to the standard. They could see that their profits would be diminished if this new bar were kept high after the war, and it might be hard to bring down again during peace time.

White women may have been part of this marginalising process, but they had little say and remained severely under-represented in the halls of power and in decisions about labour conditions. Like First Nations people, they would find that the 'freedoms' they enjoyed during wartime were once again curtailed in the aftermath of war. Their key roles in carrying the responsibilities of Australian society, in sustaining home life, caring for the old and children, injured veterans and turning the cogs of the national economy did not result in a dramatic change of status once peacetime returned. They too were subject to structural violence and societal and domestic violence rates were also high. Wherever groups are silenced or marginalised, there is likely to be an institutional framework that facilitates this condition.

William Oats wrote on 13 November 1938,

> How to meet violence – that is the problem. To meet it by violence, I am convinced is wrong. By the Cross, I am convinced is right ... but what of community reaction to community violence? Here I'm stuck. How to treat Germany, for example. I believe there must

---

[49] Clark, *op.cit.*

[50] Australian War Memorial, *Too Dark for the Light Horse, op. cit.*, p. 18.

[51] Australian War Memorial, *Too Dark for the Light Horse, op. cit.*, p. 17.

be much aversion in Germany among some of its people to the beastly ideas of the Nazi party. Surely the whole nation isn't corrupted.[52]

Oats was of course right, but we know now what a horrible end so many of these conscientious objectors met at the hands of the Nazis. Like Jewish people, those who were not heterosexual, as well as the Roma people suffered similarly. The many who participated in resistance actions risked all. So little of the extremity of the violence of World War II, especially its targeting of civilians, can even now be understood. What made the wheels of war turn as they did, with the incredible, unimaginable scale and efficiency they displayed, year in and year out? Industrial models, largely perfected by individuals in England and America, for example, with Ford cars, ironically cut the trail that Germany was following with its war and genocide strategies.

It was this routine on an industrial scale with mechanical, unthinking actions by individuals, each movement so small, which all together created hell on earth, that scholar Hannah Arendt called 'the banality of evil'. She was much criticised for this, because many imagined she was saying that the atrocities were somehow unimportant. On the contrary, her vivid expression conveys all too well the simplicity of even our own tiny, seemingly unimportant motions that together can have great, horrific impact. Perhaps today it may be how we use our own purchasing power and how we allow our tax money to be used that has the greatest impact. Yet many joke of 'retail therapy' and regard shopping as medicinal.

Eichmann, the German Nazi responsible for keeping the trains running to the concentration camps, claimed that he certainly had a moral compass. He read Kant in his spare time, and suggested that he would have felt guilty if the trains had not run on time, because that was the role assigned to him. So much for the great achievements of progress, in which the human heart becomes an appendage to the watch and the machine. But of course in truth it had become fettered to an ideology that tapped into fears and was very human in its ruthless response.

We see how the Nazis too felt that they had no choice. As twisted and morally bankrupt as this may seem from our perspective, they were worn down by a logic that blamed the Jews for the economic misery and famine they experienced after WWI. It was a simple and plausible argument for people who had long been taught that the Jewish people hoarded riches and starved their neighbours. But antisemitism was also rife in Allied countries. Many refused visas to the Jewish refugees attempting to flee pogroms in Germany. They may not have known that these same people would be exterminated, but it was clear that something very sinister was afoot. The level of persecution by Germany had clearly reached insufferably grim proportions to make the entire Jewish population, or those who could, leave their homes, their communities, break up families and flee to anywhere that would take them, willy-nilly.

Similar to WWI, WWII presented dilemmas of 'Indigenousness' for the authorities and confusion for First Nations people. The records are very poor; estimates suggest 3000-6000 First Nations men and women served. Recent figures seem to include people who did not present themselves as Aboriginal or did not identify with this background. The official records are also full of errors, so no accurate assessment will ever be established. But without minimising the life and contribution of each individual, what is most important in retrospect is not the precise overall number but the fact that a large number served.

Paradoxically in the face of Nazi racism and the rights and freedoms Australians were at least nominally protecting by fighting, the prejudicial policy that the Diggers be 'substantially of European origin' was reinstated. This did not deter many who are recognisably Aboriginal in photos from entering

---

[52] Oats, *op. cit.,* p. 29.

the forces. In 1940-41, they made significant contributions to the campaigns in the Western Desert, Greece, Crete and Syria. When Japan entered the war, Australia's perspective and policies changed. Aboriginal soldiers fought and died in Malaya, Singapore, Papua, New Guinea, Bougainville and Borneo.[53]

Bert Beros, who fought in WWII, wrote a poem about his Indigenous mate, Private West. The piece was written while on active service and is dedicated to West. It was likely inspired in part by the surprise Beros experienced in finding a First Nations man could make such a remarkable soldier. While deeply respectful at one level, it paints a picture of the Aboriginal man, West, as if he had transitioned instantaneously from colonial subservience in the mission (where expressions of Aboriginality tended to be outlawed) and simultaneously a traditional life untainted or disrupted by White influence, to join the services with their own very distinctive culture. This is an impossibility and far from West's reality. References to the boomerang and warrior suggest that West may still have belonged to the Aboriginal 'premodern' to which the poem implicitly refers, rather than any celebration on the author's part of the unique cultures of First Nations. He must have been, in fact, a man of his time, when Christian, colonial and 20th century influences would have had profound effects on his upbringing.

Describing West's bravery as that of a warrior suggests a term very rarely used to characterise white Diggers, and again implies that West drew his courage from his Aboriginal roots. Beros specifically said West was 'still' a warrior, as if that was what one could expect of any Indigenous man. Reference to the 'War God' may be a throw-back to Beros's own Greek culture and the classical notion of fighters, but also suggests a plurality of gods such as the author might have supposed existed in his mate's Indigenous spirituality. Yet if he were taken as a young child to live in a mission, or even born there, chances are great that he would have been Christian. There is no doubt that West's smiling face hid much pain, and his tolerance of hunger concealed a lifetime of coping with it, to which the author Beros is oblivious. The use of the term 'Abo' is 'othering' and remains derogatory but in this case probably serves the poem's structure.

Contrary to Beros' anticipation of a new, more open Australia, had he survived the war, West would have suffered significant racism, not a warm welcome, at most RSLs. He would have waited a lifetime yet for full emancipation. Striking is that the relationship between the two men was close enough that West could share his sense of the injustice concerning Aboriginal people being pushed out of city centres and prime real estate, and of not having any political representation. This is as much a sad reflection of the racial segregation of Australia at the time as it is a sign of the sensitivity Beros had for his friend, West. The author sees his mate as a man among men, high praise in this case. Beros wrote,

> He came and joined the colours,
> When the War God's anvil rang,
> He took up modern weapons
> To replace his boomerang,
> He waited for no call-up,
> He didn't need a push,
> He came in from the stations
> And the townships of the bush.
>
> He helped when help was wanting,
> Just because he wasn't deaf;
> He is right amongst the columns
> Of the fighting A.I.F.

---

[53] Clark, *op. cit.*

He is always there when wanted,
With his Owen gun or Bren,
He is in the forward area,
The place where men are men.

He proved he's still a warrior,
In action not afraid,
He faced the blasting red-hot fire
From mortar and grenade;
He didn't mind when food was low,
And we were getting thin,
He didn't growl or worry then,
He'd cheer us with his grin.

He'd heard us talk Democracy
– They preach it to his face –
Yet knows that in our Federal House
There's no one of his race.
He feels we push his kinsmen out,
Where cities do not reach,
And Parliament has yet to hear
The abo's maiden speech.

One day he'll leave the Army,
Then join the League he shall,
And he hopes we'll give a better deal
To the aboriginal.

Written at Donadabu Rest Camp (near Moresby) by Sapper, H.E. "Bert" Beros, RAE, AIF Pte. But there is more to West's story, and here we see a man whose true colours show, his core loyalty to a First Nations mate. When his Aboriginal friend was killed in the Owen Stanleys, West went naked and stalked the Japanese machine-gun pits, into which he hurled grenades. He died from illness after the campaign. He was well remembered by the men of his AIF brigade, the reader is told.[54] Beros both consciously and unconsciously holds an important mirror to the condition of an Aboriginal soldier. West was fighting his own war-within-a-war, determined to avenge the loss of an Aboriginal brother even unto death. This war-within-a-war consisted of Indigenous people attempting to protect themselves and one another, the land to which they belonged, their attempt to achieve a status that afford them the full rights of citizenship, the assumption that they experienced no racism among their peers or from superiors, and the desperate struggle to cope financially given their lifelong and inter-generational marginalisation. Two generations on from this war, the fallout from the added twist on disadvantage that it imposed can be seen in such indicators as astronomic rates of poverty, incarceration, family breakdown, loss of culture, early mortality, diabetes and other health conditions, mental ill-health and addiction.

Among the Indigenous forces, in 1944 Reginald Saunders became a commissioned lieutenant, although undoubtedly recognisable as Aboriginal, and noted for his service in North Africa, Greece and Crete, as well as New Guinea. By this time Pilot Officer David Paul, who had become a bomber pilot in the Royal Australian Air Force (RAAF), was shot down over the Aegean Sea in 1943 and imprisoned by the Germans. While still a prisoner of war he was awarded the Distinguished Flying

---

[54] From *The fuzzy wuzzy angels, and other verses,* by Sapper H.E. Bert Beros, Sydney, F.H. Johnston Publishing, (1943), as cited in The Australian War Memorial, *Too Dark for the Light Horse, op. cit.,* p. 8.

Cross in 1944. In the same year Sergeant Len Waters became the RAAF's first Indigenous fighter pilot, serving in Indonesia. Tragically, a year later in August 1945 another First Nations Flight Sergeant, Arnold Lockyer was shot down over Celebes in the same territory and was killed by his captors six days after Japan's surrender, and presumably just over a week after the atomic bombs fell on Hiroshima and Nagasaki. Needless and vengeful violence by this point had become a routine part of this inhumane war.[55]

Australia's next military action was as part of the British Commonwealth Occupation Force (BCOF) in Japan. Ostensibly a peace mission, the three battalions that served here were, largely by proximity, immediately committed to Korea when war broke out there in 1950. There were a number of Aboriginal soldiers, including a sergeant and two corporals, serving with this force.

The Korean War involved about 17,000 Australian personnel in the UN multinational force, including up to 35 Indigenous men, from 1950-57 (although the war officially spanned 1950-53). By its end a 'demilitarised line' stretched across the peninsula only a few kilometres from where, at the start of the war, its dead twin lay. The horrors of this war included an enormous number of civilian casualties, torture and atrocities committed by both sides, and the use of bacterial warfare by the US, including bombs containing plague, typhoid, anthrax and other diseases.[56]

The Korean War was called 'the forgotten war' because it has received very little media attention compared to other wars then or since. It was one of loyalty and fulfilling the commitments of alliance from Australia's perspective. In June, 1950 the North Korean army crossed into the southern zone. Two days later the US mobilised air and sea support for South Korea. The United Nations Security Council called on all members to assist. Australia honoured its commitment, supplying the 77 Squadron of the RAAF and the 3rd Battalion of the Royal Australian Regiment, both stationed nearby in Japan. We were among nineteen countries that contributed, conducting bombardments, escorts and blockades. Four more sent medical assistance. Compulsory military training, called 'national service' was reintroduced in 1951 and lasted until 1959, when it was abolished as a drain on the Regular Army's finances and manpower.

The human costs were significant for all concerned. It is estimated that there may have been between four and five million casualties during the Korean war, including civilians and the losses of every participating nation. Conditions were often extremely harsh, with cold reaching minus 50 degrees and frostbite commonplace, afflicting all concerned but the north more than the south. The Americans mobilised 6.8 million personnel, lost 54,000 soldiers including 33,000 in direct combat, while 339 Australians were killed and more than 1500 injured by the time the conflict ceased. Across the British Commonwealth forces, about 1263 deaths were incurred and a further 4817 were injured. Although fighting ceased in 1953, in calculating injuries, the long-term mental, social and economic impacts of post-traumatic stress were not taken into consideration.

The war went to some extent under the radar for Australians, since there was no question of conscription or mass mobilisation.[57] Estimates vary widely about the toll to North Koreans, and the ongoing conditions of closure to the world greatly limit information gathering, but somewhere between 900,000 and 30 per cent of the population are considered to have died. Countless more have died subsequently as a result of knock-on effects of the war. Many Chinese, possibly more than half a million, were also killed.

In Australia there came a blanket of silence at the end of this war. Australian scholar Gavan McCormack has spoken some sharp truths concerning this quiet: 'Perhaps the most inhuman response of

---

[55] Clark, *op. cit.*

[56] Gavan McCormack, *Cold War Hot War*, Sydney: Hale & Ironmonger, 1983, p. 147.

[57] 'Australians at War', Government of Australia, http://www.australiansatwar.gov.au/throughmyeyes/ko_main.asp

all is to have been involved and then to have simply forgotten'.[58] He echoes the concern of the World War I Diggers that by wiping the memory slate clean, we immediately begin to prepare ourselves for the possibility of the next war. Finally the silence was broken when in 1981 the first volume of Robert O'Neill's *Australia in the Korean War* appeared, which sparked a larger conversation about this unusual war. The lack of discourse or explicit commemoration is particularly poignant and pointed today given the vehemence of Anzac celebrations. In 1983, McCormack's own book, *Cold War Hot War An Australian Perspective on the Korean War* appeared. McCormack shows how Australia's role vis-a-vis its south-east Asian and Pacific neighbours changed as a result of its engagement in Korea. He argues:

> The Korean War was in a very real sense a definitive moment in the genesis of the modern world, though for all its importance it has received little scholarly attention, almost none in Australia till very recently, and it passed out of the public mind almost as soon as the ceasefire was signed in 1953 and the Australian troops were withdrawn. But the continuing saga of the Korean people, whose experience of the twentieth century has been one of almost unbroken tragedy and manipulation in the interests of one or another outside power, compels our attention now as then . . . What was elsewhere a 'cold' war was, in Korea, a conflagration that killed between three and four million people and created a nation of refugees. It was in Korea that U.S. Cold War policies moved from containment to 'roll back', and as a result of Korea that the relationships between the powers in Asia were crucially modified. The Taiwan problem is a legacy of the Korean War . . .[59]

The UN/US force initially understood itself as defending South Korea from invasion by the communist north. However Australia played an important peacebuilding role by shedding greater light on the politics and complexity of the conflict. The United Nations Temporary Commission on Korea, UNTCOK, was led by Australia, and also included Canada, China (Taiwan), El Salvador, France, India, Philippines, and Syria. It was led by the Australian, S. H. Jackson, who took a strong and internationally courageous position in steering Australia away from giving any blessing to what he saw as an intolerable and intolerant American-driven puppet government in the South. He went so far as to press for the commission to enter North Korea, but he could not gain consent from the necessary authorities. He held the radical view that 'any election that is held must be held in relation to all of Korea'.

The Australian government, once aware of the 'narrow and undemocratic' political base in South Korea, backed this position. It is notable that that although fighting under American supreme command they were willing to diverge diplomatically in a significant way. It may have been Australia's role as UN mission leader that afforded this measured independence. Australia supported Jackson in its instructions to him, as well as in representations to London and the other Commonwealth capitals. There was a deep-seated concern not to do anything to aggravate or institutionalise the north-south division. As a result of this Australian intervention, the matter was sent back to the Interim Committee of the General Assembly. The head of the Australian mission in Tokyo, Patrick Shaw, wrote on 11 November 1947,

> Real power is apparently in the hands of the ruthless police force which works at the direction of the G-2 section of the American GHQ and Syngman Rhee and Kim Koo . . . Korean prisons are now fuller of political prisoners than under Japanese rule. The torture and murder of the political enemies of the extreme Right is apparently an accepted and commonplace thing . . . the American G-2 is too concerned with the suppression of the Left to enquire too closely into the methods adopted by their Korean agents.[60]

---

[58] McCormack, *op. cit.*, p. 167.
[59] McCormack, *op. cit.*, p. 15.
[60] Australian Mission in Japan, department despatch No. 29, 11/11/1947. AA 19/301/1208 as

For his part, Jackson described the American role further and with grave implications. However, the Commission lacked the power to compel any change in this situation. As an ally of the US, Australia was forced to contribute to the veneer of legitimacy of the Rhee regime, but did what it could to witness to the contrary. Jackson reported with dismay on 29 January 1948 '. . . the American Military Government is supporting the rightists and treats anyone who is not a rightist as at least a near communist . . . Several spokesmen for the parties have said that a free election is impossible because the rightists with the aid of the police have the whole situation under control. This is probably very near the mark.'[61] It is surely lamentable that few Australians are aware of this admirable period of diplomatic peacemaking by our nation.

Korea was a war of almost constant contact. The Australian army had become multicultural, including servicemen from the full range of backgrounds represented by Australian citizens. But it must be recalled that inclusivity in the forces meant an equal right to die. Private Joe Vezgoff remembered one incident:

> We were about a mile forward of the battalion, with the responsibility of racing back when we saw any large troop movement on our front. I, of Russian origin, and George of Chinese, caused some consternation when someone back at battalion headquarters asked who was in the forward outpost. 'A Chinese and a Russian', came the reply![62]

While most Indigenous servicemen were in the army, at least one was aboard the HMAS Condamine in 1952-3. Two were known to have been killed in battle, S.K.J. Lenoy and T. Hazel, while Torres Strait Islander Corporal Charles Mene was decorated with the Military Medal.

Yet not all ethnicities were treated equally. The renown Reg Saunders returned to military service as captain at the battle of Kapyong, leading a company of the 3rd Battalion, Royal Australian Regiment.[63] While in this capacity, a classic snapshot of life for the family of the eminent Indigenous leader was reported in an Australian newspaper:

Officer's wife lives in squalor

```
Melbourne - Mrs Dorothy Saunders, wife of the first full-blooded Aborig-
inal to be given the King's commission, is living with their three baby
daughters in one squalid room in North Fitzroy while her husband fights
in Korea. In this room of a condemned house - the only one that a war
hero and his family could find in years of searching - the youngest baby
has been bitten by a rat, and there are great gaps in the broken, sunken
flooring. A patch of mud lies at the doorway, where the floor had been torn
right away. Lieut. Reginald Saunders, the 'real Australian officer', won
his commission and distinction for his race by AIF service in the Middle
East and New Guinea.[64]
```

Reg Saunders had two great regrets to the end of his life. One was that he was refused a place in the

---

cited in McCormack, *op. cit.*, p. 41
[61] Australian Representative to UNTCOK, departmental dispatch No. 3, Seoul, 29 January 1948. AA 19/301/1208 as cited in McCormack, *op. cit.*, p. 41.
[62] https://www.awm.gov.au/exhibitions/korea/ausinkorea/, accessed 11/2/16.
[63] Clark, *op. cit.*
[64] *Reg Saunders: an Indigenous war hero*, p. 51, http://trove.nla.gov.au/ ndp/del/article/130288638, accessed 10/2/2016.

coronation contingent, despite public pleas on his behalf and his many years of loyal service at one front after another. But his greater and more bitter dismay was that he, like all other First Nations people was never considered eligible for the soldier settlement scheme. Many servicemen returned to the 'camps', often to urban ones, which were degraded catch-all baskets for those Indigenous people who had lost contact with their own people and culture. Levels of stress and anxiety were high, as reflected by elevated levels of violence and alcohol abuse. The cruelty was sharpened by the fact that Saunders' traditional lands were being assigned to other returned service personnel.[65]

In addition to the great civilian death toll during the Korean war, vast numbers became refugees, many of whom subsequently perished from residues of biological warfare and their displaced condition. Conditions were harsh for the soldiers too. Lieutenant General Sir Thomas Daly, a British officer recalls:

> I remember the dust, the heat, the enervating humidity, the bitter cold of winter when the men slept with their boots on and weapons cradled lest they should be found frozen in an emergency; the soldiers on listening post, lying silently on the frozen ground trying desperately to remain alert, knowing they were responsible for the safety of their comrades. I remember long nights in my command post . . . listening to the sounds of battle in the valley, anxiously awaiting reports from units involved in life and death situations and for news of success or failure and of the inevitable cost . . . Best of all, I remember the lovely spring dawn when the harsh landscape was suddenly transformed; walking through wildflowers . . . to visit our men, tired but cheerful Aussies returning from patrol, taciturn Geordies from Durham, cheeky Cockneys from London Town.[66]

Australia's 'spoils' from the Korea confrontation were significant. It won much recognition from other nations, and over 600 decorations among Australian personnel. Most importantly in terms of geopolitical standing, Australia sealed the Australia, New Zealand and United States Pacific Security Treaty (ANZUS). After the war, Australians remained in Korea. For the first four years they served as military observers. This has continued under the Australian Military Attaché.

In order to maintain the numbers of those enlisted, national service was not discontinued until 1959. This 'need' arose because coincident with the Korean War, the Australian government became involved in the 'Malayan Emergency' (1950-60). Led by the Far-East Strategic Reserve, of which Australia was a key part, it provided protection, including air coverage based in Singapore for most of that period. Regular army tours served from 1955. The defence presence turned into a low-level military confrontation when Indonesia challenged the newly formed Federation of Malaysia. The 'Confrontation' which stretched from 1960-63 focused on Borneo, where Indonesia had established land borders with Malaysia. Of the regular army soldiers, 19 are known to have been Indigenous Australians.[67]

In his memoir, 'They were foremost Australian soldiers' Col. Max Carroll recollects the eminent contributions of some of his First Nations troops during the Malayan emergency. They were all Queenslanders as was most of the platoon. He reflects back on the year of training in the Australian camp of Canungra as well as their year or so in active service in Malaya. With regard to Private N.G. (Noel) Brown, who was 19 or 20 at the time,

> As I came to know him better my respect for him increased. He was an extremely good soldier in the bush, using all of the natural skills he inherited . . . he proved to be a first-class soldier on operations. There is one instance . . . in which my platoon had to take a

---

[65] *Reg Saunders, op. cit.*
[66] Australian War Memorial, 'Out in the Cold', https://www.awm.gov.au/ exhibitions/korea/ ausinkorea/, accessed 11/2/2016.
[67] Clark, *op. cit.*

surrendered terrorist back into the bush in a hurry to get to an arms dump that he had revealed during his interrogation. It was essential that we got there first, before his fellow terrorists woke up to the fact that he had absconded and could reveal where the weapons were cached . . . I took the terrorist, a Chinese interpreter, an Iban soldier who was a Sarawak Dyak (these people were used as trackers) and Noel Brown as the other Australian soldier . . . This emphasises the trust I had in him . . . As darkness was descending the Chinese interpreter . . . sprained his ankle. I left Brown with him and I pushed on with the terrorist and the Iban. We eventually recovered the weapons and came back in the dark, picked up Noel Brown and the Chinese interpreter and made it back to the platoon. The point I want to make here is that out of a platoon of [between 16 and 50] Australian soldiers I selected Brown because I trusted his bush craft, and I also trusted his ability as a soldier to back me up if I had any trouble with the others . . . In all the time I knew Brown he was never up before me on a charge. He knew just how far to go. Nevertheless, he was a first-class field soldier and I have never had cause to change that view.[68]

We learn from this that Brown's superior officer valued his capacity to work as a team player but also his independence. Clearly there was a significant measure of trust between Brown and Carroll. It is also evident that Carroll noted the distinctive skills Brown had as a result of his cultural upbringing, and saw these as highly effective contributions to the platoon. However these capacities he attributes to Brown's ethnicity, not to personal attributes. Brown is profiled according to his race, a familiar position for Australian First Nations people. Their war would not end until they could be seen as individuals with depth and unique traits that run beyond a stereotype. However this kind of testimonial probably provided a necessary stepping-stone on the path to that end. The process of change was to be extremely long. Carroll goes on about another First Nations man he commanded.

. . . I'd put Ken [Private K.H. (Kenny) Williams] at 6 feet, solidly built and a very impressive character. Again quick, a most competent Bren gunner and thoroughly sound and reliable soldier. There were never any disciplinary problems with Ken, which is more than I can say for a number of his colleagues from other Australian states of Caucasian origins . . . there was a solid reliable streak to Ken, and I would rate him as NCO potential. I lost track of these people after I returned to Australia at the end of 1959 . . . We served together as young men in the closeness that a fine platoon makes possible. Trust is complete at this level, you have to rely on your fellow soldiers, and rely on their instincts. A professional officer is always proud of a good platoon for it shows the results of hard training . . . We won the champion platoon of the battalion in 1958, being assessed as the best platoon in the battalion in training and operations. Soldiers such as Noel . . . and Kenny made this possible.[69]

During this period, Australia had overlapping involvement in regional conflicts. The Vietnam War (1962-73) was Australia's longest until its recent Afghanistan commitment. Vietnam was not a popular war from its beginning. In an era in which a cultural revolution was going on in all Western countries, the Cold War was by now transparently ideological. With a shortage of volunteers, Australia's Liberal government reintroduced National Service in 1964, probably anticipating its next move: in 1965 it extended these powers to force national servicemen to serve overseas. From 1965 to 1972, 15,381 national servicemen were deployed, with 200 killed and 1279 wounded. The scheme was abolished on 5 December 1972 by Gough Whitlam's newly elected Labor government[70] which had a better pulse on the will of the people. Many found conscription a total violation of their democratic rights.

---

[68] Col. O. M. Max Carroll, Australian War Memorial, *Too Dark for the Light Horse, op. cit.,* p. 20.
[69] Carroll, *op. cit.*
[70] Australian War Memorial, 'Conscription', *op. cit.*

During the Vietnam war, Quaker Charles Stevenson noted 'Quaker Service Australia has consistently divided earmarked funds for Vietnam equally to both north and south for civilian drug supplies in the Quaker tradition of recognising the human needs of the enemy'.[71] It was important for those seeking to remain neutral, those with the foresight, to realise that the war would not go on indefinitely, and the human lives, communities and societies would have to be rebuilt. It is never soon enough to begin.

Like each of the previous 'Australian' wars, Vietnam had its own unique characteristics. Its guerilla nature resulted in fewer psychological casualties on the battlefield. Yet the impact of fighting in an area where unexpected dangers were always present from landmines, surprise attacks, and even 'friendly fire' meant that immediate and delayed stress reactions were common. Of the 60,000 Australian Vietnam veterans, about half have had compensation claims recognised for post-traumatic stress disorder (PTSD), depression or anxiety.

A large number of First Nations peoples was among the Australian Vietnam contingent, in all areas of the forces, mainly army, but again firm numbers are not known. At least seven Aboriginal servicemen were killed, possibly more, and a number injured.[72] The personal recollections of Col. Max Carroll from the battlefield reflect on the performance of Aboriginal service people. As a white senior officer it is his words that have endured and must stand in for the voices and records of the many First Nations individuals who served in so many capacities and in experiences ranging from very positive and affirming to others who were left with disappointment, dismay and horror.

Social conditions have suppressed most of the first-hand accounts of Indigenous troops who served in Vietnam as elsewhere. Many soldiers of all colours were not well educated, having had little chance at schooling, and what they had was often interrupted. It was quite common for them to have a mate write a letter home. The language used would have betrayed that the author was probably not the family member who signed the letter. Others would have remained silent because their families moved often, avoiding authorities who continued to round up children for residential schools, and economic conditions drove people to travel in search of work. Some knew their families could not read letters, or did not have mailing addresses or postal boxes, and so regular contact was not possible. In yet other examples, letters were sent and preserved but have either been kept private or subsequently lost. The practice of journal writing would also have been less common among First Nations service men and women and their families.

It seems that all existing records in the public domain express appreciation and a sense of (qualified) equality with the Aboriginal service people, albeit maintaining stereotypes. Surprise is reflected that they were well behaved, and showed substantial heroism. There is more valuing of their bush skills by far than of the intellect that drove these skills. There were moments, or for some people, whole wars in which they were treated with condescension if not worse. The retrospective impressions changed for those who did return home and found themselves excluded from drinking with their mates, entering many RSLs, finding themselves short-changed on pay, benefits and recognition. Of course the matter of citizenship would remain moot for a long, long period after the war. In a passage that seems clear of the kind of patronising appreciation that was more common, Carroll recalls,

> During my tour of duty in Vietnam (1966–67) with the 5th Battalion of the Royal Aus-
> tralian Regional (5RAR) my time as OC of both Support Company and A Company (a
> rifle company) allowed me to serve with a further four Aboriginal soldiers . . . Corporal
> N.J. (Norman) Womal was a Queenslander, he came from Bowen and is buried in the
> Bowen cemetery. He was one of my NCOs in the Anti-Tank Platoon. He was smart, well

---

[71] Australia Yearly Meeting of the Religious Society of Friends (Quakers), *this we can say Australian Quaker Life, Faith and Thought* (2003), Charles Stevenson, S. 3.95.
[72] Clark, *op. cit.*

turned out, always immaculate in presentation, and a good instructor. I had cause, whilst in Australia, to send Norman to run a short course of a few days for some Royal Australian Air Force ground defence people on the 106 mm recoil-less rifle with which the Anti-Tank Platoon was armed. He went off on his own taking his stores and weapon with him. The letter of commendation and appreciation that I received subsequently from the Royal Australian Air Force warranted me parading him, and reading to him the contents of the letter. It also allowed me to thank him personally. Being a shy person, he was embarrassed, but that was Norm Womal, a first-class junior leader. He was most effective in the field and I had cause to see his work at close quarters when he was in my company. On 17 October 1966 at a place called Nui Thi Vai ... We were ambushed as we were sweeping up a ridge line and the signals officer was shot in the chest. The Anti-Tank Platoon, which had been leading the battalion headquarters group, had been allowed to pass through the VC ambush before it was sprung. I summoned the Anti-Tank Platoon to back down to try and take out the enemy position from above and it was during this action that Womal was hit. He was shot in the throat and, although mortally wounded, he literally held his throat together with one hand whilst he was lying in an exposed position and continued to direct the fire of his machine gunner, relaying information to both his platoon commander and myself. It was because of this extremely courageous action that we did not suffer further casualties. He was still alive when we recovered him but he died as he was being evacuated by helicopter. Everyone within 5RAR respected Norm Womal; he was a first-class junior leader and, as a result of his actions on that day, was awarded a posthumous Mention in Despatches ... Had he lived, there is no doubt in my mind Norm Womal would have been awarded a Military Medal. It was a privilege to serve with such a fine soldier.[73]

Another young soldier gave exemplary service in Vietnam as Carroll further reflects. It is gratifying here that the skill demonstrated by both soldiers was attributed to their own capacity rather than an innate racial ability. Davis was a 'full blood' from Atherton, North Queensland. In late March 1967 his company was building a large wire fence in a location between Dat Do and Phuoc Loi.

Suddenly, in a firm quiet voice, Davis called out for everyone to stand still and not move. In the middle of the group, barely protruding through the sand, were the three prongs of an M16 jumper mine. It was obvious that the [Viet Cong] had estimated the line that our fence was going to take, and even though this area had been cleared beforehand, this mine had been missed. If it had not been for Davis' sharp eyes I estimate that all of the group, including myself, would have been casualties. Everybody carefully recovered their weapons and gingerly walked away from the area, having marked the locality of the mine for our sappers to delouse. B Company, who replaced us on the fence a few days later, was not so lucky. They had a young officer named Rinkin killed when another one of these jumper mines was activated. It was Davis' sharp eyes that saved the lives of many of his mates. I also owe him my life.[74]

More recently, the Department of Defence claims to have made significant progress in eliminating discrimination in the forces, in areas such as pay, gender and racial inclusiveness. However, most First Nations enlistment in recent times, which props up these statistics, has been in the formation (beginning in the 1980s) of three Army Reserve regional force surveillance units. The units include the Pilbara Regiment, the 51st Battalion, and the Far North Queensland Regiment. The staffing of these is dominated by Aboriginal and Torres Strait Islanders.[75] While there is no doubt that First Nations people have plenty to contribute to these NORFORCE units, they do help explain why there is a

[73] Carroll, *op. cit.,* p. 21.
[74] Carroll, *op. cit.,* pp. 21-2.
[75] Clark, *op .cit.*

strong racial bias of the higher levels of the Australian Defence Force. Reservists rarely draw the attention required to move into senior and most responsible positions.

The sheer scale of commemoration of World War I, the number of 'Australian' wars in its wake, and the atrocities against civilians in which Australia has been directly or indirectly involved suggest that little has been gained or learned. Put differently, a deceptive conclusion of victory had been prematurely reached. More and better fire-power has not been the answer to threat. In part we have seen, in 9/11 and the Iraq War, as well as the ongoing Afghanistan War, a serious misperception of threat. Greater confidence and investment in working for peace, not through the barrel of a gun, but by unarmed face-to-face building of relationships of trust, does not seem the primary method employed by Australian foreign policy leaders of both major parties. This is not to suggest that Australia plays no role in diplomacy, but her close alliance to America, which goes so far as to hosting military bases on the Australian mainland, leaves little room for independent thought or action. As has been seen by events such as the Bali bombing, and the specific mention by IS in Syria of the need to kill Australians as part of their strategy of warfare against the West, Australia is not seen to stand apart but rather in line with what the Islamic extremists have come to so resent as Western imperialism.

Chapter IV
War and Resistance at Home

The face of war in our time is so awesome and terrible that the first temptation is to re-coil and turn away. Who of us has not despaired and concluded that the entire specta-cle of war has been the manifestation of organised insanity? Who of us has not been tempted to dismiss the efforts of those working for peace as futile Sisyphean labour? Medusa-like, the face of war, with its relentless horror, threatens to destroy anyone who looks at it for long. Yet we must find the courage to confront the abyss. I deep-ly believe that war is a sickness, though it may be mankind's "sickness unto death".[76]

– John Stoessinger

If we cannot look at war, neither can we afford to look away. The ripples of its destructive forces carry on and on through peacetime and into the most remote corners of our earth and our lives. To under-stand the place of World War I we must first look beyond it in Australian history, to the beginning of its first modern war. This is the nameless one to which historian Henry Reynolds has devoted two books, and can only be recognised in the larger categories of scholarship as the 'Australian Civil War'.

> . . . the contribution of Aborigines and Torres Strait Islanders to the armed forces in the many wars since Federation has been increasingly recognised and commemorated . . . While this is to be welcomed, it draws attention away from the armed conflict that was the central feature of the relationship between settlers and the Indigenous nations. Ab-origines who fought for the white man are remembered with reverence. The many more who fought against him are forgotten . . . it will be unconscionable to indulge in a crescen-do of commemoration and ignore the fundamental importance of the war between set-tlers and Indigenous nations within Australia. This is the forgotten war of conquest that saw the expropriation of the most productive land over vast continental distances, and the transfer of sovereignty from the Aborigines to the British government and its successive colonial administrations. This is the war that made the nation, not the fateful invasion of Turkey at the direction of the imperial government.[77]

---

[76] John G. Stoessinger, *Why Nations Go to War*, 3rd ed. New York: St. Martin's Press, 1982, p. 204.

[77] Henry Reynolds, *Forgotten War*, Sydney: NewSouth Publishing, p. 6.

As this volume suggests, it becomes impossible to consider a single war in isolation in the history of any country. We cannot understand Australia as a country without grappling with its relationship to war and to peace. It is impossible to wrap our heads around the ongoing conflict in Afghanistan without knowing about previous conflicts and invasions that fostered hostilities, brought intolerable anguish, and provided arms and hostilities that continue to erode the stability of life there.

If we consider the subtext of the political culture of memorialisation, much is revealed between the lines. For example, in its resource kit, 'Too Dark for the Light Horse', the Australian War Museum includes ideas about how school children might delve deeper into the history of warfare. In a small segment suggesting they might set up their own museum or memory box, the following advice is given: 'Gather material: Ask around your local area for relevant material; these may include medals, badges, discharge certificates, photos, old cigarette tins, uniforms, diaries, letters or you could record some oral histories.'[78] Combined with the memory box that has been lent by the War Museum, which contains photos of Aboriginal soldiers, badges, Indigenous women and girls knitting warm clothing at a mission, a corroboree in traditional dress with enlisted white soldiers in uniform watching, images of military vessels, et cetera. it is clear that the students are to build up the ideas that have already been presented to them, the now-hackneyed themes of war at home and away – with brown faces added. But to capture the colour spectrum of war is to include much that would not be according to the War Museum's recipe.

One of the ongoing silences in the record is the assumption that wars have no impact on the relationships between Indigenous service people and their communities. There is rather an assumption that they have their traditional culture and land to which to return, a deceptive notion since the rules of enlistment meant that most often it was First Nations people who were fair, mostly of mixed race, and had been 'Westernised' who were acceptable in uniform. This paints a very different picture from the deep respect expressed by comrades and superiors for the tracking and bush skills of Indigenous men in battle. Arguably, many of those who served did so because they had already been deprived of their country, people, culture and or livelihood by the White majority. Many more had been dispossessed from Country, to which they belonged, and where they thrived on the foods and age-old economies of exchange, hunting, gathering, and as we now know, agricultural land management under Laws that governed diplomacy and independence.

Children are to take away from the 'Memory Box' exercise the lesson that every good Aborigine participated in the war effort as they could. Not one actively resisted the conflict in any way, nor even harboured secret sentiments that resources being poured into these war efforts might have been better spent compensating First Nations for their losses and improving their quality of life. Somehow they had forgotten the massacres and dispossession of their people and were grateful to white Australia even unto death. But this imputed enthusiasm for war did not mean that they had become fully worthy or qualified as Australians (hence justifying their non-payment or severe underpayment, for example, for work as trackers and coast watchers, and informal companies which deceived its men into thinking they were enlisted), and so backs up the history which did not count them in the census or afford them the vote until more recent times.

Ultimately, the War Memorial invites students to weave First Nations people into the dominant narrative, rather than to interrogate it critically. In lieu of scrutinising the impressive documentation in the resource book and elsewhere, which provides considerable evidence of injustice toward Indigenous people throughout the First and Second World Wars and beyond, children are led back to the myths with which most likely began. This suggests, sadly, that the 'Memory Box' project may be ultimately a grand, expensive and unfortunate failure, or worse, yet another surface exercise in the celebration of militarism as the core of the national identity, overlaid by surfing, the Sydney Opera House, kangaroos, and a surplus boomerang.

---

[78] Australian War Memorial, *Too Dark for the Light Horse, op. cit.,* p. 32.

When moral convictions stood in the way of enlisting, people struggled to find the language that expressed the strength and directions of their commitments. Many held their silence, just as so many Australian veterans have come back from all fronts with laconic demeanour and states of mind too complex for words. One British pacifist, Corder Catchpool, was among many imprisoned for almost three years. He wrote, 'We conscientious objectors are often called cowards and shirkers ... Loyalty to principle prevents us from expressing loyalty to country in the same way as the soldier, but I dare to hope, none the less, that we are still patriots.'[79]

With the inclusion of women and First Nations soldiers in Australian World War I commemoration, and war service workers, comes a new exhortation, from Chloe Mason's perspective: "We must not forget those who were ridiculed, jailed and worse for daring to fight for peace". Their contribution is a source of both consolation and inspiration for the future. There were others, among them many women and First Nations Australians, who chose to avoid the war effort entirely by turning their backs on opportunities to enlist directly or in supportive industries. These people are of course large unrecorded, since they did not enlist, yet their quiet but important witness also placed a restraint on the conflagrations of war. Often this was a significant personal expense given employment was difficult to acquire.

Although a truth that has generally been silenced in the larger historical narrative of World War I, Australia remains far from united in its position vis-a-vis its wars. Throughout all its years of conflict, the country has been divided in its sentiments. Both those unspoken and those loudly voiced became differences creating rifts in communities, families, and the society at large. Some divergences dating back to World War I continue to underlie segmentation in the civil society to this day. Branches of families lost touch with one another as they turned their backs on 'he who was too cowardly to fight' but in fact who had chosen the courageous and lonely road of the war resister. In some families young people may have simply disappeared rather than face the disapproval of their loved ones, church, or community for going against the predominant leading, one way or another.

In the UK, compulsory military training before World War I was opposed by Quakers and other pacifists. Any man taking such a position or was imprisoned for refusing the training was offered support by Friends. Spies were active in reporting those who gave voice to conscientious objection. Chloe Mason reported that her own family members were imprisoned as a result. In Australia, as a result of the rejection of adult conscription, it was the compulsory training of children that provided the most fertile ground for voluntary recruitment but this also became a flashpoint for resistance. Controversially, children were legislated into the preparations for war because it was too much of a political hot potato to do so with adults. To some Australians this meant the government was taking advantage of the lack of political clout and vulnerability of children.

The *Defence Act 1903* was one of the first pieces of legislation passed by the new Commonwealth government, and it gave the government the power to conscript for the purposes of home defence. The legislation did not allow soldiers to be drafted for overseas service. It was used as a way to train the minds and bodies of potential soldiers, with no age limit, so that they would respond readily if the call came for an overseas fighting force. Indeed it would transpire that this was an accurate gamble, however unjust in the view of many.

The Universal Service Scheme was the first system of compulsory military service in Australia, and included underage schoolboys. The legislation for compulsory military training was introduced in 1909 by Prime Minister Alfred Deakin, and was passed into law in 1911. Already by February 1913, 35 boys in Melbourne area alone were detained at Queenscliff Fort for non-compliance. The legislation

---

[79] T. Corder Catchpool, *On Two Fronts*, 1918. http://c.ymcdn.com/sites/ www.quakers.org.au/ resource/resmgr/WW1_poster/ WW1_Exhibition_banners_Part5.pdf accessed 14/12/2016.

was strongly contested, particularly in the early years of World War I when it seemed possible that conscription might be extended to include overseas service.[80]

One young man was sentenced to 53 days where another was put in solitary confinement on gruel, bread and water alone. Some served two or even three terms in detention. Neither were conditions lightened for those underage. Quaker Tom Roberts, aged 16, had been seriously ill and managed to delay his sentence briefly. However he soon found himself in Queenscliff. There little regard was given to his wellbeing or even life chances. The record shows:

> A few days later, the parents visited Tom and found that, on refusing to drill, he had been put in the guard-room for two days, and was then committed to solitary confinement on "half-rations" for seven days. Tom Roberts was threatened with further periods of solitary confinement if he continued to refuse to drill. Widespread coverage in the press, and questions asked in parliament, eventually resulted in Tom Roberts' release. The government promised to abolish solitary confinement for trainees.[81]

During the war years there were over 27,000 convictions for non-compliance, including over 7000 youth placed in continuous detention.[82] This was harsh punishment indeed for what was either a matter of conscience of the young people or a question of respecting their parents and religion or following the dictates of the state.

The need to formulate a corporate position on national issues such as race and defense policy was becoming pressing as Federation approached. For some, this was legislation that could not in good conscience be obeyed. At their national meeting in that year, Australian Quakers anticipated and made public their readiness for civil disobedience, stating 'As those who desire to remain law-abiding citizens of the Commonwealth, we are reluctantly compelled to declare that if these proposals are passed into law we shall be bound by our Christian consciences to refuse to yield them obedience'. The Peace Committee of London Yearly Meeting of Friends (Quakers) sent a concerned deputation to Australia in 1912 to help in the struggle against the compulsory clauses of the *Defence Act*.[83] Quakers contended that the preparation for war would only create division, not prevent war. In particular they believed that children ought not to be taught the necessity of war, much less its glory.

Tessa Bremner noted that 21,000 boys from various religious denominations were prosecuted between 1911 and 1913 for refusing their cadet service. Some parents were convicted for not allowing their boys to be registered. Two Queensland Quaker families moved from the town into the country because the compulsion did not apply to those living more than five miles from the nearest training centre. In South Australia, an Anti-Military Service League was founded, later renamed the Australian Freedom League by Quakers including John Hills and Percy Fletcher in 1912. Fletcher, editor of its journal *Freedom*, assisted in establishing branches in Melbourne, Hobart and Sydney, though it remained strongest in South Australia. There was a number of women's branches among them. Such early efforts against child conscription laid the groundwork for the successful 'No' vote in the conscription referenda of 1916 and 1917. Nevertheless, the law on cadet service was in effect until 1929.[84]

---

[80] Australian War Memorial, https://www.awm.gov.au/encyclopedia/ conscription/, accessed 11/2/2016. Also http://c.ymcdn.com/sites/ www.quakers.org.au/resource/resmgr/WW1_ poster/WW1_Exhibition_banners_ Part3.pdf accessed 26/10/16.

[81] http://c.ymcdn.com/sites/www.quakers.org.au/resource/resmgr/ WW1_poster/WW1_Exhibition_banners_Part4.pdf accessed 26/10/2016.

[82] http://c.ymcdn.com/sites/www.quakers.org.au/resource/resmgr/ WW1_poster/WW1_Exhibition_banners_Part4.pdf accessed 26/10/2016.

[83] *this we can say, op. cit.,* s. 7.12

[84] *Ibid.*

Despite the peace witness of Quakers, the compulsory military training for boys and the penalties associated with failing to participate had a significant impact, as Chloe Mason describes. Many of those who were of age to enlist had been pressured and socialised to do so. Therefore about one third of young Quaker men enlisted. For others, this was regarded as 'backsliding from the peace testimony' which Friends had held since the 1650s. However, Quakers are not bound by rule but by individual conscience, so such judgments were harsh and adversely impacted the lives and continued association of such men with the Religious Society of Friends. It was also interesting for the commemoration research committee to discover evidence that geographic variation underpinned the extent of supportive networks for young men of enlistment age.

During the war, a wave of strikes and two campaigns around conscription created particularly bitter divisions among communities and families. The pre-war period was also a time when the tide was turning in Great Britain: numerous strikes were threatening to grind the economy to a halt just when large scale industrial preparations for war were proceeding. But urban life was for many Brits one of poverty, sickness and disease. Many skilled industrial workers were required to put in an eighty hour week. The long-disinherited were asserting their claims while the ruling classes went about their expensive and gay lives, largely uncomprehending of the paradigm shift that was shortly to come upon them too.[85]

Australia's biggest socialist group was the Victorian Socialist Party (VSP), which included future prime minister John Curtin. Despite a membership of 2000, the VSP was stunned by betrayal when its own members refused to strike, and by news of European socialist parties obediently following their governments' edicts to enlist.[86] So much for the workers of the world uniting!

The most successful union effort was made by the Industrial Workers of the World (IWW), commonly known as the 'Wobblies'. First established in the United States in 1905, they went on to take root in Australia in 1911. Their first major anti-war rally in Australia was held on Sydney's Domain on 8 August, 1914. A week later during a follow-up event, they sold 400 copies of their *Direct Action* paper.

The Wobblies based their opposition to war on class terms with strong, direct language. 'WAR! What for? For the workers and their dependents: death, starvation, poverty and untold misery; for the capitalist class: gold stained with blood of millions, riotous luxury, banquets of jubilation over the graves of their dupes and slaves. War is Hell! Send the capitalists to hell and wars are impossible.' The Wobblies hit some home truths with this message: some industries did flourish during wartime, and some people were greatly enriched. It was true that campaigns such as Gallipoli were hopeless affairs from the first hours, and yet the British leaders insisted that the men fight on, with horrific cost to human life and limb on both sides. Unsurprisingly, after the news of Gallipoli arrived in Australia, more effective strike efforts became possible.[87]

> . . . rats in the same field-grey as the invisible enemy, that were as big as cats and utterly fearless, skittering over your face in the dark, leaping out of knapsacks, darting in to take the very crusts from under your nose. The rats were fat because they fed on corpses, burrowing right into a man's guts or tumbling about in dozens in the bellies of horses. They fed. The guns, Jim felt, he would get used to . . . they meant you were opposed to other men, much like yourself, and suffering the same hardships. But the rats were another species. And for him they were familiars of death, creatures of the underworld . . .[88]

---

[85] National Library of Australia, *On the Idle Hill of Summer*, BBC film, *op. cit.*
[86] Salmon, *op. cit.*
[87] Salmon, *op. cit.*
[88] Malouf, *op. cit.*, p. 81.

The increasing cost of living seemed unjust and at odds with the many sacrifices that Australians were making. It is perhaps little wonder that the Broken Hill coal miners were successful in winning a 44 hour week as a result of their 1916 strike. This paved the way for further success in their 1919-20 strike.[89]

Preparations for the 1916 referendum led to bitter and socially damaging divisions between those in favour of conscription and those opposed. In Melbourne, Curtin of the Wobblies, as well as Adela Pankhurst and Vida Goldstein, were amongst those who led the 'No' campaign with such groups as the Victorian Socialist Party and the Women's Peace Army. In Broken Hill, the Labor Volunteer Army was formed, led by Percy Brookfield. In the elections of the following year he was elected member in the New South Wales parliament for the area.[90]

But the defeats were many. Not surprisingly, there were concerted political efforts to squelch the momentum of the labour movement in its anti-war efforts. Preceding the conscription campaign of 1916, 12 Wobbly leaders were framed by the New South Wales government, charged with plotting to burn Sydney and sedition. Their jail terms extended from five to fifteen years. Due to public outcry, these leaders were released in 1920, by which time the IWW movement had dissolved.[91]

Yet many fought on. The railway workers in Sydney's Eveleigh and Randwick railway workshops staged a strike in August 1917 in opposition to a card system, a protest that was not put down until late September. This card system was eventually implemented across Australia.

The union movement received reinforcements from returned soldiers who were disgruntled with the treatment they had received abroad and their paltry reception and compensation at home. Strikes continued therefore in the wake of the war, into 1919 and 1920. The maritime workers, Fremantle lumpers and miners of Broken Hill earned hard-won victories. Some soldiers and unionists joined the Communist Party of Australia after its formation in 1920.

Prime Minister Hughes made a second expensive attempt at conscription, facing a seemingly exhausted public. However, the referendum that eventuated in December 1917 sent an even clearer message of rejection than did the preceding one. Undeterred, the new government of 1917 passed the *Unlawful Associations Act*, which allowed them to ban the IWW. As Tessa Bremner notes, other new legislation was passed as a political backlash against those who opposed the war in any form. It became an offence to say or do anything that might prejudice recruitment. In Britain conscientious objectors had to choose between alternative service, such as the Friends Ambulance Unit, and were known as 'alternists'; or 'absolutists', who refused to serve entirely and could be imprisoned. There is now a memorial to conscientious objectors in Tavistock Square, London. Australia has no such memorial to those who paid a very high price for following their conscience in favour of peace.

The Russian Revolution put a further nail in the coffin of the Australian war campaign. At the 1918 federal Labor Conference, an anti-war resolution was passed.[92] Even at the political level, the message was now getting through that a large segment of the Australian public opposed the war.

While those who served in the armed forces were generally silenced by their commitment, according to Guy Hansen some senior officers did manage to express disillusionment as they were less subject to censorship than troops. However, the personal and political views up and down the ranks are well reflected in their private papers, with diaries being most revealing. It was not uncommon to have second thoughts about enlisting once one saw the reality of what was occurring at the front.

---

[89] Salmon, *op. cit.*

[90] Salmon, *op. cit.*

[91] Salmon, *op. cit.*

[92] Salmon, *op. cit.*

'Listen Wizzer,' Jim began again, 'we've got t'get outa here and find the rest of the platoon.' 'Not me,' Wizzer said, springing to the alert. Just that, but Jim saw that he meant it, was in no way abashed, and assumed in his own frank admission of cowardice that they were two of a kind. Jim began to be alarmed. He tried in the dark to locate his rifle. He had stopped hearing the noise overhead. There were so many ways of being afraid; you couldn't be all of them at the same time.[93]

What were community reactions to the threat and outbreak of another World War? First Nations peoples were divided over whether to serve, particularly after seeing the outcomes of the First World War. There were those Aboriginal organisations which, in 1939, hoped that by serving, their claims for citizenship would be better received. For this reason, they pushed for the formation of First Nations battalions which would maximise popular exposure of their contribution to 'the cause' across Australia. When the number of lives lost through innocent efforts to survive on their own lands in the face of the white invasion is considered, and the additional count of those who died defending their way of life and territories is added, is seems paradoxical that they might have to choose to sacrifice even more of their numbers to establish themselves in the eyes of what had long since become a white majority. Then there were many others who entirely opposed service by First Nations people.

> William Cooper, the Secretary of the Australian Aborigines' League, argued that Aborigines should not fight for white Australia. Cooper's own son had been killed in the First World War, and Cooper was bitter that Aboriginal sacrifice then had not brought any improvement in rights and conditions. He likened conditions in white-administered Aboriginal settlements to those suffered by Jews under Hitler, and demanded that the Aborigines' lot be improved at home before they take up 'the privilege of defending the land which was taken from him by the white race without compensation or even kindness'.[94]

In his senior years, Bill Oats acquired a handle on some of the questions that vexed him as a young man. Today his words very aptly reflect on Australia's race politics and its endemic domestic violence as well as the regional and global contexts:

> We need to have a much deeper concept of peace than the negative assumption that it is simply an absence of war. Peace is an organic concept, living and creative, and concerned with the relationships between people and groups of people. Peace is the state of health of the body politic, but more fundamentally peace is a matter of the spiritual, mental and emotional health of individual bodies . . .The biggest threat to the future of humanity is not the atomic bomb, but the provincial mind, the limited outlook, the myopia which prevents us from seeing beyond our own immediate interests . . .especially in our attitudes to people who are different from ourselves in colour, in religious creed, in political affiliation, in educational opportunities, in abilities. Acceptance of others is not merely tolerating others. It is an affirmation of the importance of variety and difference. The most primitive reaction to the fact of difference is one of fear – the other is difference and therefore a threat, a danger.[95]

For every bead on the string of major World War II events that remain burned in the memories of subsequent generations, such as the Holocaust and the atomic bombs, there are thousands more that have become invisible to us, we the generation of both 'peacetime' and perpetual war. For many of us, it is the precious stories of relatives and their war experiences that somehow keep our connection to past conflicts alive. This is as important for pacifists and conscientious objectors as for those who feel or felt that war was justified. Australian Robert J. Burrowes recalls the fate of his uncle after whom he

[93] Malouf, *op. cit.*, p. 91.
[94] Australian War Memorial, *Too Dark for the Light Horse, op. cit.*, p. 16.
[95] William Oats, 1990, *this we can say, op. cit.*, S. 3.105

40

was named. Such chilling accounts bear telling witness to the paradox of war.

> Bob was a soldier in the 34th Fortress Engineers of the Australian Imperial Force (AIF). He was captured during the fall of Rabaul on 22 January 1942, held prisoner and half-starved at the Malaguna Road camp until he was put on the Japanese prisoner-of-war ship *Montevideo Maru* in late June. On 1 July 1942, the unmarked and unescorted *Montevideo Maru* was torpedoed off Luzon by the *USS Sturgeon*. The ship sank in six minutes. All 1,053 Australian prisoners of war were killed: it was Australia's largest single loss of life in a single incident during the entire war.[96]

Probably few Australians would cite this as a major loss of the war. Quakers, like most people of decency around the world, were horrified by the atomic bombs, no matter what the Japanese troops had done. Sensible people could see that they were in the service of an Emperor whom they had been trained to believe was God, and they were told that there were only two choices: victory or death. Quakers wrote to the Japanese Friends:

> Dear Friends in Christ,
>
> We want at this time to send you a message of loving sympathy and deep regret for the suffering and devastation which have come to you as a result of war. We have been reminded that we are members of one another, and that in a very real sense the world is one. We long to be able to share and to lighten the burden which is yours, and we look forward to a time when we can once more find joy and inspiration in fellowship with you.
>
> Here in Australia, after our forest fires, the tree trunks stand gaunt and blackened, with leafless boughs held up to heaven. In time, new leaves appear and the trees once more are green and beautiful. We have the promise, 'Behold I make all things new'. May you find courage and strength to build once more on the firm foundation laid in the past, and be sustained by the knowledge that Friends the world over feel at one with you and are holding you in their thoughts and prayers.[97]

Paradoxically, in our time, war between nuclear superpowers is suicidal: there can be no winners. Today's hydrogen bombs are far more powerful than the bombs dropped on Japan in 1945. Nuclear warheads are useful for deterrence, perhaps, but much less so for actual confrontation with the most powerful of enemies. This is why the Cold War occurred, with many hot wars used as surrogates to avoid the direct confrontation that could not be allowed to happen between the USSR and America. Wars that drag on, wars in which superpowers often do engage, are most often those with a range of smaller powers, often with forces other than nation-states being key actors. The current Syrian War is a good illustration of this. The preparedness and willingness to wage war, in other words the logic of deterrence carried to the next step, makes the possibility of actual confrontation much more likely.

States justify to their own people the continuous building and rebuilding of their arsenals by curious means, even if some taxpayers return home in body bags to make the point. Disarmament has consequently become a key focus of anti-war activists. A world without major disputes may never exist, but the facility with which a 'minute-man' can press the button, in which drones strike civilians, hospitals, schools, orphanages, and other clearly non-strategic targets with impunity can be greatly reduced. This would allow time and space for negotiation and the strengthening of the global political community in which the tool of choice is diplomacy rather than the arsenal.

A particular thread of disarmament logic focuses on arms control. This implies stabilising existing arms stocks (albeit allowing for continuous updating of arsenals) and the prevention of arms build-ups and races. However, this approach can be an eventual source of mistrust because reported counts

---

[96] http://robertjburrowes.wordpress.com accessed 20/03/2016.
[97] Australia General Meeting, 1925, *this we can say, op. cit.,* S. 3.92.

and weapons do not always correspond to the reality, or are not believed to be accurate representations of the holdings of a particular state. When mistrust runs high then politicians do not think the best of one another, particularly if they are locked into an ideological perspective that paints others with a different hue.

The Iraq war presents a poignant example of this trend. The Americans and British alleged that they had intelligence confirming that Saddam Hussein's regime held unreported 'weapons of mass destruction' and connections to al-Qaeda. That government refuted this but to no avail. Despite the invasion and monumental destruction, none was found. The British government has admitted that it had 'inaccurate information' but has never come clean to say that this was simply a way of duping the public into agreeing to go to war, that it simply wanted to overthrow the Hussein government. Saddam was clearly a dictator, and estimates of how many of his own citizens he killed run to 250,000,[98] but this was not the imputed cause of the invasion. Indeed it could not be: the US remains very friendly with other authoritarian regimes.

John Stoessinger has identified a number of elements that seem to many war-resisters as key causes of war. He suggests that only settlements based on equality are likely to hold, and this kind of respect is rare. Where it exists, parties are unlikely to engage in violent conflict to resolve their differences. Misperception is a key incentive for violence as assessed by Stoessinger. Typical manifestations are the distortion of leaders' images of themselves, their adversaries and their intentions, as well as of the powers of both sides. This obviously occurred in the case of the Iraq war. The confident expectation of triumph after a brief campaign is a common result of these misperceptions. Many individuals and countries have gone into specific wars only because this expectation was so 'certain'. Thus there is a kind of accidental circumstance that contributes to the outbreak of war: the assassination of a duke, the illusion or suspicion that weapons of mass destruction exist, the assumption that an arch-terrorist is hiding, like the 'red under the bed' somewhere under the wary eyes of those whose land has been too often ravaged, or even where peace reigns. Sadly it is often during warfare that revelations occur and misperceptions are gradually exposed, but often much too late for all its victims, including fighters, civilians at the warfront and in faraway communities.

Two things become clear to those who, however reluctantly, feel a sense they cannot shrug off the need to struggle against all warfare. Firstly they believe that there has been far more than enough warfare in the world to demonstrate its ultimate futility: that one battle leads to another and another, and one war is merely a segue to the next. Indeed war prepares a ground of bitterness, mistrust, and desire for revenge. This might be called 'an eye for an eye' logic. Because of the misperceptions and accidents upon which wars are built, they do not exist on firm ground and cannot be won, no matter the fire power deployed. There are no winners.

Secondly, the destructive nature of wars, particularly the extraordinary devastation wrought by modern weaponry, is such that no ends can be justified by such means. This has become particularly true as technology has increased in scope and capacity to do damage to enormous and distant landmasses and populations. The environmental impacts defy measurement, but we know that Europe will never look as it did before WWI, that global warming has been hastened by warfare, and that some terrains, for example in Vietnam, have been rendered uninhabitable. Often this destruction is of such long duration that it becomes a health and environmental reality with which generations have to live. In 2018 there are still children being born with severe malformations as a result of residue toxins and the

---

[98] Human Rights Watch, 25/1/ 2004, 'War in Iraq: Not a Humanitarian Intervention', https:// www.hrw.org/news/2004/01/25/war-iraq-not- humanitarian-intervention accessed 19/3/2016.

ill-health of parents. There is simply no rebuilding of cultures, civilisations, communities, and biota that have been extinguished by war. Therefore there are no defensive justifications for it, and offensive wars have long been disavowed by the United Nations and all but the most totalitarian or misguided regimes. However actions speak louder than words.

Furthermore, the major investment in the preparations for war is costly, 3-5% of gross domestic profit in many democracies and above 10% in a number of countries in the Middle East and Africa.[99] Between 2002 and 2012, North Korea spent about one quarter of its GDP on arms, according to the US State Department.[100] While figures may be sketchy, it is known that poverty is rampant and human rights few in this state. Peacebuilders are convinced that were such money dedicated to making a just peace, righting the wrongs of the past and providing for those most disadvantaged, there would be much less likelihood of war. It is not only leaders who wage war. They require 'willing' or at least less-than-rebellious troops. Sometimes this is accomplished by such measures or threats of force and cruelty that little choice is apparent. It is by playing upon real or alleged injustices and disadvantages, often assigning blame to the 'adversary', that such forces are raised. We have also seen how serving in armed forces can provide opportunities for education, advancement, enfranchisement and recognition for marginalised groups. Among these, we may particularly note the cases of women and First Nations peoples in Australia. Such promise is not always realised, and there can be many hidden costs.

But other than in totalitarian states, the public will not tolerate or cooperate with warfare that it deems at odds with its interests. This is one of the reasons why so many civil wars are being waged in the world: groups of peoples feel they are not being represented by their governments and others, and that violence is their only or final option to get past this condition. They may become quite vulnerable to populist leaders who spearhead movements that promise to do away with the old guard and to uphold and rebuild along the lines of the people's dreams. This of course is what Hitler did, but few imagined that his dream would go down such a dark path, dragging the German public with him under totalitarian conditions. Even in a wealthy country such as the United States, this is the appeal of individuals such as Donald Trump, or in Australia of Arthur Calwell, Joe Bjelke Petersen or Pauline Hanson, to many who feel marginalised. Such leaders hold up simple answers, scapegoating innocent parties, often at great cost, and many are willing to believe these accounts. They usually come with 'easy' promises and 'solutions', on the surface: build a wall, send them 'home', rebuild the industrial jobs, and so on. However such claims are empty, even destructive, may incite violence, and draw publicity away from the more nuanced discussions of which they are capable. For example, how can jobs be provided in a post-industrial economy?

The dream of most pacifists is that the world will transcend the current global order that seems to depend so fundamentally on the balance of military might. One of the darkest conspiracy theories is that global warming has itself been caused, not by the massive overuse of carbon fuels, but as a political tool to force countries into a new world order in which they would work together.[101] It is presumed that the United Nations has been a central player in this conspiracy, supported by those who are calling for dramatic changes in emissions, including the Australian Labor Party and the Greens.

It is unfortunate that more information and rigorous science have not been embraced in such climate change debates. Of course a drastic reduction of greenhouse gases will likely cause a pinch in lifestyle. But it will also bring business opportunities, and the hope that human and other life will be greatly

---

[99] World Bank, http://data.worldbank.org/indicator/MS.MIL.XPND.GD.ZS accessed 2/3/2016.
[100] *Korean Times,* 'N. Korea spends quarter of GDP on military 2002-2012: US Data', 1 April 2016, *http://www.koreatimes.co.kr/www/news/nation/ 2016/01/485_194556.html*, accessed 16/9/2016.
[101] https://www.youtube.com/watch?v=YHCD6GQ7dCw accessed 2/3/2016.

extended. Consideration is not given by those subscribing to the conspiracy theory to the role of military interventions in increasing pollution levels, often to entirely toxic levels. Publicly available information, such as the fact that the United Nations does not tax but merely calculates and request quotas as contributions from its members, is also ignored. Perhaps most troubling is that the majority of those who are convinced by this line of thinking live in the United States, which also spends the greatest amount on its military in absolute terms. It is also very influential in deciding where violent conflicts will occur around the world.

Such conspiracy theories appeal to those who feel threatened. They resent the prospect that their way of life may need to change, or that changes they have experienced are permanent. They see the 'freedoms' that they enjoy in a prosperous society as prone to erosion. The freedom to own and drive large consumers of fossil fuels, such as the private 'Hummer', a military vehicle adapted for road use, is one they want to defend. The right to own not only one but often several large homes filled with electronic devices, and cooled or heated 365 days a year is one they are willing to fight for. The protection of these freedoms is one of the reasons that the American presidency was established to be weak, having few powers, compared to the British monarchy.

The 'freedom' for citizens to bear arms (also a reaction to the dominance of the monarchy at time of US independence) is resulting in over 10 deaths per 100,000 per year, often of close family members, in America. It is a right apparently worth defending with violence (by stockpiling weapons in the home).[102] One recent example was shocking enough to make Australian headlines, but is in fact representative. In 2015 about 265 American children shot someone.[103] This statistic highlights the cruelty of exposing children to a world in which the use of arms is the norm and a source of 'fun'. One example is worth considering, fortunately where there was no death, but which should send out a chill. Darren Boyle for *Mail Online* reported,

> A high-profile pro-gun activist was shot in the back by her four-year-old son after he found her pistol lying on the back seat of her truck just 24 hours after she boasted about his shooting skills online. Jamie Gilt, 31, who posts about firearms on her social media accounts was driving through Putnam County, Jacksonville, Florida, on Tuesday in her truck when she was wounded after the toddler picked up the weapon and shot her in the back. It came just a day after she said the youngster would get 'jacked up' before a shooting practice on a page dedicated to her musings on Second Amendment rights. On the profile 'Jamie Gilt for Gun Sense' she wrote: 'Even my 4 year old gets jacked up to target shoot with the .22'.[104]

---

[102] https://en.wikipedia.org/wiki/List_of_countries_by_firearm-_related_death_rate accessed 2/3/2016.

[103] Adam Lidgett, 'Accidental Gun Deaths Involving Children are a Major Problem in the US', *International Business Times*, 01/06/2016 http://www.ibtimes.com/ accidental-gun-deaths-involving-children-are-major-problem-us-2250568 accessed 22/08/2016.

[104] Darren Boyle, *Mail Online*, 14/3/2016, http://www.dailymail.co.uk/news/article-3484064/Pro-gun-poster-girl-shot-four-year-old-son-driving-Florida-boy-pistol-seat-truck-truck.html. #ixzz42qNBo09x accessed 16/3/2016.

Chapter V
Impacts of War: During and After

> I think of Anzacs when the dusk comes down
>   upon the gums – of Anzacs tough and tall.
> Guarding this gateway, Diggers strong and brown.
>   and when, thro' Winter's thunderings, sounds their call,
>   like Anzacs, too, they fall...
> Their ranks grow thin upon the hill's high crown:
> my sentinels! But, where those ramparts frown,
>   their stout sons mend the wall.[105]
> – C.J. Dennis

Wars make impacts, often permanent, on the people who experience them. This poem, written in about 1932, illustrates the central place that the Anzac experience had in the author's mind and heart. Although Dennis is writing ostensibly about his garden, the Anzacs are his primary analogy. They continued to cast a shadow across his life until his untimely death in 1936. Many veterans found their experience of war unspeakable in post-war Australia, which had moved on to new social, economic and political realities. There was guilt for many returnees: survivor guilt for the mates who did not come home, echoes of questions 'Why me? Why me when others, fine blokes, didn't make it?' There was guilt for being found insufficient, as breadwinners, as husbands, sons, fathers, and lovers, for those who came back damaged by the war, not the larger-than-life heroes portrayed in the media.

> ... he tried not to look at the place under the blanket where Eric's feet should have been, or at his pinched face. Eric looked scared, as if he were afraid of what might be done to him. *Isn't it done already?* Jim asked himself. *What more?* 'One thing I'm sorry about,' Eric said plaintively. 'I never learned to ride a bike.' He lay still with the pale sweat gathering on his upper lip. Then said abruptly: 'Listen, Jim, who's gunna look after me?' 'What?' 'When I get outa here. At home 'n all ... I got no one, not even an auntie. I'm an orfing.'[106]

Graham Walker, a veteran of the Vietnam War and active worker for the Vietnam Veterans Federation, made a presentation during the Anzac Conversations which he entitled 'The Other Side of

---

[105] C. J. Dennis, 'Green Walls' excerpted from *Selected Verse of C. J. Dennis*, Angus & Robertson, 1950, as reprinted in *My Country op. cit.*, p. 525.
[106] Malouf, *op. cit.*, p. 85.

the Anzac Story'. He began by referring to post-traumatic stress as an 'epidemic' that began on the war front in 1914, and became known as shell-shock. Returned soldiers, Walker notes, faced an uncomprehending public. Many families and communities found that a generation of young men was crushed, either gone with no funeral possible or returned in body, part or whole but with a mind that was decidedly damaged by trauma and sometimes the effects of gas. The military and the government made light of these problems, and did not offer compensation to most but simply deemed them 'unfit' and argued their mental disorders were a liability to the Armed Forces, not caused by the line of duty. Families were left empty-handed and damaged.

The suffering of those debilitated by trauma during the war set an example: they were subsequently regarded as 'weak' by family and community. Pensions were frequently denied to deserving soldiers, Walker indicated. Many others succumbed at some later stage after returning home and had no compensation. Vera Brittain spoke of this destruction of men and their souls as 'a crime again civilisation'.[107] This may have been the germ that eventually sprouted the 'crimes against humanity' concept.

There was no compensation for this 'epidemic' which would frequently bring on lifelong difficulties. It was to those at home incomprehensible why the peace of Australia and reunion with loved ones would not bring recovery. Flashbacks went on, disrupting sleep and daily life. Mood swings were commonplace. The inability to concentrate or relate to people around them led to frustration and mistrust. Often injured men could not work, or could only take light jobs rather than the heavy work they had been expected to shoulder upon their return. What had happened to the soldier from the front, expected to come home heroically proportioned? 'Angry disposition' was repeatedly cited as a reason for friction, loss of jobs, frequent moves, and marriages ending. Younger brothers or cousins had sometimes 'usurped' their roles within the family, which was also demeaning and even enraging. 'Violent behaviour' (after all the purpose of war) affected families but was not seen as related to shell-shock or implicating the government.

'Shell-shock' was especially associated with heavy artillery bombardments. Walker listed the symptoms as far more than physical: mental impairment, paralysis, insomnia, blindness, headaches, deafness and tremors among others. The authorities initially saw this as malingering, moral weakness or a genetic predisposition. In any case the fault lay with the soldier. It was not until many decades later that the medical profession recognised that like many diseases no one was immune, and that the cause lay with the trauma of war and no individual weakness. It should be noted that medical staff, non-combatants serving other roles near a front, and civilians were also casualties of this epidemic. Even some who never left Australia could suffer from it if they or their families were hard enough hit by the effects of the war, such as many casualties in a single family. More recently we have seen the heavy mental and emotional costs as an epidemic of post-traumatic stress syndrome (PTSD) has hit those who have suffered trauma through abuse, in particular child sexual abuse. In total, 10 per cent of Australians are likely to suffer from this condition during their lifetimes, according to a 2013 ABC story; second only to depression.[108]

> Potentially traumatic events are powerful and upsetting incidents that intrude into daily life. They are usually defined as experiences which are life threatening, or where there is a significant threat to one's physical or psychological wellbeing. The same event may have little impact on one person but cause severe distress in another individual. The impact that an event has may be related to the person's mental and physical health, level of available support at the time of the event, and past experience and coping skills.[109]

---

[107] Tessa Bremner, *op. cit.*

[108] Melissa Brown, http://www.abc.net.au/news/2013-08-27/ptsd-depression-mental-illness/4915164 accessed 16/12/2016.

[109] Australian Psychological Society, https://www.psychology.org.au/ publications/tip_sheets/

It is now well known that post-traumatic stress disorder (PTSD) has an effect on brain function so that the very primal 'fight or flight' mechanism in the amygdala dominates. The mind cannot recognise even a non-threatening stimulus as a mere echo of a memory thus it becomes a retraumatising event. If a victim does not receive appropriate therapy, as has been the fate of most of Australia's Armed Forces personnel suffering PTSD until recently, then the rest of the brain and its logical and other rational and emotive functions are compromised. These pathways are literally starved for blood circulation while the amygdala dominates. The effect on behaviour is that a sufferer will be highly sensitised to stimuli that in any way repeat patterns associated with the trauma: smells, sounds, tastes, as well as sight and texture. Effectively, a sufferer continues to be at war. It becomes very difficult for such a victim to sustain concentration on daily events, responsibilities, and even conversation. Such a condition can be very painful and lead to great distress, depression, other mental disorders and even suicide.

For want of proper care, many veterans have become debilitated by a pattern of self-medicating through substance abuse that has been a consistent but quiet companion on every war front with the continuation of this pattern at home. Although a variety of drugs has become associated with war and veterans, alcoholism has been a particular scourge in Australia, often heaped on top of physical disability. This country has a more serious problem with alcohol abuse than almost any other Western nation, except the UK, according to the World Health Organisation, with 6.17 per cent of men suffering from it in 2004.[110] Alcoholism is not only associated with war, of course, but alcohol is the cause of 15 deaths daily, or over 5550, according to a study by the ABC.[111]

Heroes cannot be shattered by the hell of war, it is said. Yet the evidence suggests the contrary. Sane people are precisely those who are often sensitive to the horrors of war. Their humanity is severely knocked about by witnessing, or worse, being party to inhumane acts. About a third of all veterans are known to have been permanently incapacitated by PTSD following the Vietnam War. 'Suicidality', thinking about, planning, or attempting suicide has a much higher incidence for these veterans than in the wider community. This can be attributed to a range of factors, including frequent and graphic flashbacks, insomnia, crippling headaches, and guilty feelings, as well as social recrimination. Such symptoms are impacting and will continue to assault the health of soldiers now serving and those who will enlist or be called up in the future. Untreated symptoms bring many to find life unbearable.

Troops returning from overseas have found a changed Australia to which they have trouble relating. Having left for the 'Great War' and others, often in a wave of popular enthusiasm, some or much of which may have caused them to enlist, veterans encountered a more sober tone with the heavy losses incurred, and sometimes an openly critical public. Having seen something of the 'old' world, or diverse cultures, the homeland of their dreams now appeared to some as a poor, new cousin.

Australia was not only at war overseas, but within itself. As in Europe, the old order had fallen away. The world of firm, unquestioned beliefs, in which fathers were the undisputed heads of households, as described in the bible, was no more after WWI. Social divisions were rife and sometimes dangerously physical in nature. Class divisions that had melted in the trenches were very present in the new Australia where the lower classes had developed a sense of their rights, and an indignant sense of entitlement to a share of the pie. The 'squattocracy' of landowners was no longer secure. The world had also turned with speed, and soldiers of World War I especially had only intermittent access to news.

trauma accessed 13/9/2016.

[110] http://gamapserver.who.int/gho/interactive_charts/substance_abuse/ bod_alcohol_prevalence/atlas.html accessed 19/9/2016.

[111] Simon Santow, 'Australians die each day from alcohol-related illnesses...: study', ABC RN, 31 July, 2014. http://www.abc.net.au/news/2014-07-31/15- australians-die-each-day-from-alcohol-related-illness:-study/5637050 accessed 19/9/2016.

Technology in some areas had gained significant ground, and this too could be bewildering. New figures had taken leadership roles at all levels.

> It was all so new. So many things were new. Everything changed. The past would not hold and could not be held. One day soon, she might make a photograph of this new thing. To catch its moment, its brilliance up there, of movement and stillness, of tense energy and ease – that would be something. This eager turning, for a moment, to the future, surprised and hurt her. *Jim*, she moaned silently inside, *Jim, Jim*. There was in there a mourning woman who rocked eternally back and forth; who would not be seen and was herself.[112]

Women had become accustomed to being heads of households, having responsible jobs, managing the family budget and cash, and raising, educating and disciplining children as well as caring for aged parents. The returned soldier would often attempt to claim his role back as head of the household, but women were not ready to yield their hard won and hard earned 'rights' easily. Much conflict ensued. The women in turn felt that returning males should have been grateful for the way their mothers, wives, girlfriends and daughters had stepped into their big shoes so ably. In some cases, wives had become lonely, or had been misinformed that their spouse had died in combat, and had made other liaisons. There could be children from such relationships. Many a soldier came home to find himself truly displaced.

The Soldier Settler Scheme offered a new start and many returned servicemen took up farming in regional Australia with the help of land grants or assignments and substantial government loans. About 40,000 ex-soldiers took part. The conditions varied, it seems, according to rank, duration of service as well as different records and accounts. That it was a hard life, soldiers and their children consistently reported, and inexperience, debt and the harsh physical environment were ominous obstacles.[113] Graham Walker concluded that overall the scheme was a failure.

Before heading onto the land, many veterans benefited from three to six months of training in agriculture. However, this was frequently not enough or not made available. Town and city men had no idea what to expect or where their shortfalls would lie. Farming to this day looks deceptively simple. Most in the scheme were provided with an initial block of land, with a frame house and a tank for water. Many new farmers found that the block was too small to be tenable, and had to move several times, or to appeal for additional land. Some got no house, found the land was swampy and snake ridden, or entirely devoid of water. One recalled how all the soldiers in his area were trained to grow apples and pears. However, this meant that there would be no yield in the first five or six years, and they were all in competition. So they grew potatoes under the saplings to try to get by. Falling prices further exacerbated the conditions of the settlers.

Isolation was another major problem for many of these ex-servicemen, who had lived shoulder-to-shoulder day and night for years with their comrades. Transport and schools were distant dreams. One family, the Griffiths, got 540 acres initially, but found it insufficient to raise a family. A son recalled in an oral account that as children they did jobs incessantly, there was no church, nor any other activities as a family or in the community. It was pure drudgery. None of his siblings finished high school, and little wonder, he felt. His father seemed invariably angry. He recalls it being hard to cope with this. Shortages of funds led to a deep frustration at the father's incapacity to care adequately for his family. Interestingly, Griffiths Jr. recalled that his father was nervous around horses, and that this was very unusual for a farmer. Little could he imagine what his father might have experienced in relation to horses on the battlefield. The soldier's son concluded, 'Life was miserable. If not for the

---

[112] Malouf, *op. cit.,* p. 134.
[113] National Library of Australia, *op. cit.*

grace of God then why . . . ?'[114] It is little wonder that, as Walker points out, suicides were common.

Despite the memorials and plethora of 'Lest we forget' reminders, the darker side of war, including death and bereavement have not been sufficiently emphasised, according to Stanley. Yet with our current understanding of the impact of shock and trauma, we realise that a death brings a shattering of lives with ripple effects that impact everything from the economy, family survival and unborn grandchildren. For many family members the gaps of loss are unspeakable and damaging. Often there was little or no support for them and the 'stiff upper lip' was expected, no matter what they were suffering.

The Keepsakes collection holds the personal papers of Hugo Throssell, who married writer Katharine Susannah Prichard after the war. Throssell had been a farmer from Western Australia who was awarded the Victoria Cross for his action at Gallipoli with the 10th Australian Light Horse Regiment. Yet he was deeply disturbed by his experience of war and became a socialist and pacifist upon his return, speaking often in public venues. During the Depression, like many other returned servicemen, he fell into debt and suicided in 1933 with his service revolver. He had never recovered from the trauma of the war despite or perhaps underscored by his public aversion to it and what may have been desperate attempts to redeem himself from his own 'patriotic' acts as a soldier, which he later regretted bitterly. Prichard kept his wartime notebooks and press clippings of his celebrity.[115] Midlife was a time for many veterans when it no longer seems possible to hold on, when dreams seem definitively dashed, and when the hope that returning home would be a balm to their pain had faded.

A cablegram sent on 4 August 1914 by the Governor General Ferguson, who had arrived in Australia himself for the first time only on 18 of May of that year, stated 'There is indescribable enthusiasm and entire unanimity throughout Australia in support of all that tends to provide for the security of the Empire in war'.[116] While ties of sentiment, history and conviction lived on for many, it seems the Governor General had not yet familiarised himself with Australia and was significantly out of touch with the complex realities that were unfolding.

The low rate of initial recruitment, the peace and union movements gathering energy, the very real need for male labour to keep farms functioning effectively and productively were all factors tempering unanimity. It is little wonder that his enthusiasm was not universally shared. While many did feel loyal to the Empire, others believed that Federation should afford a degree of autonomy. The distance from Europe and the Middle East was another reason not to go rushing in, especially when Britain and its geographically closest allies were numerous and well equipped. Many were not of a like mind with Ferguson, and spoke out against the war. But Quakers and those who shared this perspective were slandered as unpatriotic, and the general mood was that they should be ostracised.[117]

Yet there was a superficial agreement with the Governor-General's proclamation, as the political parties attempted to outdo one another in promising an all-out effort, however untested by popular opinion, which was in many pockets quite resistant. Domestic politics continued to dominate the agendas of many. Political power seemed within the grasp of the Labor party of New South Wales, and they felt betrayed by their leader, Holman, who shelved the people's demands in favour of the war platform.

What all the parties shared was a relative innocence about matters of foreign affairs and war in particular. The politicians therefore tended to take the easiest path: to follow the edicts from London.

---

[114] National Library of Australia, *op. cit.*

[115] National Library of Australia, *op. cit.*

[116] As quoted from Scott, E. *Australia during the War* (Sydney, 1936), cited in Greenwood, Gordon, *Australia A Social and Political History*, Angus & Robertson, 1955, note 1, p. 258.

[117] Tessa Bremner, *op. cit.*

Having been isolated from geographic threat, and protected by the British navy, they were inwardly focused on the task of building the new country and were not seasoned in diplomacy of a global scope. Furthermore, Australians felt no great bitterness toward Germans, and counted a good number among their own lot. It was only later when they learned of German aggression and the human cost of war that bitterness took hold.[118]

The conscription campaigns of 1916 and 1917 were anything but civil in many quarters. Strong feelings and acrimony spread to beatings. At confrontational meetings in Sydney, speakers were attacked with eggs quite regularly and there was no respect for property. General riots broke out. Banners were pulled down, and effigies of the Prime Minister were burnt. It was a time of high drama when families and neighbours played out their own loyalties and moral convictions against one other.

For a large number, war took a particularly ugly form.[119] Officially in the interests of security, the Australian government interned thousands of men, women and children in camps around the country. Many were citizens of countries at war with Australia, and considered 'enemy aliens' but a significant proportion of other internees were not. The National Archives include extensive holdings about people who spent the war in detention and about government policy.

Internment camps were run by the army along military lines, although the quality of life varied between the camps. The personality and approach of the officer in charge seems to have been the most significant influence. However there were significant distinctions according to climate, the original purpose for which the camps were built, and the level of isolation.[120]

During World War I these were often called concentration camps. Some were located in repurposed institutions such as the old gaols at Trial Bay and Berrima in New South Wales. The largest in this war was at Holsworthy (Liverpool), located west of Sydney.

During World War II by contrast, prisons were the first institutions used, for example Long Bay in NSW, as well as inpromptu accommodations such as the Keswick army barracks in Adelaide and Northam race course in Western Australia. Camps were established at the Enoggera (Gaythorne) military base in Brisbane, Dhurringile Mansion in Victoria, and Liverpool military bases in Queensland and New South Wales. However, many camps were bursting as the numbers detained grew. Purpose-built camps were constructed at Tatura (Rushworth) in Victoria, Hay and Cowra in New South Wales, Loveday in South Australia and Harvey in Western Australia.

Most internees during both World Wars were nationals of 'enemy' countries who had already taken up residence in Australia. In World War I, the internment policy was comprehensive: all those who originated even in childhood in countries opposed to Australia were interned. While at first the policy focused on those who still held citizenship in such countries, it was then was expanded to include those who were naturalised as British or Australian subjects. The government then went a cruel step further, to detain descendants of migrants born in enemy nations, as well as others who did not fit this description but were considered nonetheless to be a security risk. This may have included people who showed compassion or solidarity with those bound for internment, or those who sheltered potential internees. It also included 'sympathisers' for causes other than the one for which Australia fought, and anti-war activists.

---

[118] Greenwood, *op. cit.* pp. 259-60.

[119] National Archives of Australia, 'Wartime internment camps in Australia' http://www.naa. gov.au/collection/snapshots/internment-camps/ introduction.aspx accessed 29/1/2016.

[120] Cate Connolly, 'Britons finally learn the dark Dunera secret,' *Sydney Morning Herald*, 19/5/2006, http://www.smb.com.au/news/film/britons-finally-learn- the-dark-dunera-secret/2006/05/18/11475457055.html accessed 12/9/2016.

Australia interned almost 7000 people over the course of World War I. Of these, about 4500 were considered 'enemy aliens' and British nationals of German ancestry already residing in Australia.

In World War II, three reasons were found to intern people. The first was to identify and prevent residents from assisting enemies, as well as providing a deterrent to those not incarcerated. Among those deemed undesirable were members of the radical nationalist organisation, the Australia First Movement. As the tone of public opinion shifted during the course of the war, all Japanese were interned, as much to appease public opinion as to enhance security. Italians were included, particularly those from the north of Australia, where it was imagined they might be more likely to assist the Pacific war effort in some capacity. Just over 20 per cent of Italian residents were interned. There were also nationals of about 30 other countries, including Russia, Portugal, Hungary and Finland. Again, about 7000 residents were interned, including more than 1500 British nationals, during World War II.

However, Australia also housed 8000 overseas internees sent by allies for the duration of the war. Many of these were Germans and Japanese from Britain, Palestine, Iran, Singapore and Malaysia, the Netherlands East Indies (Indonesia), New Zealand, and New Caledonia. Overall, between 12,000 and 14,000 people were interned in Australia during WWII, including many women and children. Families were very often separated, with women and children either not in camps, or distributed to different camps from their male relatives.

Among the most infamous of internee shipments was that of the *HMT Dunera*. After delivering New Zealand troops to Egypt, the *Dunera* was deployed to assist in bringing some of these foreign nationals to Australia. After the fall of France, men of German and Austrian origin in Britain were rounded up as a precaution.[121] In what Churchill later regretted as a 'deplorable mistake', the distinction between those who had fled Nazism and those who had been suspected of helping in the invasion of Britain was blurred. All were grouped together as 'enemy aliens.'

On 10 July 1940, 2542 detainees were embarked aboard the *Dunera* at Liverpool, having been told they were bound for Canada. They included 2036 anti-Nazis, most of them Jewish refugees, frequently called 'Jewish swine' on board.[122] Some had already been torpedoed while on the Arandora, with great trauma and first-hand experience of loss of life.[123] The rest of the Jewish contingent had fled after experiencing cruel persecution, hardship and family separation.

The *Dunera* was to bring yet another form of torture. The total complement of the ship, including guards, was almost twice its official capacity. Detainees were frequently abused, beaten and robbed by the guards even of their documents and false teeth, many of which were thrown overboard. The refugees were kept below decks for the entire 57 day voyage except for 10 minute exercise periods. During one such, the guards smashed beer bottles through which the internees had to walk barefoot, in addition to the sewage that already flowed freely on deck. With a shortage of hammocks, many had to sleep on the floor soaked with human waste. There was only one piece of soap for every 20 men, and luggage was stowed so there was no change of clothing. Dysentery became rife; one refugee tried to go to the latrines on deck at night and was bayonetted by a guard. The ship was torpedoed in the Irish Sea but the weapon failed to detonate.

The experience has been documented by film, books and on dedicated websites.[124] Many eventually famous athletes, scientists, musicians, artists, authors and others were aboard, and they have frequently reflected on their horrific *Dunera* experiences.

---

[121] *Friendly Enemy Alien,* film, 2006.

[122] Connolly, *op. cit.*

[123] *Wikipedia, 'HMT Dunera,* War Service' accessed 1/29/2016.

[124] *The Dunera Boys,* film, 1985.

Upon arriving in Sydney, the medical army officer was appalled, and his report led to the court martial of the officer-in-charge, Lieutenant-Colonel William Scott. Meanwhile the ailing and emaciated refugees were transported by night train to Hay and Tatura for internment.[125] While on board the train they received food and fruit, and Australian soldiers offered them cigarettes. Once interned, the refugees administered their own township and created Hay currency and an unofficial university. When the Japanese bombed Pearl Harbour, these *Dunera* detainees were reclassified as 'friendly aliens' and released by the Australian government. Hundreds were recruited into its army and roughly 1000 took up the offer of permanent residency at the end of the war. Most of the rest made their way back to Britain, and several returned to East Germany.[126]

Prisoners of war represent a distinct category, members of enemy forces who had surrendered or were captured. Records in the National Archives have to some extent muddied the distinctions between the different kinds of detainees. Yet in many cases they were held in the same camps. However the rights of these two groups were different. Prisoners of war could be forced to work while internees could not, but were meant to be paid for any work they did.

The camps were closed at the end of each war. After World War I, most internees were deported. During World War II, the situation was different, because many internees, particularly Italians, were released before the armistice. Others were released as soon as hostilities ceased. Internees of British or European background were permitted to stay in Australia, including those who had been brought by British authorities. Most of the Japanese were 'repatriated' in 1946, no matter whether they were Australian-born or not. This would have brought great hardship as they were unused to Japanese culture and in some cases did not know the language. Japan at the end of the war was in a state of great disarray and economic hardship. Integrating into this society at such a time without a social safety network would have been extremely difficult. Mere survival was questionable.

It is important to note, without in any way excusing it, that internment was not unidirectional. Hundreds of Australian civilians were interned overseas by the Japanese in the Asia-Pacific region. However, in both wars Australia projected itself as fighting for democracy and freedom. It is paradoxical that such vast numbers of innocent people, and others who were no longer in uniform, were deprived of all rights and kept interned or detained under the noses and in among the very Australians who supported the struggle for these values. This is yet another way that war gives birth and credence to its own illogical contradictions and resentments.

One of the miseries that was imposed while Indigenous Anzacs were busy overseas was the 1915 power of the Aborigines Protection Board to act *in loco parentis* over all children of First Nations background, with no right of appeal. Although the stated objective was the 'protection' of these children's health care and right to education, in fact they were deprived of their belonging, often never reconnecting with their people, and prevented from speaking their own languages. In the process there was no watchdog to oversee the treatment of the children, to mitigate its harshness, or prevent the sexual and other abuses that we now know were widely inflicted.

While the overwhelming sense seems to be one of outrage regarding the 'stolen generation', some Indigenous people thought their children would be better off integrated into white schools, where they were convinced that a higher quality education was to be had, and the children would learn to assume the same equality at home as the Diggers had on the battlefield. However the Australian authorities were either intent on keeping a glass ceiling on First Nations people, or expected that intellectual limitations meant they could not advance beyond primary education. Either way they were prevented, in the main, from securing secondary or tertiary education. On the few occasions when such opportu-

---

[125] Connolly, *op. cit.*
[126] Connolly, *op. cit.*

nities were offered, Indigenous Australians were made to feel beholden to their colonisers.

> In the case of Mick Flick, an Aboriginal serviceman who had fought in France for four years with the 29th Battalion, this power was used repeatedly as a threat to stop his persistent protests against the refusal of Collarenebri Public school to admit his six children (Flick 1988). In New South Wales by 1920 an almost totally segregated education system was operating for some 1,100 Aboriginal pupils in 35 separate Aboriginal schools. A syllabus introduced for Aboriginal schools in 1916, while including reading, writing and arithmetic, stressed manual training for a life of labour in primary industry as its special feature. A high school education was never viewed as a possibility for Aboriginal children.[127]

In 1919 Australia's troops brought home an unwelcome guest; a severe strain of influenza. While there was low resistance generally to this unknown cocktail of infection, this was particularly true for the First Nations peoples who were displaced, deprived of their traditional bush tucker and Indigenous and Western medicines were hard won. Their accommodation was nothing short of miserable, and social security payments were still denied them. In short, their health was already poor and immunity compromised. They had little idea how to cope with the heavy colds, fever, headaches and aching limbs characteristic of the flu.

Legitimate fear of the authorities drove many away from government care and into hiding in the bush. Eighty-seven residents died at Barambah and thirty-one at Taroom Settlement, where more than half of the 400 residents contracted the disease within 24 hours. Even C.A. Maxwell, the superintendent at Taroom, died in the epidemic. The Chief Protector estimated that there were at least 298 Aboriginal deaths as a result, mainly in the southern camps. The total losses in New South Wales were 4266 for the first half of 1919, but the number of Indigenous deaths is not recorded. The following year was to bring more grief, as 105 First Nations people died of the flu in the Torres Strait and Cape York.[128]

At home, First Nations women were busy in both wars. In World War II they helped to salvage aircraft from the bush, while others worked in factories. It was a time of change for Australians, white and Aboriginal, as they came into greater contact with one another. The army had employed First Nations people in pastoral positions similar to the stations, under systematically poor conditions from 1933 on. They demanded long hours, offered inadequate housing, diet and medical care, and little pay. But as the army took over from the Native Affairs Branch during World War II, conditions almost miraculously improved in all areas. Sanitation, adequate housing, limited work hours, healthy food, and medical care in army hospitals made a vast difference.

The young Quaker Bill Oats saw more 'action' at the end of his war than he anticipated. In June 1940, having played a key role in evacuating the remainder of his Geneva school to France and then England, he found himself almost broke and longing to return to Australia, or at any rate to leave Europe. At the end of July he was invited to report to the Children's Overseas Reception Board (CORB) in Liverpool with 48 hours' notice. They were arranging exile for English children to the safety of the colonies, with the need to travel through what had now become treacherous seas.

The Chief Escort, a retired headmaster, appointed Oats as Deputy for his ship, the *Batory*. She proved to be a luxury liner, built for 300 passengers, but all the signage was in Polish. Furthermore, the ship was divided for safety into three sections with bulkheads completely closing one from another. There was a maze of interior corridors and the signage was 'Double Dutch' for the children. Oats had 14 boys in his personal charge as well as being the Deputy Head for the other thirty-four groups, amounting to some five hundred members. After standing for hours to board without refreshment,

---

[127] The Australian War Museum, *Too Dark for the Light Horse, op. cit.*, p. 13.
[128] The Australian War Museum, *Too Dark for the Light Horse, op. cit.*, p. 11.

and being sorted eventually into cabin groups in ways that would bunk each child close to his or her guardian, Oats realised that his troubles were only beginning.

Seven hundred officers and men bound for Singapore had also boarded, making the ship a very possible and 'legitimate' target for the enemy in terms of war, however much Oats disagreed personally with such conventions. The children were confined to the lower decks, third class. It turned out that their bags had been tossed willy-nilly into the deep forward hold. The ship met rough seas almost immediately upon leaving port, so it became difficult to retrieve luggage. Fortunately in the initial stages the children were still enjoying the lark of the outing, and not disturbed by the inconveniences that were looming large for Oats and the other escorts. The children were instructed to sleep in their clothes for the first night, with 'SHOES OFF'. They were aged 5-15, and it was all a strange but exciting world for them. Unfortunately, it took a full week to ensure all the young passengers had their clothing, and a miserable week it was as they were all seasick.

After being confined below decks for almost a week, Oats surfaced to discover that the *Batory* was part of a great Atlantic convoy. There were some sixty ships, among them a dozen liners such as the *Empress of Britain* and the *Stratheden*, and a collection of slow moving cargo vessels. They were all zig-zagging towards America via Greenland, not the most direct line for Australia. Then, just as suddenly, one morning about only a fifth of the ships remained. These had turned south while the rest had gone on to the west. The *Batory* was truly starting its voyage. Clearly it was to be a long one.

Oats concluded that his charges would need a program for the coming extended journey to Australia. Having been promised all the needed accessories for their trip, he discovered they had been equipped only with some Bibles and a collection of Laurel and Hardy films. Routine was required for meals and for occupying the children. Oats conducted a survey to discover the skills of the escorts, and found that there was 'a galaxy of talent, including a vivacious ballet mistress, several trained kindergarten teachers, scout and guide leaders, primary and secondary teachers'. It was thus possible to have discrete programs for three age groups. Seniors had the option of Literature, Sketching, History, Australian Geography, First Aid, Physiology, French and English. Following a compulsory siesta, there were afternoon deck sports, scout, guide and cub meetings, and 'hosing rosters' in the tropics for cooling off.

The real saving grace for Oats as for the children and other escorts was the discovery that they could 'sing their troubles away'. With a robust staff such as he had, as well as the sharp memories of many children, there was much sharing. Sing-songs in the dining room after dinner, in what had to double as a recreation area, became a nightly affair. Individuals and groups were soon planning special skits. A very popular presentation was an enactment of 'Waltzing Matilda' by the escorts. They even learnt a Polish national song for the crew, but eventually, foiled by the language, had to be content with an English translation of the lyrics. The rapport between the children and their mostly quite young escorts grew strong, and helped to soften the homesickness and sense of anxiety about those left behind and their own futures. These fears were legitimate, and some would never see their families again.

Other troubles encountered by Oats and his charges were water rationing; a strict policy of no contact with the soldiers that he managed to soften with their participation in the sing-songs; and impetigo (from mandatory life-jacket usage), which was highly infectious. First landfall was to be Freetown in West Africa, requiring quinine to be administered to stave off malaria, only to discover that they were barred from shore leave. Next stop was Cape Town, where they did have several days away from the ship.

The escorts had radioed ahead for help and they received it in trumps. They departed South Africa for Australia with a library of 1000 books and enough toys and books to entertain all as well as to make personal gifts to each young passenger. An abundance of fresh food, including 8000 oranges, 3000 buns and 2000 cakes, ice cream, 300 pounds of sweets and much more came in addition to personal lunch boxes. They were overwhelmed by the warmth of hospitality, as locals would take the children off on daily outings and bring them faithfully back for the nightly head count. A picnic was arranged at the showground, in which the children distinguished themselves with their singing and appetites, but did not stop short of asking 'What's on for tea?' as soon as they reached the *Batory*.

An unexpected stop in Bombay resulted in a concussion for one child, who had to remain in hospital. The primary request from escorts was for shoes. Many of the children had come on board hurriedly, with old shoes, others had grown quickly, and some were lost. And a ship in the tropics made for different needs to aerate and protect their feet. It seemed impossible to get the number needed, until as if by magic at ten pm a bicycle taxi pulled up at the Taj Mahal hotel, transferred the sandals to a taxi, and the ship sailed with them at midnight. The next day, they were still in Bombay harbour, and it was discovered that 500 sandals, not 500 pairs, had been delivered. However, due to the ship's delay, Oats, like a dog with a bone, got special shore leave and went straight back to his 'friend' at the bazaar. The salesman explained that he had the rest of the sandals behind the curtain, and had expected to deliver them in two lots.

The delay allowed the injured larrikin to return from hospital to the ship, somewhat the wiser about breaking the cardinal rule of not sticking heads out of portholes. In Singapore a group of lads went missing, and were found with four minutes grace before the sailing of the *Batory*, playing in a nearby rubber plant. Oats looked back on the experience as a maturing one for himself as for the children and other escorts. 'We'd been ten weeks afloat, ten weeks into which I'd crammed … almost a lifetime of experience – of children, of human nature, of people under great stress, of living one day at a time, of discovery of unexpected resources within young and old to meet anxiety and separation, of laughter and singing as a tonic for frayed nerves.' No doubt this experience equipped him for the uncertainties in his later career including being a teacher and school principal.

The ship reached Fremantle on 9 October 1940 and Melbourne on the 16th. They had been ten weeks afloat on what came to be known as the 'Singing Ship', another of the lesser-known heroic ventures of the Second War. There have since been criticisms of the scheme, which took children from their parents and so far from home, in some cases resulting in permanent separation. The Blitz had hit London not long after their departure, but a ship carrying 70 children on the same route as the *Batory* crossing the Atlantic had been torpedoed and sunk shortly after the *Batory*'s fleet had veered to the south. Indeed, since naval losses became so severe, the program was suspended, at least as far as the Antipodes were concerned, so the *Batory* was to be one-of-a-kind. It had come by grace to Australia, with the adult escorts probably feeling much the same relief as many asylum seekers feel when they see the Australian naval vessels approaching their boats today.[129] Fortunately they received a warmer reception.

Australia is now dotted by perhaps thousands of commemorative plaques, memorials and cenotaphs around the country, including over 900 in Western Australia alone. These are formal, some might say in many cases visually soulless, inscriptions that record the passing of local men, and in a few cases women. Some are much more creative sculptures. For the veterans of World War I, and their families and friends at home, these monuments took on great importance. In many, perhaps most cases, the bodies of the fallen were never recovered, so there were no graves to visit, no places to lay flowers on birthdays, anniversaries of weddings or death. Monuments and plaques designated a physical place where such rituals might occur.

Importantly, Anzac Day and Remembrance Day were established as times set aside for recollection. The first Anzac Day was held on 25 April 1916, just a year after the Australian landing on Gallipoli,

---

[129] Oats, *op. cit.,* pp. 137-149.

and long before anyone knew when the war might end. There were many ceremonies around the world. In Australia there were ceremonies and services of various kinds. In London, dubbed 'the knights of Gallipoli', more than 2000 Australian and New Zealanders paraded through the streets. In Egypt it was a lighter occasion; a sports day in the Australian camp. After the war, Anzac Day became the day of commemoration for the more than 62,000 Australian veterans who had died by many means in the war.[130] Many rituals, from the dawn vigil, memorial services, ceremonial parades, to drinking and games such as 'two-up' fell into place by the 1930s. With the onset of World War II, far from paling in significance, Anzac Day began to serve to commemorate the fallen in all combat situations in which Australia engaged.[131] It has remained a day of primary importance in the national calendar, because of its dual role as a designated time of commemoration of the dead but more significantly as an overtly patriotic celebration of nationhood.

The eleventh hour of the eleventh day of the eleventh month of 1918 was the day the violence ceased on the Western Front. It was a moment of stunned silence. Over 70 million people had been mobilised, and between 9 and 13 million were dead, with probably a third of these having no known grave. The former Allies chose to memorialise this by initially calling the occasion Armistice Day. Two minutes silence was instituted across the British Commonwealth, at 11.00 am, as suggested by Australian journalist Edward Honey. In 1920 the day was given further significance when it became the occasion for the burial of an unknown soldier, brought back from the front, with full military honours. At the end of World War II the name was changed to Remembrance Day to incorporate all conflicts and commemoration of all war dead. In 1993, Australia added new significance to the day when the remains of an unknown Australian soldier, exhumed from a military cemetery of First War France, was re-entombed in the Hall of Memory at the Australian War Memorial.[132] However Remembrance Day continues to be overshadowed by Anzac Day, and is not a public holiday.

The popular memorialising of World War II necessarily took a different form. Although in many smaller centres the names of the dead were added to the World War I list, or the local monument was modified to add pillars or an opposing side where more names could be added, the 'Lest we forget' cenotaph continued to be important as a focal point for Anzac Day and Remembrance Day.

However, public sentiments had turned to practical landmarks as commemorative contributions to communities. These created work as well as opportunities for all citizens to benefit, and the Commonwealth Government encouraged private contributions by allowing tax deductions for any gifts to projects that could be described as war memorials. There was a sudden proliferation of memorial parks, memorial swimming pools, memorial libraries, memorial community centres, memorial fountains and all manner of other structures of use, attractiveness and dignity.

The creativity soon extended to schools and churches, and the Garden Club of Australia suggested a Remembrance Driveway from Sydney to Canberra. Set up as islands of plantings along the highway, this became a national project that stayed in the memory of school children who were involved, as well as adult associations. The emphasis was on native plants and trees. Plantings went on for subsequent wars. In 1954 Queen Elizabeth II and Prince Philip launched the Driveway by planting two plane trees in Macquarie Place, Sydney.[133]

Because of the scope of the Second World War, as well as Australia's more direct and varied involve-

---

[130] State Library Victoria, http://guides.slv.vic.gov.au/c.php?g=245248&p= 1633071 accessed 15/2/2016.

[131] https://www.awm.gov.au/commemoration/anzac/anzac-tradition/, accessed 13/2/2016.

[132] https://www.awm.gov.au/commemoration/remembrance/tradition/, accessed 13/2/2016.

[133] Neil Radford, *Dictionary of Sydney*, http://dictionaryofsydney.org/entry/ war_memorials_to_world_war_ii_and_later_conflicts, accessed 14/2/2016.

ment, many memorials also sprang up for losses associated with specific tragedies, such as the stunning event of the sinking of the *HMAS Kuttabul*, with 21 Australian naval personnel on board, when it was torpedoed in Sydney Harbour by a Japanese submarine.

Unique to World War II was the explicit memorialising of the contribution of women as a distinct group. While in a few places their names were added to the fallen in World War I, numbers were small and the public had not perhaps fully understood how much women were exposed to the dangers and horrors of the front. In Sydney's 'Rocks' the Australian Army Nurses Memorial provides something of a late corrective by noting the contribution in all wars of the nurses. Not far away in Jessie Street Gardens, a Service Women's Memorial was erected in 1990 for those who enlisted in World War II. Plaques in the Chatswood South/Artarmon Uniting Church focus uniquely on the contribution of 200 women who served in the Middle East during World War II in Voluntary Aid Detachments.[134]

Prisoners of war (POWs) are another group who are remembered with special structures, as the bodies of those who perished were almost never returned. As Neil Radford reports, Australian prisoners of war held by the Japanese built a pulpit themselves for the war memorial chapel at the Army's School of Military Engineering at Casula, south of Sydney. They were able to source Changi marble (from the Changi Peninsula in Singapore where the Japanese ran seven POW and internee camps) and wood that originally served as sleepers on the Burma-Thailand railway, in a poignant tribute to their fellow detainees. Memorials to honour those who died as POWs on the Sandakan death march of 1945 and in Sandakan, North Borneo exist in Burwood, Kirribilli and Turramurra.[135]

It may be the very brevity of the white Australian story that has caused it to make so much of the wars that happened largely offshore, while impacting the fabric of society, indeed likely every family, in some way or other. There was a longing to make tangible the losses, the disappearances, the questions, the sense that all that was promised had not been delivered, and what was most precious had not been protected, but on the contrary, for too many, so much had been taken away. Many Australians found themselves significantly worse off at the end of a war than at the beginning. They were also shorthanded and therefore less income supported the family. Overall the tangible benefits tended not to materialise.

Yet no number of little monuments or cenotaphs around the country would suffice. It was already during the First World War that journalist Charles Bean began envisioning an even larger legacy: the creation of a war museum that would serve simultaneously as a memorial. It would be a place of remembrance but also one where detailed records of Australia's experience and contribution could be housed. It would be fair to say that this institution has had the most formative, and in the view of some, single minded imprint upon our understanding of World War I and of the Australian experience of war. It contributes a great deal to the recollection and fostering of knowledge of all the conflicts in which Australia has been party. Bean was not a pacifist and neither has been the institution whose inception was due to his imagination. For many, as Peter Stanley noted in his comments, the Australian War Memorial has contributed too much to the celebration of war and its achievements, and far too little to the counter-narratives that expose the darker sides of violent conflict.[136]

Despite the energy and investment in memorialisation, this perennial activity carries with it not solace but discomfort for many. Recently, one Quaker realised that her exercise class was moving enthusiastically to the beat of the American song 'The Sinking of the Bismarck', an event in which over 2000 lives were lost.[137] All too often, memorials are celebrations of the heroism of the soldier, sailor,

---

[134] Radford, *op. cit.*
[135] Radford, *op. cit.*
[136] National Library of Australia, *op. cit.* See also Peter Stanley.
[137] Pamela Leach, personal anectdote.

or airman in battle. They are festivals in which the drums of war are heard and the hawks circle. The Australian Armed Forces are good at making a splash at local events, often by bringing in hardware: naval vessels offer popular conducted tours, and children enjoy climbing around and in vehicles and tanks.

For those whose experience remains one of pain, loss, or moral outrage such as the pacifist, memorial events and related celebrations of militarism feel too close to dancing on the graves of the dead, or attending public executions or stonings for amusement, as was popular for many centuries.[138] The horror of war is too often missing, the sense of 'never again' has morphed into a vengeful sentiment that is likely directed at the latest 'enemy' to have been constructed by the propaganda machine, and the dogs of war strain to be unleashed.

There are other ways of remembering warfare. One is to visit the place where it occurred. This is increasingly possible with air travel within the reach of so many and cooperation between former enemies now frequent. Pilgrimages to Gallipoli have become quite commonplace for many Australians, paradoxically given how far flung it was for the Diggers themselves. Quaker Di Bretherton visited Vietnam from Australia in 1986 expecting to see 'the place where the war had been'. She found herself one of a party of only six 'Westerners' visiting the country at that time.

> It is painful to converse with an innocent child who struggles to close his lips around a syllable because his face has a crater down the middle of it. It is one thing to accept such a burden as an accident of nature, another to fear that it is an end result of American, and by extension Australian, foreign policy . . . I had also thought the effects of Agent Orange would be limited to those who were exposed at the time, not giving sufficient thought to the fact that in Vietnam the chemicals have entered the food chain. The local people do not receive an occasional exposure to sprayed chemicals but rather live all the time in the sprayed environment, eat food grown in the sprayed soil, drink water that has run off sprayed land, eat fish that have been reared in the run-off water. Indeed the fate of many of the chemical drums, in a make-do post war culture, was to be recycled as household water tanks.[139]

There is no great celebration associated with Vietnam for so many Australians who were involved or touched. Even as the war progressed, the growing hostility of the public had a negative effect on the returning soldiers. Some heard rumours on the field of a disgruntled populace at home. Gradually a more nuanced understanding has emerged that separates the role of soldiers from the political decisions about going to war. Yet the mechanisms of war do not turn without the energies of the Armed Forces, of individual men and women.

Returned soldiers from Vietnam hold a range of positions about the war in which they fought. The effects of the chemical Agent Orange are now better understood. Agent Orange was a mixture of diesel fuel and dioxin, a toxic defoliant used both to clear forests so that enemy forces could not hide, and to deprive the very productive Mekong Delta of food crops. It was sprayed by aircraft. Soldiers affected by Agent Orange are now eligible for medical support and compensation. Graham Walker indicated that the Department of Veterans Affairs is better prepared to help returning soldiers and their families but the Repatriation Scheme is still far from ideal. This remains an injustice for current servicemen and women.

> It was that intense focus of his whole being, it's *me*, Jim Saddler, that struck her with grief, but also the thing – and not simply an image either – that endured. That in itself. Not as

---

[138] *The Monty Python Flying Circus* depicts one such biblically based occasion in its darkly humorous film, *The Life of Brian*.

[139] Di Bretherton, *op. cit.*, pp. 8-9.

she might have preserved it in a shot she had never in fact taken, nor even as she held it, for so long, as an unbroken image in her head, but in itself, as it for its moment was. That is what life meant, a unique presence, and it was essential in every creature. To set anything above it, birth, position, talent even, was to deny to all but a few among the infinite millions what was common and real, and what was also, in the end, most moving. A life wasn't *for* anything. It simply was.[140]

Wars have challenged human capacities to survive to their limits, and have demanded accelerated scientific creativity. Living in close quarters, often with poor nutrition, little opportunity to wash, and very limited access to toilets was a toxic cocktail. The added presence of decomposing corpses and rats sealed the fate of too many soldiers and nearby civilians. Outbreaks of predictable and surprising diseases were among the unfortunate results. At home, families, friends and neighbours with little immunity fell prey to the illnesses brought from overseas, where previously Australia had the benefit of being relatively cut-off from contamination.

This sad condition at home and away did provide additional motivation for medical advances, many of which were documented in the *Medical Journal of Australia*, launched in 1918.[141] During WWI, infection was a primary killer at the front as at home. The time it took for an injured soldier to reach a surgeon was sufficient for gangrene to set in. Infection was a greater scourge than the enemy during that era. To address tuberculosis, there was an understanding that isolation was essential to break the chain of infection. Quarantining of arriving ships and the construction of sanatoriums were measures that contributed to a reduction of contagion.[142]

The pan-European outbreak of Spanish influenza in Europe began in 1918 and killed more people than the war that preceded it. The return home of soldiers seems to have been the primary means of infection for Australia as for other countries.[143] While the Commonwealth used the same type of policy to isolate the illness as it did for tuberculosis, notably isolation and quarantine, eventually the illness swept a devastating tsunami across the country. It was a virulent strain. More than 12,500 Australians died of flu between 1918-1919. This came at a time when morale was sapped by losses, poverty was widespread and access to ample food had been compromised by the reduction of the farm workforce and the need to supply the front. Hospitals were stretched beyond capacity, and makeshift arrangements sprang up across the Commonwealth. In Melbourne, for example, the Royal Exhibition Building was converted to fit the purpose, and 4046 people were treated there, of which 392 died. While the pandemic was an epic tragedy for Australia, it brought advancement of a kind.

> … for the newly-founded Commonwealth Serum Laboratories (CSL), it provided a huge burst of public support and recognition which facilitated CSL's development, expansion, and success. CSL was established during WWI to respond to Australia's need for vaccines, serums and anti-toxins, all of which were imported. The war limited the availability of manufactured medicines and facilities for shipping them. Australia was feeling its isolation acutely; clearly, independent production was vital to ensure public health needs could be met. Almost immediately after opening in 1918, CSL poured all its efforts into battling the coming onslaught of Spanish flu. By March 1919, CSL had packed and produced three million doses of flu vaccine. While accounts of its efficacy suggest that it did somehow reduce mortality, the vaccine was actually derived from a mix of bacterial strains,

[140] Malouf, *op. cit.,* p. 132.

[141] Yvonne E. Cossart, 'The rise and fall of infectious diseases: Australian perspectives, 1914-2014', *MJA* 2014: 201 (1 Suppl): S11-S14. https://www.mja. com.au/journal/2014/201/1/ rise-and-fall-infectious-diseases-australian- perspectives-1914-2014 accessed 17/9/2016.

[142] Cossart, *op. cit.*

[143] Cossart, *op. cit.*

reflecting the mistaken belief that influenza was caused by a bacterium.[144]

Syphilis was another disease brought home by Australian troops, in greater proportion than most other Allied forces, with horrific consequences. The stigma associated with it, as a sexually transmitted disease, meant people with no obvious symptoms avoided treatment. Making reporting compulsory for troops had little effect. It is estimated that 5 per cent of mental illness hospital admissions and 60 per cent of aortal aneurisms in Victoria were caused by this illness at the time. It was easily passed on, so 10 per cent of pregnant women tested positive for it. However, only female sex trade workers were required to be screened. During the postwar period, the Australian National University was founded and contributed in significant ways to research relating to infectious disease control and eradication.[145]

Another disease that took firmer hold in Australia in the post-WWI period, paradoxically because of better hygiene, was poliomyelitis. Victims were older when they contracted polio and lived with it for longer, and as a result more advanced neurological symptoms became commonplace, rather than the infant mortality and quick death that had long been associated with the illness. Leg braces were common sights, as well as people with uneven and shriveled limbs. Some sufferers had weak diaphragms and respiratory paralysis, demanding the use of a mechanism known as the iron lung.[146] Its introduction in 1937 required patients to live in the misery of a ventilator capsule similar to a casket with only their heads projecting outside.

Polio became a 'notifiable' disease in Tasmania in 1911, and by 1922 across Australia medical professionals were required to report new cases to the authorities. In 1938 the condition had reached its peak with over 39 patients per 100,000 in the population. During WWII troops did contract the disease while in service. Franklin Delano Roosevelt who had also caught it at the age of 39 (before becoming US President), was paralysed from the waist down and became a strong advocate for a cure until his death in 1945 (by stroke). It was not until 1956 that Dr Jonas Salk discovered a non-toxic, deactivated vaccine. Dr Percival Bazely brought this back to Australia and widespread immunisation was initiated with the assistance of the CSL. Today there are an estimated 400,000 polio survivors in Australia, and still the very occasional outbreak when the infection comes from one of the few countries where it is still active.[147]

WWII brought, by necessity, the accelerated development, production and use of antibiotics. First to come were sulpha medications, with penicillin following closely. Howard Florey, the Australian scientist, played a key role in its development, which remains one of the greatest contributions of this country to medicine. This drastically reduced the number of deaths by pneumonia on the front and gradually also at home. For tuberculosis, compulsory x-ray screening was introduced for troops, to identify the infection and enforce required treatment. After WWII efforts at eradication cast a wider net to the civilian population,[148] and with antibiotics tuberculosis is now rare except in impoverished pockets, notably among First Nations people.

War is a menace to public health, mental and physical. In addition to the Armed Forces it has been responsible for a very large number of 'secondary' deaths, of Australians not at the front but nonetheless unavoidably targets of infection. Great advances in medicine were necessary to assist the population in moving beyond these invisible, deadly enemies. But it must be remembered that the cost of these

---

[144] Museum Victoria, 29/5/2009, https://museumvictoria.com.au/about/mv- news/2009/museums-flu-history1/ accessed 17/9/2016.

[145] Cossart, *op. cit.*

[146] Cossart, *op. cit.*

[147] Polio Australia, https://www.poliohealth.org.au/polio-timeline/ accessed 17/9/2016.

[148] Cossart, *op. cit.*

achievements was enormous: Australia, like other nations, was dragged into the business of resolving these puzzles of science in order to preserve what was retrievable of its precious, and in some respects very vulnerable, population.

Chapter VI
Agony and Passion: Artistic Responses to War and Peace

Many cultural expressions and wartime reactions have become woven into the fabric of Australian identity. Those with long memories of the music, visual media and literature of war hold a special sense of connection with the threads that bind them to this land and its people, who have also been shaped by Australia's war history. Whether they agreed or disagreed with any particular war, each work is manifest as a form of cultural expression and has contributed to a rich, robust and tangible legacy of 'Australian-ness' that was at the time of Federation a much more fragile thread.

Before World War II, in addition to the obvious Indigenous art, which went mostly unnoticed and was not foundational to the country's identity at the time, the vast majority of Australian artistic and literary depictions concerned two subjects: humans and nature (settlement), and humans and the 'motherland'. There were also intermittent themes regarding relationships with convicts and Indigenous people, but these raised such conflicted feelings that there was less public expression concerning them. From World War I on, many more themes enter the grand narrative of what it is to be Australian. Australia at war is of course a primary one. But there are many that interpret the implications of these wars. Some of these include the impact of war, life overseas, new cultures as they become familiar to traveling Australians, those in service overseas or manifest in Australia, the new faces of labour and the family, the depiction of challenges of daily existence, as well as relationships and conflicts between groups.

Australians were afforded fresh horizons that in turn offered mirrors on themselves. The national kaleidoscope was well and truly evolving. Each of the forms that war-related cultural expression took had its creators and its interpreters, formal critics but importantly also audiences and their adversaries. In other words the debates of each era were seen, and continue to be understood from many sides. Knowledge and experience of this expanding culture became a common bond.

The arts, especially the visual ones, were often able to pass under the guardian radar of hardened ideological views and official positions to catch up shared emotion, experience, and to bring what was fractured into conversation. Within the segmented and layered realities of Australian society, the arts wove people into a unique culture that played a significant role in consolidating the nation. Yet threaded into this legacy were images that caused significant discomfort. These were often the missing voices, the challenges to the dominant thinking, to the patriotic and militaristic ways. This was a region in which women have had greater scope to play significant roles. As Di Bretherton writes, describing the creation of *As the Mirror Burns*,

> My attitude to making the videotape, and later the film, was very much like one of holding a baby. I did not see it as my own baby, or even think I was the real parent. Rather I was like a midwife who helped the film to give birth to itself ... The arts can speak symbolically, and so have been called the language of the unconscious, the vehicle for metaphors, dreams and visions ... one of the strengths of using the arts is that they cross cultural barriers and find common ground, even when an understanding of each other's language is limited.[149]

The National Library's 'Keepsakes' exhibition shows how the private correspondence and journals provide some of the most vivid literature to describe the experience of war, though it was sadly often lost or being suppressed, and has never reached, nor was it mainly meant, for a public audience. Fortunately for the historical record and contemporary study, William Oats' mother, Mabel Rosalie (Nicolle) Oats, kept all his letters from the early period of World War II, and in his aging years he chose to publish the collection. On 1 September 1939, he wrote vividly of the preparations for war. One can't help wondering at the details. Did the men eventually slump over on one another's shoulders? Did the baby have a father while growing up? What was the mechanism that made the men fall so innocently into line? But then, they might not yet have been born at the end of the War to end all Wars. In a passage entitled 'A Hasty Return to Geneva' he notes,

> I came back across France on the night when the French ... were being called up. Stations were in black-out hues, trains travelled in darkness, but a perfect moonlit night seemed to underline the unreality of it all ... All stations were crowded with men returning to their units, a silent and determined lot ... the other seven in my compartment just had empty looks. I chatted with one of them in the corridor. He was a decorator by profession, had left a wife and one-month old baby. 'Fatalism' was his main summing up of the mood of the French soldier. 'Look at these men', he said. 'In times of peace they will be squabbling, arguing and even fighting, but when their nation's in peril, they will march in step and fight like the very devil.' The Russian Pact was for him a stab in the back of France, because it meant that Germany had access to raw materials and petrol ...[150]

For an Australian population, many with limited education, cartoons and photos in newspapers could be consumed in a breath, from the oldest to the younger members of the family. Such images certainly played a role in generating ongoing support for the war in some quarters, eliciting or highlighting a mix of patriotism, temptation for adventure, 'easy' money during a time of hardship, and fear. Fear, it is said, is the midwife of war. However, for others the photos especially may have clinched their convictions that the war should not be fought, should not continue, or that Australia should withdraw. After all, contrary to propaganda, as the struggle wore on, Australia had not been threatened by the 'Huns' who clearly had their hands full with the several fronts on which they were fighting, as well as with the naval battles. There would be no danger to Australian territory from these alien forces in WWI.

The campaign of fear and hatred against the Germans is given powerful expressed in the cartoon characters drawn by Norman Lindsay, which play an important role in the 'Keepsakes' exhibition.[151] The horrific portrayal of ogre-faced Germans bearing down on innocent Australians is racist, brutal and distorted. They did not represent reality at the time of WWI, but would have played powerfully on the heartstrings of those who had struggled so hard and so recently to build this new nation and their place within it. Without excusing the consequent ill-treatment, both official and unofficial, of

---

[149] Bretherton, *op. cit.,* pp. 38-9.
[150] Oats, *op. cit.,* p. 83.
[151] National Library of Australia, *op. cit.*

those Australian residents and citizens of German extraction, we begin to get a hint of why this might have occurred.

The construction of the 'Huns' as an inhuman and heartless 'alien' force now sounds like the stuff of computer games, in which it is right and good to eliminate aliens. 'It's ok mum, they're not human', parents are told. In contrast to Lindsay's ogres, the modern day aliens or zombies are faceless although they have distinctly human, black forms. The dehumanising of the enemy, whether German, Austrian, Hungarian or Turkish, was an important first step in desensitising young Australian warriors to go into battle and destroy these unknown threats. The 'Diggers' are seen as standing strong, not lying dead, fearful or abandoned in some foreign trench. At home neighbours belonging to these ethnic backgrounds had their humanity eroded, which engendered at least Anglo-Australian submission with regard to 'enemy' internment.

Fellow cartoonist Will Dyson's contribution brought dignity, even 'an almost beatific vision of the Australian soldier' according to the National Library. Working for London's *Daily Herald*, he was a harsh critic of Prussian militarism and German nationalism. Both threatened the fabric of Europe under the nuanced analysis of his pen. A publication entitled *Kultur Cartoons* brought together some of his best work in 1915. As Australia's first official war artist, he depicted conditions on the front lines through 1916 and 1917, including the Somme and Ypres. Here, the Diggers were raised from the mud as noble warriors, faces clean and shining in their lamps and firelight. These were also collected in a large format book, *Australians at War*.[152] His scenes of the battlefield did challenge the 'public' version of the war, according to War Memorial art curator Anthea Gunn. Such alternative perspectives are now welcomed, she emphasises.

Some artists used cartoons to express criticism of war efforts. David Lowe, in particular, showed up the conflicts in the community and satirised leaders like Billy Hughes. Even soldiers were keen to get copies that were published in Lowe's *The Billy Book*, according to Guy Hansen.

Another important new medium for wartime reporting was photography. Frank Hurley, who reached fame through his participation on the Mawson and Shackleton expeditions to Antarctica, also took powerful photos at the World War I front. They brought a more vivid and authentic account, but for that reason barely palatable, of the horrors of war than did the cartoonists. Although Hurley lost face by altering his pictures, for example by adding a cloudy sky from another location to enhance the drama of a battle scene, his photos remained true and powerful to his audiences. His post-production modifications can be likened to the kind that are commonplace with digital photography, yet they effectively cost Hurley his reputation. However, this did not mitigate the punch of seeing from home the scale of death and decay, not only of human life but of landscapes that appeared as deserts or unearthly environments. His images from Passchendaele became etched in the memories of three generations. Trees, still standing but burnt and lifeless, hinted at farms and countryside that had not so long before flourished. The Australian connection to the land would have embraced the powerful impact of these photos, associating more reality to the destructive nature of warfare than had ever been possible to date. Perhaps for some, images such as these would have evoked the grotesque or gothic aspects of raging bush fires, great forces that show no mercy. Many of Hurley's glass plate negatives are in the Keepsake collection.[153]

Photographs played other roles in World War I, as we have already seen. But the Keepsakes exhibition shows that they were also of strategic importance. Australians pilots risked all to fly reconnaissance missions to gather intelligence about enemy positions. Photographs were pieced together to create mosaics of battlefields, which with the assistance of stereoscopes took on a three-dimensional quality.

---

[152] National Library of Australia, *op. cit.*
[153] National Library of Australia, *op. cit.*

Knowledge of enemy positions, targets, and artillery bombardments came to be dependent on them.[154] In these early days of flight, when aircraft were fragile skeletons and the pilots themselves ill-prepared, with little experience and often only map and compass by way of navigation equipment, this was perilous work. Many pilots were lost through disorientation, weather, and of course enemy fire.

Anthea Gunn, art curator at the Australian War Memorial, in her presentation to the 'Anzac Conversations: Lessons Learned' series, underscored the War Memorial's sense of a mandate that incorporates all the sides of war. She emphasised that many people have come to value the War Memorial over the years, especially those who spend the time to appreciate its offerings. For example, paintings that show the suffering and agony of war are now more prominently displayed, including for example those depicting the stress on horses at the front. For many people, compassion for animals seems to be more accessible, as they are universally regarded as innocents in such situations. Gunn focuses on an iconic painting of the Gallipoli slopes by George Lambert as one that has been well accepted, despite some inaccuracies such as troops wearing slouch hats.

Other paintings also have pride of place in the collection. For example, Arthur Streeton emphasised nature as the context in which war took place in his canvases, creating a 'conversation' with photographer Hurley's works. Too old for the war at its beginning, when he was living in London, he volunteered for the Royal Army Medical Corps. He worked as an orderly alongside other notable Australian artists, including George Coates, A Henry Fulton and Tom Roberts. Eventually discharged as medically unfit, Streeton lobbied and eventually was appointed as an official war artist for Australia in May 1918, when he was sent to France. There he worked around the Somme until mid-August 1918, and in October again travelled from London to France, this time focusing on the destruction around Peronne. While in France he made many drawings, watercolours and paintings, including places where the Australians lived, worked and fought, as well as landscape studies, panoramas and still life images of wrecked machinery. Even these depict a strange but palpable agony.[155]

For the completion of his contract as war artist, he painted a large landscape in the Somme Valley, at the opening stages of the second battle. A peaceful rural setting occupies the foreground, while an artillery barrage can be seen in the distance. By the time he returned to Australia in 1920, he was both popular and famous, and was knighted in 1937. Despite the power and vividness of his depiction of the destruction of landscapes, buildings, machinery, and of death itself, Streeton had a telling insight to share about what could and would be depicted of war. In fact, he concluded, it was indescribable in any medium to anyone who has not witnessed it. He wrote to Baldwin Spencer that 'true pictures of battlefields are very quiet looking things. There's nothing much to be seen – everybody & thing is hidden & camouflaged – it is only in the illustrated papers one gets a real idea of battle as it occurs in the mind of the man who's never been there'.[156]

Partly because of the disproportion of men at the front, but also the lack of respect for women as artists among other vocations, they are less well represented in the cultural record. Yet there were many who took strong stands and expressed these in personal and sometimes political ways. Hilda Rix Nicholas (1884-1961) stands out as one of relatively few internationally celebrated female Australian artists of the First World War period. Originally from Ballarat, she studied under Frederick McCubbin and exhibited with the Victorian Artists Society in 1904-06 before moving to London with her mother and sister, following her father's death, in 1907.

There she briefly studied drawing before traveling extensively in Europe, where she was very prolific

---

[154] National Library of Australia, *op. cit.*

[155] Australian War Memorial, *Arthur Streeton,* https://www.awm.gov.au/ people/P10676828 accessed 3/2/2016.

[156] Australian War Memorial, *Arthur Streeton, op. cit.*

and had substantial successes. One work was hung at the Salon de la société des artistes français in 1911. After wintering in Spain and Morocco, her one-woman exhibition sold, among others, a pastel to the French government. Keeping studios in Paris and at the artists' colony of Etaples, she exhibited with Les peintres orientalistes français in Paris in 1914. With the declaration of war the family escaped to England, but tragedy would continue to follow Hilda. Her sister died in September and her mother less than two years later.

Major George Matson Nicholas of Melbourne found and admired her paintings abandoned in France. In October 1916 they married in London. In an occurrence that was all too frequent, but incredible in Rix's circumstances, Nicholas returned to France three days later and was killed in action the next month.

Hilda Rix Nicholas turned from sunny canvasses of a bygone world of light and innocence to several years of furious outpouring of grief and anger, depicting the morbidity, death and dark sacrifice of her war years. Yet throughout she captured a heroism that reflected her personal loss and the Digger as larger than life. At her first opportunity, in 1918, she returned to Australia, and exhibited frequently in Melbourne and Sydney. Her works of the period have been described as capturing a spiritual dimension of war, which coincided with the now legendary deeds of the Anzacs and a consolidating patriotism.

This energy became more positive as she gradually found restorative peace in the Australian landscape, but combined this with continued patriotic energy. The invitational, bucolic quality of her new works turned out to be widely welcomed, perhaps for her cheerful, healing vision, in Europe as well. Returning to France in 1924, her exhibition on Australian subjects the following year was much acclaimed. One oil work was purchased for the Musée national du Luxembourg, and soon after another was hung at the Royal Academy of Arts, London. She became an associate of the Société nationale des beaux-arts (New Salon).

In the following years the light returned to her palette, her paintings and drawings of Australian life and landscape toured England, and offered successful stimulus for migration to her homeland. This was particularly true for north-country men and women whose postwar lives were pinched by shortages and industrial unrest. Back in Australia in 1928, Hilda married Edgar Wright, a grazier, and produced her only child, Barrie Rix, in 1930. Living at Knockalong station near Delegate, New South Wales, she settled down to painting the people and setting of her rural environs. She was debilitated by Parkinson's disease by the mid-1950s and could no longer see to work. However her legacy by any measure was vast and significant. In a life beset by troubles, from which Hilda rose and rose again, her final tragedy is that despite being a most deserving candidate, her name is not known among the most noted and gifted of Australian artists of all time.[157]

Another successful woman artist who dedicated herself for a time to the depiction of war was Nora Heysen (1911-2003), the first woman to be awarded the coveted Archibald prize. She was appointed Australia's first female official war artist at the rank of captain in 1943, charged with painting women in all their roles in the war. She went round to the army, the navy and the air force, attempting to capture women in action. She painted scenes from field hospitals where soldiers languished, their lives in the balance. The stress on the women who worked in such situations could never be adequately recognised, as they struggled to keep up cheerful dispositions while suffering from trauma, exhaustion, and demands that went far beyond their training.

In 1944 Heysen began a seven-month stint in New Guinea, where conditions were far from ideal for painting, returning home only when she was driven by severe dermatitis. Undeterred she began

---

[157] *Australian Dictionary of Biography,* 'Nicholas, Emily Hilda' http://adb.anu.edu.au/biography/nicholas-emily-hilda-7837 accessed 3/2/2016.

depicting the activities of the army medical units at Sydney hospital, and then in May 1945 moved north to Queensland. There she painted the RAAF nursing sisters serving on medical evacuation flights. In total, she painted over 170 works of art in her capacity as official artist. After the war, she continued to paint but sought anonymity, although she traveled widely. She made a notable contribution to Australian art in her own capacity, and as the fourth child of Hans Heysen would have had a high bar to confront.[158]

Some artists have dedicated themselves to the theme of war. For example, for Napier Waller who designed the Hall of Memory mosaic tiles, this became a life-long project. The War Memorial has focused increasingly on depicting war and peacekeeping around the world. Perhaps one demonstration of the Memorial's commitment to broadening its interpretations of war came with the appointment of Ben Quilty as the official war artist for Afghanistan. Quilty is well known for his strong paintings and wide range of genres, from portraits, figurative subjects and still life to landscapes. Masculinity, national identity and mortality have been common themes for him. After three weeks in Afghanistan, attached to the Australian Defence Force, he was commissioned to record and interpret the experiences of Australians at Operation Slipper in Kabul, Kandahar, and Tarin Kot, as well as at Al Minhad Airbase in the United Arab Emirates. Quilty came home strongly motivated to depict all he had learnt and seen. The result was a series of large-scale portraits that capture the raw emotional and psychological consequences of military service, along with the intense physicality of these soldiers.

Another medium with popular appeal in depicting war has been poetry. At the time of World War I, Australian literature was still in relative infancy, with most of it, as with the visual arts, relating to the struggle between early settlers and the forces of nature. A cynical and anti-establishment tone had been typical, as legends were built of the Eureka stockade, the heroics of a Robin Hood casting of Ned Kelly, and songs such as "Waltzing Matilda" that flouted the authority first of Britain and its officers, and later the face of official home rule. Also derided was the 'squattocracy', or upper class landowners for whom many ordinary Australians found themselves working, under very harsh conditions. They had hoped to leave class distinctions behind when they came to Australia, only to find they were firmly entrenched here too. Arable or ranging land, for example, was increasingly scarce, while the squatters kept cattle stations of incomprehensible magnitude.

Poet Leon Gellert served in Gallipoli where he was wounded and evacuated to England, and then discharged as unfit in June 1916. His *Songs of a Campaign* (1917) was an anthology whose popularity extended to three reprints in its first year of publication. His homesickness itself must have pulled at the heartstrings of Australians, who so missed their family members overseas. Gellert's horror and disbelief at the realities of battle were powerfully recalled in his writing.[159]

> *The Jester in the Trench*
>
> "That just reminds me of a yarn" he said;
>   And everybody turned to hear his tale.
> He had a thousand yarns inside his head.
>   They waited for him, ready with their mirth
> And creeping smiles, – and then suddenly turned pale,
>   Grew still, and gazed upon the earth.
> They heard no tale. No further word was said.
>   And with his untold fun,
>   Half leaning on his gun,
>   They left him – dead.[160]

[158] Australian War Memorial, 'Nora Heysen', https://www.awm.gov.au/ exhibitions/fiftyaustralians/23.asp accessed 3/2/2016.

[159] National Library of Australia, *op. cit.*

[160] The Jester in the Trench' from *Songs of a Campaign*, Angus & Robertson: 1917 as cited in *My Country: Australian Poetry and Short Stories*, Leonie Smith, ed. Ure Smith Press, Vol. 1, p. 508.

Another poet who recorded unflinchingly the deep paradox of war was John Shaw Neilson. He himself lived in grinding poverty, was poorly educated, and did not serve in the war, both because of his failing eyesight by his early 30s, and his strong unionism. His involvement with the union occurred during his shearing years when he and his father would move and work together around the countryside. As his eyesight worsened, he spent more time in road building, which was crude and required little precision. Although his life was cut short by heart disease, he left a rich legacy of poetry, and several more volumes were published after his death. Many of his poems have also been put to song.

The Soldier is Home

Weary is he, and sick of the sorrow of war,
    Hating the shriek of loud music, the beat of the drum;
Is this the shadow called glory men sell themselves for?
    The pangs in his heart they have paled him and stricken him dumb!
        Oh ! yes, the soldier is home!

Still does he think of one morning, the march and the sun!
    A smoke, and a scream, and the dark, and next to his mind
Comes the time of his torment, when all the red fighting was done!
    And he mourned for the good legs he left in the desert behind.
        Oh! yes, the soldier is home!

He was caught with the valour of music, the glory of kings,
    The diplomats' delicate lying, the cheers of a crowd,
And now does he hate the dull tempest, the shrill vapourings –
    He who was proud, and no beggar now waits for his shroud!
        Oh! yes, the soldier is home.

Now shall he sit in the dark, his world shall be fearfully small –
    He shall sit with the old people, and pray and praise God for fine weather;
Only at times shall he move for a glimpse away over the wall,
    Where the men and the women who make up the world are striving together!
        Oh! yes, the soldier is home.

Simple, salt tears, full often will redden his eyes;
    No one shall hear what he hears, or see what he sees;
He shall be mocked by a flower, and the hush of the skies!
    He shall behold the kissing of sweethearts – close by him, here, under the trees
        Oh! yes, the soldier is home.[161]

The most popular of the Australian World War I poets was C. J. Dennis, who sold widely and remains a household name even now. *The Songs of a Sentimental Bloke* of 1915 sold over 60,000 copies in its first year, a vast number by any standards in poetry publication. Dennis appealed to mass audiences with his clever use of the slang of the times, honouring working Australians. A special pocket edition of this work was sent to troops serving overseas. His two sequels address the emotional impact of the war, and they too achieved mass popularity: *Ginger Mick* (1916) and *Digger Smith* (1918).[162] In *The Push* Dennis captures the almost accidental causes that led Australians to the front, and the unifying effect of being in uniform and valuing one's mates at the deepest level, as they face death together.

---

[161] John Shaw Neilson, from *Collected Poems of John Shaw Neilson*, Lothian, 1934.
[162] National Library of Australia, *op. cit.*

Excerpts from *The Push* by Dennis:

Becos a crook done in a prince, an' narked an Emperor,
    An' struck a light that set the world aflame;
Becos the bugles East an' West sooled on the dawgs o' war,
    A bloke called Ginger Mick 'as found 'is game –
Till they shed their silly clobber an' put on their duds fer fight.
Yes, they've shed their silly clobber an' the other stuff they wore
    Fer to 'ide the man beneath it in the past;
An' each man is the clean, straight man 'is Maker meant 'im for,
    An each man knows 'is brother man at last.
Shy strangers, till a bugle blast preached 'oly brother'ood;
But mateship they 'ave found at last; an' they 'ave found it good.

So the lumper, an' the lawyer, an' the chap 'oo shifted sand,
    They are cobbers wiv the cove 'oo drove a quill . . .

Ev'ry feller is a gold mine if yeh take an' work 'im right;
    It is shinin' on the surface now an' then;
An' there's some is easy sinking, but there's some wants dynermite,
    Fer they looks a 'opeless prospect – yet they're men.
An' Ginger – 'ard shell Ginger's showin' signs that 'e will pay;
    But it took a flamin' world-war fer to blarst 'is crust away.[163]

Poetry has been an effective instrument of anti-war and peace movements. Valerie Nichols was the Convener of Quaker Service Australia, then Quaker Service Council Australia between 1976 and 1986. She was moved to write the following poem while returning from Cambodia where she and other mainly Australian Quakers were doing service work, including running the Cambodian English Language Training (CELT) project:

On coming home from Kampuchea (1984)

I could cry for these people
but tears will not come. So many things destroyed, so many people,
so many pillars of dead houses standing like naked   begging agonised
fingers
clutching at empty air.
Cry for the travesties of homes that now squat meagre on wide
concrete bases,
flimsied in palm leaf. They will not last, but they will have to do
in the thin hungry scrabble to survive.

I could cry for these people
for the long haunted years of dwelling in caves and tunnels,
for brutalizing rain of bombs that made young girls and boys
grow into merciless savages,
whirled by the whipping winds of ideologies,
turning against their own people.

I could cry for these people
now, walking numb,

---

[163] C. J. Dennis, 'The Push' from *The Moods of Ginger Mick,* Angus & Robertson, reprinted in *My Country, op. cit.,* p. 513.

pretending, hoping to be real again -
mind-wounds and aching memories of suffering unexplained
the shadow of a demon and demoniacal cadres' raging whips.

Unscathed by the terror and the pain
which ravaged this once-lovely land, these gentle people,
I am a dazed onlooker, dismayed and sick, marvelling
that creatures so bruised can lift themselves to their feet again.
Old women with their eyes mercifully blank,
Young women lined and old, mainly their eyes alive,
watching over precious children.

Theirs is the burden, mine the onlookers' emotionality.
Tears will not come to comfort my tight aching throat
as I look at shattered femurs disintegrating on the ground
(too far gone to collect and display)
beside a chequerboard of gaping holes, unearthed mass graves,
so many empty piled skulls,
so many children's garments in filthy heaps,
so many bloodstains showing on the floor of the horror prison,
Tuol Sleng,
so many ordinary faces in the weird display -
photos of torturers as well as victims.
How can I understand the WHY of it? but the sight
prickles the nape-hairs in broad daylight,
as the smell of whistling sorcery in the evil dark of the spirit's night.

After the horror, the torture prison,
and the mind-paining, heart-jabbing boot-in-the-guts misery of one
hour there,
It was a blessed relief,
a merciful return to sanity,
to find a group of children at the gate,
just a knot of giggling, peeping, curious kids
ready to burst out laughing at a foreigner, given the slightest chance -
God's good gift of young green grass
springing in a desert place.

William Oats used this poem as the title piece for his book on Cambodia: *I Could Cry for Them: An Australian Quaker response to the plight of the people of Cambodia*. It is noteworthy that Pol Pot's regime of terror was instigated and gained ground because of the American bombing of the north of the country. It is said they dropped twice the level of fire power of all that was used in the course of World War I, in an effort to sever the supply lines of the Viet Cong. This led to a vehement hatred of all things American and Western, and gave Pol Pot the ideological fuel to destroy everything that reflected Western style development or industrialisation. But of course there was less and less connection to this logic as the killing fields were steeped with more and more blood and bone.

In her biography of editor Beatrice Davis, Jacqueline Kent makes significant observations about the impact of war on the Australian literary world.

It seems bizarre to say that the Nazi onslaught on Europe was of great benefit to Angus & Robertson and indirectly to Australian literature. But it was so. U-boat attacks on British shipping soon made the export of British goods, including books, a perilous business.

For the first time British publishers allowed their Australian counterparts to print under license their own editions of English and American books. This was a reversal of current policy: some years before, British publishers, who dominated the Australian market, had formed a cartel to prevent Australian-owned publishing companies from acquiring separate rights in British-originated books. They also agreed not to buy the rights to a U.S.-originated title unless those rights encompassed all the territories of the British Empire, including Australia. This cosy arrangement also meant, ironically, that Australian writers published overseas received inadequate 'export' royalties in their own country.[164]

Kent goes on to reveal a second reason why World War II brought a boon to publishing. The Australian government decided upon an aggressive publishing strategy of books and pamphlets for both civilians and service personnel. However, not having the capacity to print these in the quantities they desired, they turned to Angus & Robertson and its printers Halstead Press for assistance.

'For the duration of the war, Angus & Robertson became Australia's de facto Ministry of Information,' Kent remarks. While the chief editor may have been delighted with the turn in fortunes of the company, editor Beatrice Davis was less than enthused. 'Beatrice, however, was able to contain her joy. She now had to edit a stream of books, booklets and pamphlets in leaden prose with such titles as *A Manual of Elementary Drill, Food Shipments from Australia in War Time and Diesel Engine Practice*' observes Kent. Davis's own caustic remark was 'I must sweat over execrably written technical works on such subjects as poultry breeding or the wool industry or diseases of the ear, which is apt to make me very cantankerous'.[165]

With the attack on Sydney Harbour, Angus & Robertson were forced to follow the rules of the defense authorities. They had slit trenches dug outside the Press offices in Surry Hills, but these could not protect the number of staff inside. A new, bigger shelter was made from rolls of paper in the store room: about as fire-proof as fire itself! At the publishing arm, 89 Castlereagh Street, a similarly hazardous arrangement was made with the air-raid shelter in the basement. The fact that a bookshop was highly flammable, and the staff would have to descend three steep flights of wooden stairs without being burnt or asphyxiated defies the imagination. Fortunately of course no call came for the use of these facilities.[166]

The government had yet more hurdles in store for the company. Although it had huge and deemed-urgent need for publication, its new National Economic Plan stood in the way of purchasing much needed printing machines. As well, paper was in very short supply – importing being out of the question. Even the 'poor quality, yellow-grey paper made in Burnie, Tasmania, was in short supply.' Costs also skyrocketed, with paper prices increasing by 350 per cent between 1939 and 1947.[167]

Yet despite the odds, WWII was a heyday for Australian literature. Other large projects included the Commonwealth Literary Fund's Australian-Pocket Library, a series of accessible, inexpensive editions of Australian books for the servicemen. They published 25,000 of each edition, and included twenty-five titles, amounting to 625,000 volumes.[168]

The public itself had a new, voracious appetite for true stories about the war. Here journalists who had enlisted took pride of place. In *Behind Bamboo*, journalist Rohan Rivett wrote a gritty account of his life in Japanese prison camps and on the Thai-Burma railway. It eventually sold 43,000 copies. George

[164] Jacqueline Kent, *A Certain Style: Beatrice Davis, A Literary Life*, Camberwell, Victoria: Penguin, 2001, pp. 56-7.
[165] Kent, *op. cit.*, p. 57.
[166] Kent, *op. cit.*, p. 58.
[167] Kent, *op. cit.*, pp. 58-59.
[168] Kent, *op. cit.*, pp. 59-60.

Johnston, another journalist, wrote an account of the cruiser HMAS Sydney serving with the British Mediterranean fleet, entitled *Grey Gladiator*, which sold 14,000 copies. With this success he quickly delivered *Battle of the Seaways, Australia at War* and *New Guinea Diary*, all of which sold with success. Other works of significance focusing on Australia during the wartime era included works by Tom Hungerford, including *Sowers of the Wind* about Japan, *The Ridge and the River*, describing Bougainville, and *Riverslake*, examining conditions faced by postwar immigrants.[169]

Lawson Glassop, another journalist who was working in Cairo when Rommel's army was positioned to take North Africa, wrote *The Rats of Tobruk* which was eventually substantively edited by Beatrice Davis and retitled *We Were the Rats*. This work caused Angus & Robertson great headaches. In Glassop's attempt to report accurately the words and emotions of the soldiers, he depicted an unusually raw and realistic image of what happened in such situations. He also went AWOL to meet with editor Davis and suffered badly for it. There was a string of problems in getting this work to its readers, but it was eventually very popular, selling 10,000 in the first year. However, complaints of obscenity in the book resulted in court cases and it being pulled from the shelves until 1961.[170]

A number of other works might have seen the light of day but for the rather conservative publishing ethos of Angus & Robertson. Eventually the successful but controversial author, Kenneth Mackenzie, turned to publisher Jonathan Cape with his work *Dead Men Rising* about racism in war, because Angus & Robertson saw it as 'unflattering' to Australian troops.[171] The creative process is never the work of one person, but of a great many filters and finally the audience itself who interpret its meanings and messages for themselves, judge and see the work live on or die. So the desire for 'true stories' required a certain model of the truth. Other messages, particularly anything critical, were not welcome.

One of the great classic novels of World War I was Erich Maria Remarque's 1928 work, translated by Australian Arthur Wheen as *All Quiet on the Western Front*. This work is precious in part because it offers an 'enemy' voice agreeing about the futility of war. Remarque and Wheen were both veterans of the war, Wheen having served as a signaler in the AIF. Although Wheen took liberties with the German title, his own underscores the deeply paradoxical situation that typified the First World War. While so much of trench warfare appeared orderly and fighting was in fact intermittent, the sheer horror of living, and dying, in these conditions belied that sense of calm.[172]

Theatre has been another vehicle reflecting on the experiences of war. One of Australia's most popular and critical plays, by Alan Seymour, reflects the impact that drama can have. Entitled *The One Day of the Year*, it was originally published in 1958. In this play, the intellectual son Hughie and his girlfriend Jan write and publish an article criticising Anzac Day as a big booze-up, offending Hughie's father Alf who was himself a Digger at Gallipoli. Reflecting upon his play, Seymour wrote:

> One Anzac Day during the mid-50s I was walking through the back streets of the Sydney suburb of Summer Hill. It was afternoon, and the celebrations were well under way. In lanes and alleys near pubs I saw men lying in what used to be called a drunken stupor. Broken bottles abounded in the streets ... the beery haze which had settled over the most solemn day in the Australian calendar seemed to me then somehow excessive and dangerous in that it tended to amplify the already heavy sentimentality of that day. As long as men fuzzily exchanged rich, romantic memories with wartime colleagues, so long, it seemed to me, would any sensible analysis of the individual engagements of those wars,

---

[169] Kent, *op. cit.*, pp. 60, 66-67.
[170] Kent, *op. cit.*, pp. 61-65.
[171] Kent, *op. cit.*, p. 66.
[172] National Library of Australia, *op. cit.*

and indeed of war itself, be delayed.[173]

As we have read, Charles Bean was selected in 1914 by the Australian Journalists Association as the country's official war correspondent. While such a position now seems either laughable or a travesty in light of the scale of the war, Bean proved remarkably able in the face of such a vast project. He reported on the war from Egypt, Gallipoli, the Western Front and Britain. Importantly, his focus was the achievements and characteristics of Australian soldiers, and he provided ample fodder for the media. As well as many newspaper articles, he penned diaries and books, all providing the basis for his momentous post-war 'official' history. Working largely from premises at Tuggeranong, he and his team took two decades to produce the twelve volume official history, by which time, incredibly, another world war was about to be launched.

In a paradoxical moment in Christian as in war history, there was a short cease-fire for the occasion of Christmas 1914, when troops from both sides shared Christmas songs and played football. Together they expressed weariness for a fight that was, unbeknownst to them, as yet in its infancy.[174] But this break for a recognition of humanity, and even a shared belief system with a strong teaching against killing, was one of the last on a large scale. Of course throughout the war there were countless efforts to help the adversary, through rescues, medical interventions, and companionship to the bitter end. But like the lights that were extinguished in August of that year, it was the last time that adversaries would share in song for a very long time.

Music played a vital role both at home and overseas in World War I. This is no longer surprising as we know much more about the way that music stimulates all parts of the brain and leaves it awash in dopamine. It has been shown to be therapeutic in treating the symptoms of many conditions including dementia and Parkinson's disease. Music is pleasurable to us, even in our anticipation of it. For those at home and at the war front, it provided a stimulus for relaxation and for emotional expression that so much of the time had to be suppressed for social propriety. However laughter, tears, and laughter to the point of tears all provide a satisfying release. Music was a vehicle for this 'uncorking' in a more acceptable manner than was alcohol.

It was in the early period used as a vital tool of recruitment, speaking to the heart more than the head of the young people at whom it was targeted. 'We don't want to lose you but we think you ought to go' captured an ugly irony that may have been lost on young recruits, who would have seen it as highlighting the adventure and heroism of enlisting. 'Now you've got the khaki on' underscored the uniform that would bring hoped-for honour or glory as well as deeper belonging; it too typified song themes. Sentimental music and love songs were in high demand, and despite lyrics that dreamt of Ireland or Dixie, many ditties spoke to the tender hearts of those in the trenches and at home. This adoption of wartime music from overseas became even more pronounced in later wars.

When the death toll was rising and the sheen had worn off the unmitigated popularity of World War I, recruitment songs became scarce following a decline in their popularity. This highlights the fact that this particular music was primarily targeting a working class audience, who through their union movements were loudest in opposing conscription. Sober songs were shared in the battlefield and at home, expressing the grit and dismay that after all there was no romance to war. A few lines of *Our boys at the Dardanelles* (1915) spare the audience no doubt about the conditions at Gallipoli:

> They spoiled for the fight and the battle red,
> Scoff'd death in the face and bled,
> Rush'd on amidst the shot and shell
> Into a living hell.[175]

[173] Alan Seymour, *The One Day of the Year*, Angus & Robertson, 1962, p. 3.
[174] Tessa Bremner, communication to 'Anzac Conversations', 21/06/2015.
[175] Government of Australia, 'Songs of war and peace: from heroes to loss and protest', http://

However because radios were still scarce and televisions were non-existent during World War I, Australians preserved an idealistic view of the war for much longer than populations closer to the conflict.[176] As artists and writers have suggested, no form of expression can accurately express the conditions of war.

Patriotic songs did remain popular throughout the 'Great War'. War might have become uglier but Australia itself was becoming more of an entity with each passing day. Such nationalistic songs were effective in raising morale at the front and at home, sustaining the 'war effort' despite the reluctance for both conscription and enlistment. These songs contributed to national pride, spreading propaganda, and kept up the pressure to enlist. This illustrates precisely how music (and other arts) worked at the emotions and behind the rational guard of those whose ethical commitments were increasingly conflicted or outright against fighting. Such songs also asserted the uniquely Australian identity and contribution of serving. For example, reference to 'the bold, the wild and the free' in *Hail Fair Australia* captured some distinct qualities of the new Commonwealth. Such music afforded the opportunity to identify with and contribute to the identity of the young nation.[177]

Some music attempted to express a distinctly Australian presence at the front. For example, a quote of lyrics from "Boys of Australia" ran: 'So beware, Mister Kaiser, there are more lions in the den, and the cubs will fight like tigers to the bitter end.' "To Arms, Australia" was a blatant exhortation to enlist or participate in the war effort. "Keep an Eye on Tommy" and "The Kaiser's Boast" were also popular. A variation on *Waltzing Matilda* betrayed the Diggers' very cheeky outlook on the adversary.'

> Fighting the Kaiser, fighting the Kaiser,
> Who'll come a-fighting the Kaiser with me?
> And we'll drink all his beer,
> And eat up all his sausages,
> Who'll come a fighting the Kaiser with me![178]

"Australia will be There", written in 1915 for 'those who have their backs against the wall' praised the courage of Australians while asserting its independence, to the point that it became the marching song of the Australian Expeditionary Forces, used endlessly to rally demoralised troops. One verse combines the patriotism of independence with the loyalty to England that so characterised this war.

> We soldiers of Australia
> Rejoice in being free,
> And not to fetter others
> Do we go o'er the sea.
> Old England gave us freedom,
> And when she makes a start
> To see that others get it,
> We're there to take our part.

The links to Britain remained strong, and were emphasised for obvious reasons, since Australia had arguably little reason to be in WWI other than to assist in the British war effort. "Whenever Britain calls" and "Britannia needs You like a Mother" also offered clear indications that the link to the 'motherland' was still very strong. Common to almost all the songs of this era was their need to be simple and often hearty to win success and popularity. They also needed to be memorable, so that

www.australia.gov.au/about-australia/australian-story/songs- of-war-protest, accessed 02/6/2016.

[176] Jeffrey Wood, 'Music of World War I', *The Encyclopedia of World War I*, 2005, pp. 823-25.

[177] Government of Australia, 'Songs of War and Peace', *op. cit.*

[178] Government of Australia, 'Songs of War and Peace', *op. cit.*

they could be accompanied by small instruments that went to battle, such as the whistle and harmonica, without sheet music, as well as to be sung by thousands in harmony in the cathartic fun of music hall sing-alongs. Soldier songs remained crude in no small part, longing for beer and women (often in that order). The emergence of radios was for military communication; they did not become commonplace for ordinary homes until the end of World War I.[179]

In World War I Australia, the most popular music by far was dubbed 'Music Hall', which was heard and sung in theatres round the country, mainly by the working classes. It was catchy, comical, and tended to poke fun at any target: the Black man or Jew, the foreigner, the mother-in-law or domineering wife, the upper classes, as well as amusing aspects of soldiering. Mocking the enemy was common. The lyrics were full of puns, plays on words and other sources of fun. This betrayed the critical underbelly of society toward those whose ideas or politics strayed from the mainstream. The music halls proved ideal venues for social solidarity, shirking the weight of authority, and offering affordable amusement during a grim period, a chance for women in particular to get out of the home other than going to church or facing the difficulties of shopping with tight budgets.

Music was cheap to deliver and trumped all other live performances during the period, although it paid itinerant performers poorly. Sales of sheet music skyrocketed as Australians enjoyed singing these popular songs at home, often accompanied by a piano; a single song could sell a million copies. A few singers did become big names, but none of these has stayed in our lexicons.

Toward the end of the war, the music focus changed. "Keep the home fires burning" and "When the boys come home" captured the yearnings of the people. The war had been much longer and infinitely more costly in life and limb than most Australians had imagined possible. Their fatigue is reflected in the music of the era. It gave expression to what lay heavy on people's hearts and minds: the separation and loss of loved ones and homesickness, the arduousness of boot camp, the adventures of travel and challenges of war, the endless uncertainties.

Gramophones would have been heard in resorts or parks, but most ordinary families could not afford them. It was army life that introduced many people to the gramophone, since portable models were made in large numbers to entertain the troops. An appetite for these then spread with the returning soldiers, especially those who were suffering isolation in their post-war settings. The halls themselves became more and more expansive, until 3000 seats became frequent. Empires with many halls owned by single individuals or companies became typical of the business.[180]

Music was also a vehicle of overt resistance. Although such expression was inadmissible on the music-hall stages, since it might threaten the license of the owner, or drive customers away, this genre also had a considerable following. American anti-conscription songs became popular for a while, drawing a wide audience, but these were sung at demonstrations. "I didn't raise my boy to be a soldier" was a typical jingle of this type.

These were exceptions that regarded peace not as inaction or cowardice, not as the outcome of war, but as an active means of preventing war. One 1915 song, "Why can't each nation be at peace?" included the following chorus:

> Why can't each nation be at peace,
> Instead of trying to shed each other's blood?
> Why can't we happy and contented be,
> Love one another, live in Unity?[181]

---

[179] Government of Australia, 'Songs of War and Peace', *op. cit.*
[180] Jeffrey Wood, *op. cit.*
[181] Government of Australia, 'Songs of War and Peace', *op. cit.*

The Country Women's Association of South Australia's Dowlingville Branch printed a card, to be left on seats anywhere, that quoted a verse from the internationally known "Song of Peace" set to the music of Sibelius. It not only calls for peace but also recognises the common humanity of all populations:

> . . . But other hearts in other lands are beating
> With hopes and dreams as true and high as mine
>
> O hear my song, O God of all the nations,
> A song of peace for their land and for mine.

A French folk song from the 17th or 18th century describes the impact of war: a variation of what an Aussie soldier who returned from the front of World War I or more recent wars might have found upon his arrival home. It is worth noting the commonalities as well as distinctiveness of the impacts and culture of war. In translation the lyrics are:

> The brave sailor returns from war quietly
> So badly shod and badly dressed
> 'Poor sailor where are you coming from?' so quietly
> 'Madame, I've come from war', so softly . . .
> 'Would someone bring me a glass of white wine?'
> Which, gradually, the sailor sipped.
> The brave sailor set to drinking, softly . . .
> Set to drinking and to crooning, quietly.
> And the pretty hostess cried silently.
> 'What is the matter, sweet hostess?' he inquired gently.
> 'Do you regret the loss of your white wine?' he asked
> As he continued to sip his wine.
> 'It's not my wine that I regret' she whispered,
> 'But the death of my husband . . .'
> 'Monsieur you resemble him so much.'
> 'Tell me then, pretty Hostess,' he begged gently . . .
> 'You have with him three children,'
> 'But you have six at present.'
> 'They told me of his news', she answered softly.
> 'That he was dead and buried, and so
> I married again,' she told him.
> The brave sailor emptied his glass very quietly
> Without thanks but streaming tears
> He trod his way home in silence.[182]

World War II brought several changes that affected the role of music. Although the genres were similar, ranging from the patriotic to the sentimental, hawkish to pacifist, radios and phonograph records had entered homes around Australia and the music hall era had been replaced by these and films that included news reels from the front. It was possible to get closer to the action, for performers, bands and vocalists, but also for journalists who could describe and record the sounds and voices of those doing the hard yards at the front.[183] Citizens around Australia experienced 'as if first-hand' the sights and sounds of war and were not so isolated from its day-to-day realities, if delayed. However, this is not to say that many, perhaps most, were not taken in by the propaganda machine that continued to

---

[182] It is thought that this song is considerably older than indicated, but no solid evidence survives. Translation by Pamela Leach.
[183] Syracuse University Library, 'World War II Songs'. https://library.syr.edu/belfer/programs/projects/belfer78 accessed 3/2/2016.

promote the heroism and necessity of war, and the individual duty of all to support the war effort in every manner they could.

The music during World War II maintained many of the same themes. It served in recruiting, calling men to arms and women to service. There were also bawdy ditties that mocked the enemy forces. The troops entertained themselves and lightened spirits with such music. But far fewer songs were produced, and sheet music had become almost an anachronism. Songwriters were scarcer, and there were other diversions for the populace, including films and newsreels.

Again, patriotic songs had pride of place. Now there was an emphasis on Australia's brief history as one of ongoing military heroism, to which this war was making a contribution. Among the works to this end are "Awake! Awake! Awake! Australia, Freedom's Cause" and "Australia Marches On", whose chorus runs:

> March on! March on!
> For we're all together again.
> March on! March on!
> We're ready to weather the strain,
> For there's a Call come through the Ages
> And it echoes We'll be there!
> Take up the call. Come one and all
> It's Advance Australia Fair!

The theme of continuity is prominent, although it was rare for someone to serve in both World Wars. Rather the notion is of passing the torch from father to son, and the need to be faithful to the noble military tradition that made Australia fair. Another common political trend in World War II music was to celebrate new allies and, implicitly or explicitly, Australia's recognition on the world stage. In particular, these songs fostered a sense of bonding with other English-speaking countries. For example, one song set to music the fact of common history: 'We've got a big brother in America . . . The same old blood, the same old speech, the same old songs are good enough for each....'[184]

Somewhat like the music of World War I, a sense of humour and parody also appeared in songs such as "Curl The Mo, Uncle Joe of 1944", a song about Stalin's march through Europe. One of the first songs that celebrates Australia's independent role in the Pacific also emerged:

> Aussies and Yanks know that you're a great chap,
> While you're thrashing the Hun, they're busy thrashing the Jap.

Later conflicts have been more sober and perhaps reluctant affairs. Australia was no longer in any doubt about the romance of warfare. Korea, Vietnam and Iraq prompted service but a grimmer toned patriotism. Yet the unwillingness to be passive during times of injustice was strongly felt. Songs such as "Waltzing Matilda" (c. 1895) continued their anti-authoritarian popularity, while "Downunder" (1981) and "I Still Call Australia Home" (1980) are modern interpretations of the patriotic song.

Vietnam was a controversial war that produced many anti-war songs as part of the cultural shift that was occurring in all Western countries. The folk genre that was anti-authoritarian and popular during the era captured the tenor of resistance well. Australia's first resistance song of the Vietnam era was probably written when Normie Rowe, a teen star, was conscripted.

> Smiley . . .You're off to the Asian war . . .Smiley . . .And we won't
> see you smile no more . . .No more laughter in the air . . .[185]

---

[184] Government of Australia, 'Songs of War and Peace,' *op. cit.*
[185] Government of Australia, 'Songs of War and Peace,' *op. cit.*

During and following this conflict, songwriters focused increasingly on the futility and impact of wars. There was a certain popular scorn for naive heroic ditties.

In 1969, John Schumann wrote a well-known song "Vietnam and I was only 19" about John Hunt, who was maimed by a landmine and became wheelchair- dependent. It includes the following lyrics:

> And can you tell me, doctor, why I still can't get to sleep?
> And night time's just a jungle dark and a barking M16?
> And what's this rash that comes and goes, can you tell me what it means?
> God help me, I was only nineteen.[186]

Schumann's graphic lyrics capture much more than just the hardships of war. Although they concern a veteran who was tragically disabled, his song is explicit about what were for many worse, the post-traumatic stress symptoms. He also suggests in this respect that 'it was a war within yourself', and a sense of being misled by the previous generations and their silence regarding the harshness of the front. 'The Anzac legends didn't mention blood 'n sweat 'n tears,' his lyrics reproach. Cold Chisel's "Khe Sanh" was another Australian Vietnam protest song of note. Others that have had a lasting hold are "Postcards from Saigon" by James Blundell, whose lyrics reveal the aspirations and dashed dreams of the soldiers, the conflicted sense of betrayal of comrades in coming home but of a continued conviction of the justice in fighting. Again he refers to health issues, in this case suffered by his brother in the wake of the war. Excerpts from the lyrics include:

> My brother had a dream, my brother wore the jungle green,
> My brother went to Vietnam, went for Harold Holt and Uncle Sam,
> He sent postcards from Saigon, 'I'm alright but it's all wrong'
> He felt guilty coming home …
> Why must history repeat itself time and time again?
> Close the circle and make him whole again,
> Close the circle and bring him home again.[187]

As we have seen, humour was often used as a release from the tensions of wartime. American academic and musician, singer-songwriter Tom Lehrer enlisted for several years, although without seeing action himself. His war songs became very popular in Australia. In this song he is poking fun at his own kind, people who used satire in music to highlight the political ironies of war and politics, which he later taught along with Mathematics at the university level.

> We are the folk song army.
> Everyone of us cares.
> We all hate poverty, war, and injustice,
> Unlike the rest of you squares.
>
> There are innocuous folk songs.
> Yeah, but we regard 'em with scorn.
> The folks who sing 'em have no social conscience.
> Why they don't even care if jimmy crack corn.
>
> If you feel dissatisfaction,
> Strum your frustrations away.
> Some people may prefer action,

[186] Government of Australia, 'Songs of War and Peace,' *op. cit.*
[187] http://aussie.totaltabs.com/tablature/James_Blundell/Postcards_From _Saigon_Chord_26492, accessed 6/2/2016.

But give me a folk song any old day.

The tune don't have to be clever,
And it don't matter if you put a coupla extra syllables into a line.
It sounds more ethnic if it ain't good English,
And it don't even gotta rhyme–excuse me–rhyne.
Remember the war against Franco?
That's the kind where each of us belongs.
Though he may have won all the battles,
We had all the good songs.

So join in the folk song army,
Guitars are the weapons we bring
To the fight against poverty, war, and injustice.
Ready! aim! sing!

Lehrer was writing in the 1950s and 1960s while the Cold War was raging, and after Hiroshima and Nagasaki, it seemed perfectly possible that another war of a global scale could occur. His response was to show how ridiculous it was to imagine that that the human race might survive World War III. Whether he thought that meant such an event would never transpire is doubtful as he was very skeptical about the wisdom of politicians. He called his song 'So long Mom' an example of 'World War III pre-nostalgia' because he thought if we wanted to be sentimental and patriotic about that war, which he determined was one of the driving forces behind warfare, the only opportunity would be in advance of it. Lehrer highlights the way in which wars galvanise solidarity and nationalism, and bring for many cherished memories of adventure, mateship, heroism, and masculinity which die out and are transparently false in everyday life. The fears and prospect of another war have flowed on from the McCarthy era into the 21st century.

Asked in 2006 how he was enjoying Grade 4 in his new school, a Quaker boy called Paul answered, 'Mum, it is such a relief!' 'And why is that, Dear?' responded the mother, surprised. 'Because I have been there a whole month and no one has even mentioned World War III. At my old school, it was all the boys could talk about, and they were so excited about all the weapons we're going to have. I told them 'Forget it. You won't even know about it'.[188]

Here is Tom Lehrer's song about World War III.

So long, Mom, I'm off to drop the bomb,
So don't wait up for me.
But while you swelter
Down there in your shelter,
You can see me on your tv.

While we're attacking frontally,
Watch Brinkley and Huntley,
Describing contrapuntally
The cities we have lost.
No need for you to miss a minute
Of the agonizing holocaust.

Little Johnny Jones he was a US pilot,
And no shrinking violet was he.

---

[188] Pamela Leach, personal anecdote.

He was mighty proud when World War III was declared,
He wasn't scared, no siree!
And this is what he said on
His way to Armageddon:

So long, Mom, I'm off to drop the bomb,
So don't wait up for me. But though I may roam,
I'll come back to my home,
Although it may be a pile of debris.
Remember, Mommy, I'm off to get a commie,
So send me a salami, and try to smile somehow.
I'll look for you when the war is over,
An hour and a half from now!

The late 20th century and 21st century brought a popular climate of anti-authoritarian and anti-war themes, such as Do-Re-Mi's "Warnings Moving Clockwise", Midnight Oil's "U.S. Forces" and the John Butler Trio's "Fire in the Sky".[189] John Butler's lyrics are nuanced, showing the various sides of war, its illogic and rationalising from different perspectives. In particular Butler underscores the civilian costs. An excerpt from "Fire in the Sky" captures these conflicting emotions and responses:

All came crumbling down tears in our eyes as it rained con-
fusion the whole world has changed
But I don't understand how one man can kill in the name of peace, that's ridiculous
But I understand I will defend my family, from both sides of misery
…And as those children die, pawns in the name of collateral damage
The whole world goes mad
Standing on your quicksand, the more we fight we sink
And vengeance gives us home, at least that's what we think …[190]

Glenda Cloughley, a Jungian analyst and composer, outlined for her Anzac Conversations audience the way in which her community oratorio, *A Passion for Peace* emerged from a dream about two women who have inspired her, and as a tribute to peace efforts during World War I by 1300 women from warring nations who gathered at the Hague at the International Conference of Women in 1915. The writing of the *Passion* drew on the hope of a common spring from which we all long to drink. Among the songs is an aria for Jane Addams (President of the 1915 Congress and later a Nobel Peace Laureate) emphasising the Quaker value of listening for ways our love might break the curious spell of war: 'The Ear of the Soul: While war casts its curious spell of discord, within without, the ears of the soul are listening.'

Cloughley's oratorio was presented and recorded in Albert Hall in 2015 by the 110 string cast of 'A Chorus of Women' and associated artists. The music included two levels of awareness – the underlying harmony, and the overlay of trauma and its impact in freezing time and blocking human potential. Our political systems reflect that trauma, according to the composer. *A Passion* includes songs about harmony, love, death and regeneration, stories of individuals affected by war, the psychology of the political and military leaders who lacked love as children, the laws of peace as represented in the resolutions of the Hague gathering, and a citizens' chorus 'We are all the songs of peace and freedom.'

It was argued in the discussion following the presentation on DVD of segments of *A Passion* that we tend to elect to high office many who lack love in their lives and are unable to show empathy. There was a sense that it is up to those of us who have been more fortunate to work to change the political

---

[189] Government of Australia, 'Songs of War and Peace,' *op. cit.*
[190] http://www.azlyrics.com/lyrics/johnbutlertrio/fireinthesky.html, accessed 6/2/2016.

culture. Artists of all kinds are often the people who stand up, but none of us can be silent in the face of the dangers ahead. The role of 'A Chorus of Women' has been to sing a way forward for a more positive future, and to express hope in power of building peace.[191]

Di Bretherton's film, *As the Mirror Burns* is one of innumerable Australian war films. From the newsreels of the First and Second World Wars have emerged documentaries, 'docudramas' which attempt to show true-to-life war situations through fictionalised personal lenses, actors, or subplots that add interest. There have also been many popular films that paid only casual attention to the details of a conflict without engaging it seriously, or which focus on the life or activities of a particular person.

Other films have demanded much more serious reflection from their audiences, even if the central plot or scenario is only hypothetical. Emma Campbell notes '. . . when war historians look to the cinema for a fresh interpretation of a conflict – or just for good old-fashioned entertainment – they have a glut of films to choose from. The action, glory and tragedy of war make it a popular choice for filmmakers the world over, and thousands of movies on the topic have been made since the birth of cinema in 1895.' Campbell also remarks that there are many 'anti-war films, concentrating on suffering and horror and designed to make a political or ideological statement about the futility of the endeavour.'[192]

It is noteworthy that in the contemporary era there continues to be a focus and interrogation of war in Australian films. The most tragic side of this is that people do find war exciting, and such films simultaneously appeal to those who appreciate horror films, historical and military history themes, and even fantasy, as they frequently offer larger-than-life depictions of events and actions. Computer enhancements allow for depictions from 'inside' the action in a way that is not possible when relying on traditional cinematography. However, the suggestion that this means that such recent films depict wars with greater truth or proximity to real experience is questionable. Some certainly may offer such qualities, while others simply play on the extremes of the medium without regard to authenticity. Their concern is much more significantly about the bottom line, and film remains a big industry.

Di Bretherton argues that she does not intend to tell the audience what to think or believe with *As the Mirror Burns*. She represents a variety of lenses that challenge our constructions, not only of the Vietnam War, but also of wars in general. She also interrogates related concepts such as liberation, the role of women in war and peace, and the modes of representation of history. The title suggests we must look honestly at ourselves. The thread of the film moves from observing Vietnam to finding that the Vietnamese are also looking at us. The reflection of ourselves in their eyes is confronting.[193]

War films continue to be produced because war itself is mystifying. We are interested in 'a taste' of it in an attempt to understand it better. Why are we violent? How does war come about, how and why do humans behave in the way they do under such conditions and how do they survive? Sometimes these questions relate to personal life experience, or that of family members. However, for much of the time this curiosity can simply be reduced to being human, because the human experience has so often been touched by war. In particular, Australia's identity has been and is continuing to be defined in no small part by its militarism. This generates in Australians a particular curiosity toward warfare.

---

[191] The recording can be heard at www.chorusofwomen.org
[192] Emma Campbell, The Australian War Memorial, 'Historians and Hollywood: The Best War Movies', accessed 21/2/2012, https://www.awm.gov.au/blog/ 2012/02/21/historians-and-hollywood-the-best-war-movies, accessed 24/2/2016.
[193] Bretherton, *op. cit.*, Introduction.

A sampling of the classics among Australian war films includes:

40,000 Horsemen (1941): WWI about Gallipoli, filmed on Cronulla Beach

The Rats of Tobruk (1944): WWII; North Africa.

The Odd Angry Shot (1979): Australians in Vietnam.

Breaker Morant (1980): Second Boer War. True story. The court-martial of Breaker Morant. Three officers are accused of a war crime. Legal drama and a tragic story.

Gallipoli (1981): WWI, ANZACs on the Turkish front. Intense infantry combat.

The Highest Honor (1982): WWII. True story. British and Australian raid on Japanese occupied Singapore Harbour.

Attack Force Z (1982): WWII, South-west Pacific.

ANZACS (1985, TV mini-series): During WWI, ANZACs are followed from Gallipoli to the battlefields of the Somme, Vimy Ridge etc.

An Indecent Obsession (1985): WWII, Pacific.

The Lighthorsemen (1987): Australian cavalry, WWI.

Blood Oath (1990): WWII, Indonesia. Australian POWs and Japanese captors.

The Last Bullet (1995, TV): WWII, South Pacific.

Changi (2001, TV mini-series): WWII, Singapore, Australian POW's.

My Brother Jack (2001, TV): Outbreak of WWII.

Kokoda (2006): The war in the Pacific. On the Kokda trail. Focuses on the story of two brothers.

Beneath Hill 60 (2010): WWI, Western front. Australian miners fighting in the tunnel systems.[194]

---

[194] http://allaboutwarmovies.com/2010/12/21/australian-war-movies-a-list, accessed 24/2/2016.

Chapter VII
Australians Building Peace

Britain shall remain neutral.
I hate war!
Lamps are going out all over Europe. We shall not see them lit again in our lifetime.
– Edward Grey, Foreign Secretary of Britain, August 3, 1914

War has been forced on us.
– Czar Nicholas II, Russia

There are few people who do not desire peace. Some industries and governments have high stakes in the *prospect* of war (if not its actuality) through the profit-driven military industrial complex. A few others rely on the mayhem of localised wars to exploit minerals or other resources. A small number see merit in dying what they consider the death of a martyr, and the existence of war zones enhances this possibility. However the vast majority of the seven billion earthly inhabitants do earnestly desire peace.

Jean Zaru is a Palestinian Christian and Quaker, a lifelong tireless peacebuilder and human rights activist in the most difficult of conditions. Her reflections on the Israel-Palestine dilemma surely ring true for pacifists and peacebuilders in every violent conflict. She reflects that

> Interdependence is the watchword of our era. Problems cannot be isolated from one another. World systems are interconnected, including the structures of globalisation, such as banking, commerce, communications, and armaments. In the area of consciousness, world events have pressed upon us our sense of global connections, whether in the development of a community mentality with its expectations and desires or the awareness of the economic damage of careless industrialisation. More than ever, we human beings *really do* depend on one another. My well-being and yours, my security and yours, my freedom and yours, my rights and yours are inseparable. Hearing one another in the mutuality of dialogue gives us the knowledge and wisdom to discern our close connections, to see the real implications of our situation, and to join together in positive and creative ways. As a Palestinian, I know full well that the people of Israel are not freer than we are. Both Israelis and Palestinians live in fear. Neither Israelis nor Palestinians have peace. Both Israelis and Palestinians yearn for security. Others cannot give us freedom, peace and security. No

government, no army, no wall no matter how long or high will provide for us what can only be supplied by the cultivation of mutuality and trust . . . What will bring us peace is inward transformation that will lead to outward action ... We cannot live a day without saying yes or no to death or for life, for war or for peace, injustice or justice. The choice is ours. To postpone or evade the decision is to decide.[195]

Paradoxically, we inhabit what Alan Watts calls 'the age of anxiety'.[196] We have little idea what lies ahead, and so our hearts and minds are filled with doubt. While we may not be worse off than any other age, many of the constants, the sources of security that consoled previous generations have for many people melted away or become contested ground. These include religion, which promised the opportunity at least of a happy hereafter; class, knowing how one fitted into the world, and, for better or worse, that one might continue in that role from one generation to another. Another source of stability was geographic constancy, because most peoples had been relatively settled, or migrated as a culture over many generations, up until the beginnings of mass emigrations in the 19th century, which have taken on, in leaps, larger and larger proportion and speed. Families and entire ethnicities have been splintered. The wars of the 20th and now 21st centuries have broken the floodgates entirely, so that the movement of peoples has taken on incalculable dimensions and suffering. The assurances we used to give ourselves no longer have much hold.

Into this void has come a rather empty term, 'security'. While it refers to a familiar desire for wellbeing, in fact any firm assurance of unbroken happiness for the future can only be deceptive. Youth is no barrier against eventual age. Great amounts of wealth do access medical care but cannot shelter us from war, sickness and death. Expensive arms, as this book has illustrated, have not been guarantors of peace.

As humans we are fragile and mortal; whatever, if anything, lies beyond, seems not at our behest. This does not mean we are morally free to do nothing about the future. But we may have no choice but to give ourselves over to deriving happiness and awe in the present, from our moment-to-moment engagement with one another, with nature and life, the arts, building community, learning and working, science and the unknown, with loving and being loved. And from these same places may come our diverse senses of the eternal and our inspiration to preserve what is central and good by embracing it with peace.

Yet the ephemeral desire for security has funded and fueled the biggest, scariest, and most fear-mongering of private industries humans have ever seen. We are all contributors and stakeholders. Partnering as clients, providers and customers with governments and thus their often ignorant or impotent tax-paying publics, as well as with other warring bodies and their often unwilling or unwitting supporters has achieved this outcome.

And so the 'age of anxiety' has drawn us into battle after battle, either in notion or in practice, searching for security. A lesson we have difficulty accepting is that peace is not merely the absence of fighting with arms. A truce may lead to peace, yet all too often as veterans recall it means that the air is quiet but as full of tension and fear as if battles were raging. Insecurity cuts like a knife, the more real we make it. It can lead to paranoia, trauma and very extreme responses to inflated or imagined threats.

What must characterise peace for it to have substance? As this volume has suggested, to be robust peace must entail an absence of fear. So for example, a society that suffers a pandemic of domestic or sexual violence cannot be considered at peace. While some may regard this as broadening the defi-

[195] Jean Zaru, *Occupied with Violence A Palestinian Woman Speaks*, Minneapolis: Fortress Press, 2008, pp. 128-9.
[196] Alan W. Watts, *The Wisdom of Insecurity*, New York: Random House 1951.

nition of war too far, one needs to consider the fear of such persecution and the absence of rights for victims as being quite similar to the situation of refugees who flee war-torn zones. There are difficulties obtaining accurate statistics around family violence in Australia. Even its definition is different according to state, with Tasmania lagging by limiting its definition to partner violence and abuse in contrast to any family member or carer as included by other states and territories. Family violence is thought to remain a much-underreported area of violence. Roughly speaking, it is thought that one in four women have or will experience family violence.[197] As well, the advocacy group called 'One in Three' highlights the statistic that one of every three Australian victims of family violence is a male.[198]

The World Health Organisation's 2013 study of intimate partner violence and non-partner sexual violence against women paints a grim picture. The study suggests that one in three women in high-income countries will experience such violence over the course of her life, and that while the risks are significant already in the 15 to 19 year old age group, the peak of reported violence is in the 40 to 44 age group. It is further considered that older women are much less likely to report such violence, but are not any less vulnerable to it.[199]

The impacts of this 'war' include physical and psychological trauma or injury, mental health problems, substance abuse, communicable and other illnesses (such as cardiovascular disease), irritable bowel syndrome, chronic pain, limited reproductive control, low birth weights, disability and death by homicide, suicide or disease.[200]

The experience of First Nations people in Australia has been of extreme physical, cultural, emotional and spiritual violence. To name just some such acts, the list would include murders, massacres, ethnic cleansing, forced assimilation, abductions of women and children, removal of large numbers from Country, confiscation of land, residential schools and missions that suppressed language and culture, economic marginality, denial of civil rights, institutional racism, emotional and physical abuse, and incrimination and incarceration based on racial profiling. Since first contact, Europeans have documented many instances of positive and generous welcome and assistance from Indigenous individuals and groups, but the climate established by colonialism and post-federation Australia has been far from one of unequivocal goodwill and trust toward its First Nations. In the current situation, the Indigenous minority suffers from the disadvantage of an extreme power differential in which it has little leverage.

Peace must be a condition with qualities that are mutually agreeable to all parties, offering shared respect, characteristics that draw people, groups and governments together because they find greater benefit through this condition than through armed conflict. This is only likely if the conditions of peace bring justice, which in turn entails the substantive accord of human and civil rights. It is self-evident to us that wartime erodes the rights of citizens even when the country, such as Australia, is far-flung from the war zone. But many decisions will be taken by those in power without the consent of the governed. In modern states we are told that security demands it, because we cannot always know the secrets that intelligence shares with politicians. This contrasts quite sharply with the fundamentals of democracy that suggest every adult is capable of understanding the workings and decision-making of government, and of assessing the performance of leaders.

---

[197] For example, according to ANROWS, http://anrows.org.au/publications/ horizons/PSS, accessed 18/9/2016.

[198] http://www.oneinthree.com.au, accessed 16/10/2016.

[199] WHO, 'Prevalence and health effects of intimate partner violence and non-partner sexual violence', 2013.

[200] WHO, *op. cit.*

It is interesting to consider how our First Nations managed to avoid wars of possession, while managing both the landscape and economy of the continent across cultural boundaries. Theirs was a gentle approach to governance, it would seem. Aboriginal scholar and author Bruce Pascoe notes,

> This absence demands respect, and the skills employed to bring about the longest lasting pan-continental stability the world has known must be investigated because they might become Australia's greatest export. Behind the green bough of peace brought by ambassadors of distant clans and the excitement of the trading market there must have been an intellectual musculature, not just to forge that peace, but to maintain it. Australian anthropologist, Ian Keen, says: 'The genius of Ancestral Law was that people of a wide region could agree to a body of legitimate law without there being legislation, and in spite of the autonomy of individuals and kin groups … Ancestral Law had a large discretionary component … (and) certain ritual practices tended to induce in young people a disposition to conform to shared values and norms, and to defer to people in authority.'[201]

Pascoe goes on to suggest that the decision-making processes that seemed to have overarching consensus across the very great number of First Nations make one 'think of the word democracy'. He describes how Elders achieved their roles through long processes of initiation that could not be hastened or controlled by force or inheritance. 'They earned the respect of their fellows' he suggests.[202] By contrast, the methods used to subdue and control these same groups by the colonisers must have seemed very clumsy, indeed brutish. The Whites could have been assessed as quite uncivilised in many respects that counted, in preserving the all-important peace, such as upholding the respect and goodwill of the people onto whose land they had arrived.

The moment of the creation of the League of Nations held much hope for many around the world who had come to the conviction of 'Never Again' by relinquishing the notion that war would solve conflict. In response to the Protocol for the Pacific Settlement of International Disputes, put forward by the League of Nations, Australian Quakers stated:

> As an attempt to provide for conciliatory and judicial settlement of disputes by arbitration, and so far as it secures a measure of disarmament, we approve the protocol. We believe in the pacific settlement of international disputes by conciliation or arbitration. The only true sanction for international justice is moral consent, and the only security is trust in the spirit of goodwill in all men.[203]

Their tone is a cautious, conditional one. This by no means suggests that they did not welcome peace. It is only that they worried about the various bases under which 'peace' could be secured that would be destructive of the necessary ingredients of a just and lasting peace. In retrospect who can say that they need not have worried when the authors would see within their own lifetimes the dropping of nuclear bombs on Japan. The building and use, not once but twice, of weapons of such magnitude and terror within a few days against civilian targets defies any definition of spirit of goodwill or laying the grounds for trust.

Just as definitions of peace are nuanced and varied, the means and ways to achieve and maintain peace are also many. The modern nation-state system is based on alliances and deterrence as primary foundations for peace. Deterrence employs a military threat-based logic: 'If you do not play the game by our rules, then you risk sanctions or military engagement, even invasion.' The League of Nations, founded in order to uphold the Versailles Treaty agreed upon at the end of World War I failed, we are

---

[201] Bruce Pascoe, *Dark Emu, Black Seeds: Agriculture or Accident?* Broome: Magabala Books, 2016, p. 130.
[202] Pascoe, *op. cit.,* p. 131.
[203] Australia General Meeting, 1925, *this we can say, op. cit.* S. 3.89.

told, because it 'lacked teeth', meaning the capacity to enforce its conventions and treaties militarily. However, other perspectives suggest that its primary flaw was that the peace it sought to uphold fell considerably short of a just peace. The imposition of the payments for postwar reconstruction onto the German people alone was far more than they and their war-torn economy could manage. It threw them into hardships so severe that many more deaths were incurred, and anger brewed. Yet even knowing of these conditions, the Allies did not reverse their decisions. Respect and goodwill were not present, let alone mutual trust.

The United Nations, even more than its predecessor, intentionally upholds peace and the sanctity of human life, and thus rights, as its primary values. Its organisations do remarkably effective, excellent work in promoting development, the protection of refugees, of women and children, and of Indigenous Peoples among others. With the downfall of European empires, the members of the UN include almost all the nation-states of the world and a number of other bodies have some level of inclusion, if not full membership. Yet in order to secure its core objectives, the UN Security Council operates on the basis of military deterrence. It does this first by threat and in the final instance by military action. Initially this involved inserting forces as unarmed moral presences to 'keep the peace' upon the agreement of all parties involved. However these mandates are often now greatly stretched. There is a willingness to intervene with armed forces and the blessing of the Security Council to 'build peace' in hot situations where wars are being fought.

This leaves those who want to be peacemakers by means other than militarism and weaponry an additional task of reclaiming this 'peacebuilding' term to mean something greater than control through threat of force. In particular, for those who identify as pacifists and do not regard military solutions as appropriate in any conflict, or as a response to aggression, the term 'peacebuilding' must include as viable a nonviolent path.

The United Nations makes a laudable contribution in bringing nations and other parties together for consultation. Many conventions and treaties have been signed and ratified within the member governments. Yet lamentably, as Australians know from recent national refugee policies, even such ratification, and stern critique from the appropriate UN bodies, does not necessarily influence politically-driven outcomes. So respecting such UN agreements remains largely a matter of expediency for the governments of the day. Fortunately the UN remains reluctant to turn to military action beyond the 'blue beret' peacekeepers.

One of the saving graces of the UN structures is that the General Assembly must agree to the budget of the whole institution, including that of the Security Council. However, one of the greatest Achilles' heels of this arrangement is that the largest dues are always owed by the United States, as the richest member nation. It is quick to withhold its contributions, sometimes for years at a time, if it disapproves of particular initiatives. So it would be very naive to imagine that the UN is neutral or does not struggle with political imperatives. Too often, on the other hand, the US demands the support of the Security Council to take action against an 'offender' such as Iraq, and if this is not given, then the US merely goes ahead with its military action with its allies but without the benefit of the UN's blessing, or perhaps as the US views it, the 'curse' of the UN's sway.

However, the UN often takes courageous stands and its Secretaries General have usually served as preeminent examples of peace and goodwill. Secretary General Dag Hammarskjöld (1905 –1961) was a Swedish diplomat, economist, and author, who died in a suspicious plane crash on his way to cease-fire negotiations in the Congo. Hammarskjöld was the UN's second Secretary General, who served from 1953 until his death in 1961. He is one of only four people to be awarded the Nobel Prize posthumously. US President John F. Kennedy called Hammarskjöld 'the greatest statesman of our century'. Fortunately he has been the only UN Secretary General to die in office.

As a healthy effort to balance the state-based slant of the UN, around the world UN Associations are local and national organisations supporting the work of the UN. Its associations are inspired by the opening words of the United Nations Charter, which read 'We the Peoples'. This founding phrase recognises that because

> . . . the UN is not simply a community of nations, but a community of peoples and of individuals, United Nations Associations provide a link between the citizens of the world and the United Nations by seeking to ensure that the UN is relevant to the lives of the peoples it exists to serve. Established in 1946, the United Nations Association of Australia (UNAA) promotes the aims and work of the United Nations amongst Australians of all walks of life. The UNAA engages Australian citizens in the work of the UN through a range of activities, including education programs and advocacy work. These activities are carried out by various teams including our Divisions operating in every State and Territory, as well as our National Office, which is based in Canberra. The UNAA also works in five countries in the Pacific – supporting volunteers establishing local UN Associations and running Model UN Conferences for high school and tertiary students.[204]

Much of the UN's most effective peace work lies beyond the Assembly and Security Council in the mandates and work of its various agencies, such as the United Nations International Children's Emergency Fund (UNICEF), which was set up in 1946 to help disadvantaged children in Europe and China. Its name was changed in 1950 to the United Nations Children's Fund and it was given an indefinite mandate. Its work has saved millions of lives and improved their conditions of existence. The United Nations High Commission for Refugees (UNHCR) is another body that does very effective work advocating for and protecting those who are persecuted, often in war situations. These and many other arms give the UN its most significant strength and substance, as well as informing the peace work of the UN's top bodies.

Whatever else can be said about the great powers, it was with sober hearts that their leaders stepped into the fray of World War I. The Czar still inhabited the dreamland of an autocrat whose vastly wealthy family had kept several hundred million people in penury for centuries. Yet he could see that war would be an undesirable way forward.[205] Grey did keep Britain neutral as long as he could maintain any degree of support for this, although it meant waiting until Belgium had been invaded. The lamps of which he spoke might be taken literally, referring to the devastation of war and the realisation that whole towns and villages would soon disappear from the map. He knew that countless lives would be extinguished, never to 'shine' again. Indeed, civilization as it had been known in Europe would be destroyed beyond recovery.

Just as Grey described his sense of invading gloom at the onset of WWI, Pierre Ceresole, a remarkable Swiss, made a very different kind of statement with the outbreak of WWII. He had organised 32 work camps to assist those suffering from floods in Liechtenstein between the wars, as well as providing considerable support to communities in need in India, where he became a Quaker. On the eve of a second world war, when blackouts were declared, Ceresole

> . . . had thrown open all his windows, with lights left burning, and strode down to a darkened Neuchatel market-place, where his waist-line blue torchlight, revolving slowly revealed dark listening figures slinking in the background doom. There Pierre read a message from Copenhagen Quakers urging Quakers to keep their Inner Light burning at the full while the lights were going out all over Europe. Pierre's stirring message was soon

---

[204] http://www.unaa.org.au/about-us, accessed 29/2/2016.
[205] National Library of Australia, *The Great War: For Such a Stupid Reason Too*, BBC Film, *op. cit.*

interrupted by the arrival of the Swiss gendarmes who carted him off to prison.[206]

Knowing from history the challenges he faced, William Oats noted in 1938 the dangers of pacifism for those who use it as an escape, those who are passive, in other words, rather than those who face the full moral and political weight of this path.

> There seems to me to be a great danger of sentimentalism in the ultra-pacifism which runs away from the real problems which face those who are striving to build peace. It's so easy to condone injustice and to keep on saying that everything in the garden is lovely, when all the time the garden is getting smaller and smaller and nasty noises are coming over the crumbling walls, etc., etc . . . If only Britain, instead of calling loudly about defenses, would get her own house in order, settle her appalling social problems and face immediately the Jewish problem.[207]

'The Jewish problem' in his eyes was the problem of antisemitism and how to protect Jews and their friends, not a 'Jewish' problem at all. Pacifists like others have their differences, and are fallible. It is often a desire to limit hierarchical structures and impose ideologies that leads the peacebuilders into trouble. As they work together, it is not so often the grand questions such as 'what constitutes a just peace?' that cause them to founder. Often it is the difficulty of working together with little hierarchy combined with strong principles and personalities, and the evolution of groups that come with new events and insights that brings challenges. It is this tendency to entropy that makes any groups that have survived a century or several little short of miraculous. Practicing peace inside a 'like-minded' group is already a challenge. Few pacifists are under any illusion that this is an easy project. What is peace, after all? It may be a moving aspiration in the context of particular cultural and historical moments. Di Bretherton sadly reflects,

> One of the greatest sources of disillusionment and despair in my life has been living through the destructiveness of peace groups that break down, usually in a very public way, in factional fighting and petty dispute. This of course undermines the message of peace. Already accused of being idealistic and unrealistic the peace movement sometimes seems to be bent on proving the critics right.[208]

As scholar Christian Appy underscores, the traumas of world wars have not disappeared. They have only been added to by those who have seen or participated in the horrors of subsequent wars. In the United States, an estimated 22 veterans suicide every day. The rate for vets of Iraq and Afghanistan according to one study is 50 per cent higher than that of the public at large. Appy notes that we live under conditions of perpetual wartime without this being a part of popular consciousness.[209]

What kind of 'musculature', to use Pascoe's vivid word, can be sufficient to undergird pacifism and peacebuilding, especially in the face of rampant militarism? Oats quotes from a letter he wrote home in Easter 1939, while in London. He reflects on means and ends, always a test for the nascent or wavering pacifist. Oats worries that there was a growing fear that Chamberlain's promise of 'peace in our time' is an empty boast.

> There are two approaches, [Fenner Brockway] said, to the present situation we are facing. One is the 'political', the other is the 'moral', though Quakers would probably use the

---

[206] Oats, *op. cit.* p. 92. Obviously Swiss neutrality had its own tone.

[207] Oats, *op. cit.,* p. 30.

[208] Bretherton, *op. cit.,* p. 41.

[209] Christian Appy, 'Burying Vietnam, Launching Perpetual War: How thanking the veteran meant ignoring what happened' www.TomDispatch: Tomgram: Christian Appy, "Honor" the Vietnam Veteran, Forget the War, accessed 29/3/2016. Appy teaches History at the University of Massachusetts and is the author of three books on the Vietnam War.

word 'spiritual'. If one comes at decisions from the political angle, there are times when one has to be prepared to sacrifice a point of principle (say on the question of fighting) to the ultimate aim in view ... From the moral (or spiritual) point of view the pacifist comes to certain crises when he has to sacrifice some apparent element of reason in order to be true to the thesis that the ends do not justify means. Whichever path he chooses, he is 'on the horns of a dilemma' ...[210]

David Stephens of the Honest History Coalition spoke to the Anzac Conversations group about the acquisition of influence by the arms industry, and the ways in which Australia has become an increasingly significant player on the global stage in this capacity. The country is now the world's sixth largest importer of arms, especially heavy purchases. This is a stark number if one considers that by population, Australia is the 55th largest state. Even its measure as the 10th most advantaged by per capita income leaves one pondering whether its assets are best spent on weaponry. Australia is involved in an arms race of which most citizens are unaware. This innocence is not, in itself, apolitical, as Jean Zaru might point out. The responsibility of citizens in a democracy is precisely not to be naive of what acts are carried out in their name.

According to Stephens, this history of engagement with the weapons industry has influenced Australians' memory of war and normalised the concept that war as a usual, even perhaps necessary part of humanity. He went on to suggest that the impact of this integration of the culture of war is particularly potent as it is exercised on children who are influenced by education programs and curricula that include phrases such as 'hero soldier'. This ordinariness has been imprinted to the point that war is seen by some as inevitable and the only way Australia will be safe. Airport advertising by arms manufacturers reinforces this 'obvious' logic and the notion that this choice can and should be made as easily as one chooses a hotel for a holiday, or a car rental agency.[211]

In truth of course this is part of the illusion of democratic decision-making in security matters. Very little is in the public arena, except such issues as lobbying for a contract for submarine construction, in which South Australians recently pressed hard for the jobs they imagined would result. No consideration seems to have entered the popular discourse as to the implications of building such vessels, designed for making nuclear strikes. Apparently it is so obvious that Australia needs the twelve subs that no one thought it worthwhile to publicly question the underlying premise. This would likely be interpreted as unpatriotic as the South Australians fought hard to keep the construction happening there, with the jobs that would result, over having the project go to France along with the $50 billion that is being paid to that country for the overall contract.

The popular impression that supports militarism is the view that extensive hardware and firepower are necessary in order for Australia to be responsible in fulfilling its obligations in United Nations peacekeeping and the ANZUS Treaty (New Zealand was suspended between 1986 and 2007 for declaring its waters nuclear-free, and even today is not included in its talks, which are bilateral). Indeed, it seems the Australian Defence Force is quite happy to keep such views alive.

However the arming of Australia can also be read as a tactic to intimidate its regional neighbours, which could precipitate conflict. In fact its weaponry is being used, most actively in terms of protection, not versus invaders but from the arrival of asylum seekers, incorrectly dubbed 'illegal migrants', despite their rights to claim protection as defined by the UN and ratified by the Australian parliament. Naval vessels have been involved in towing boats of would-be asylum seekers away from Australian waters and in some cases into Indonesian waters. In other cases they have monitored these vessels, sometimes from the air or considerable distance, made decisions with limited information about the

---

[210] Oats, *op. cit.*, p. 2.

[211] David Stephens, Secretary, Honest History Coalition, 'Anzac Conversations: Citizen Voices for Peace', Friends Meeting House, Canberra, 8/11/2015.

authenticity of mayday calls, and in some instances allowed them to sink.

Such actions, far from fulfilling our UN obligations, are in complete violation. Even where the navy has taken asylum seekers on board, these people seeking shelter are being removed to offshore islands, where they are placed in harsh detention conditions. This practice violates the UN Convention on Refugees, which stipulates that signatories should afford those who seek refuge the right and dignity of due process and where appropriate, protection. The principle of 'non-refoulement' requires that signatories of the Convention do not reject asylum seekers, send or return them to a place where their rights have a good chance of being violated and they risk persecution. Unfortunately the Australian offshore arrangements can be described precisely this way. Its 'outsourcing' of asylum seekers has precisely put many in the way of grievous mental and physical abuse and trauma by jurisdictions and publics who do not welcome them.

It can be mystifying to untangle the swings of public opinion. Even considerable media coverage around the plight of asylum seekers to Australia has not resulted in a groundswell of disgruntlement. Yet at other times this has happened. Di Bretherton recalls after her trip to Vietnam:

> I returned to Australia and met others who shared my opposition to the war. Hundreds of thousands of people protested in moratorium marches which stretched as far as the eye could see. The march was so long that there was a time of delay between the strains of the chant coming from the different parts of the march and the echoes from the building, as if the protest would reverberate through the whole of space. The sun shone and the stranger who walked beside me helped carry my children as they tired.[212]

Who are 'war-resisters' and 'pacifists'? While these are not identical terms, they are certainly cousins. A war-resister can be a conscientious objector, or have political opposition to a set of policies or a particular war. A pacifist is further along the spectrum, rejecting any justification for the use of violence, including war. It is paradoxical that many young people, like Bill Oats in Europe, are still discovering for themselves their inner convictions even as they are dragged off to one war front or another. Their dilemmas, shifting values and confusion make them ideal recruits, most of whose minds can be bent to the hard logic of warfare in the short term.

However, it can be the unwitting exposure to war or its consequences that makes a conscientious objector or pacifist of a person who, in effect, had it thrust upon them as the only humane, intelligent and constructive way forward by their elders. During her visit to Vietnam in 1986 Bretherton noted,

> The way the Women's Association of Ho Chi Minh City worked interested me. The women I met seemed to be lacking in bitterness, trying to pull together against the most enormous odds; to establish orphanages; to provide even classes for the children of the dust; to treat drug addiction in women, to heal and repair. The women themselves seemed to combine toughness with grace . . . When I first met with the Women's Association in Ho Chi Minh City I asked them about working together. Women who were soldiers fighting the Americans work alongside those who lived with the Americans. I was told that to hold grudges would be 'not realistic'. I would have found this attitude to forgiveness less believable if I hadn't been so well treated myself. I did not experience any ill will towards me as an enemy. The Vietnamese seem rather to value in a very positive way the fact that Australia chose to withdraw from the war.[213]

There is considerable further thought to be given to the different relationships of men and women to violence and war. The obvious socialisation of males into violence as an essential qualification for man-

---

212 Di Bretherton, *op. cit.,* pp. 2-3.
213 Di Bretherton, *op. cit.,* pp. 9-10.

hood, and in Australia, paradoxically also mateship, does not run deep enough. It was also men who sent other men to their death at Gallipoli as in every other Australian war. Bretherton's discovery that the Vietnamese women were more than ready to rebuild relationships as well as bricks and mortar seems very significant. Is there not also a distinctive kind of solidarity that characterises relationships between women? If not mateship then what is its name?

A recent revelation that women and men differ not only in their hormones and sex characteristics but by coding through every cell would seem to support the basis for diverse social responses. The realisation that women have smaller amygdalas in their brains, and may therefore be prone, in their deepest sub-conscience and most primitive organ, to react differently from men to threats or traumas, raises many questions. There may be a female genetic resilience. However these new insights in no way suggest that women are innocent of violence, whether on a domestic and interpersonal or on larger scale, and are drafted for national military service in many countries. In Australia, women have sought equality with men to enter into every aspect of warfare, and do occupy many senior positions in the Australian Defence Forces.

Diana Abdel-Rahman of the Canberra Multicultural Community Forum spoke at the Anzac Conversations of the dangers of polarising complex conflicts into an 'us versus the other' scenario in which the 'other' is cast as a force or group to be feared as 'the enemy'. This includes, she pointed out, both large overt actions and more subtle characterisations (such as the 'evil Russian' in Cold War films). She identified Islam and Muslims as well as refugees as groups now cast as 'the other' who threaten the safety of 'good' Australians.[214] The recent renaissance of Pauline Hanson suggests that this version of reality rings true for many people.

This concern harkens back to the internment of loyal Australians who descended or originated from countries with which Australia found itself, directly or indirectly, at war. It also sounds a familiar knell from the protracted era of the 'White Australia' policy (pre-Federation to 1973), during which the country permitted only white immigrants to enter. Even now, when immigration is said to be colour-blind, it is extremely economically sensitive. Wealthy people score more points for their money and education, and thus it follows that whites have, in most instances, easier access to permanent residency and citizenship.

This dream of a 'white Australia' is farcical in nature given the reality of 'brown' or Aboriginal founding nations as the first and permanent peoples. Whites were only the 'Johnny jump-ups' who have spun for themselves and the European world a convincing founding legend of their own heroism through the doctrine of 'terra nullius' in which the first Europeans found a land that was not apparently settled. Abundant evidence contradicts this convenient lie. Cook's arrival, the First Fleet, and the early settlers followed. The 'Frontier' or 'Black Wars' and massacres of Indigenous peoples constitute a secret and dirty war that was fought to clear the land for the newcomers and their exploitation of it.

As Abdel-Rahman suggests, modern technology shows that wars are not so clear-cut. For example, we can look back on the atrocities committed against Australia's First People and realise, without justifying them, that the convicts and early settlers were by-and-large disenfranchised, marginalised people from their own countries, many of whom did not arrive on these shores of their own volition. Without accepting violent solutions, one can imagine the conditions of fear and the total ignorance of the new country to which they had come. Most ordinary people sadly followed in the footsteps of the colonial power, fighting their own fear by attempting to annihilate the 'other'.

Despite widespread protest, the West initiated the Iraq war in 2003 that led to the power vacuum responsible for the extremist 'Islamic State' movement. It has been pointed out that satellite technology could have been used to destroy IS leadership. Instead the West has allowed the infestation of

---

[214] 'Anzac Conversations: Citizen Voices for Peace', Friends Meeting House, Canberra, 8/11/2015.

the region by the IS, which has increased fear and hatred of Muslims, a trend which also supports the goals of the West in Abdel-Rahman's view. For example, the West allowed Palmyra to be destroyed to make the IS and Muslims in general an even bigger enemy, she suggests. But it is not so much failing to use weapons to destroy IS in its infancy that was the strategic mistake. The much greater error was to fail to take seriously its requests and potential for creating havoc by creating strong dialogue at the outset, before violence erupted.

After terrorist events in Paris, the Australian government re-examined its policy vis-a-vis Syrians, with the fear that terrorists would pass themselves off as asylum seekers. It decided to screen the asylum claimants from Syria with extra caution, so that one year on only 3500 have been granted asylum.[215]

The Australian government's suspicion only has traction if one agrees to a prior assumption, that all Muslims look the same, and all terrorists and all Muslims are interchangeable. This is very dangerous thinking, akin to the American 'red-under-the-bed' that wreaked havoc during the McCarthy era and infected Australia as well. The notion that extremists have the same profile as genuine refugees is flawed at best, especially with all the modern methods of research and examination of asylum-seekers at the hands of Australian authorities. But it is certain that violence will increase if polarising thinking and profiling are driving government policy, both at home and abroad. Meanwhile, many vulnerable people who genuinely need a safe haven are being left in camps or other tenuous locations waiting to be accepted by one of the signatories to the UN Convention on Refugees.

The Quaker United Nations Office (QUNO), through the Quaker Houses it maintains in New York and Geneva, has been an important peace initiative for over fifty years. It works on high level policy debates, peace and stability in sustainable development, bridges between civil society actors and UN bodies, initiates and supports reconciliation and dialogue, and works to share perspectives and foster constructive engagement with emerging powers.[216] In Australia, Quaker Service Australia and the Quaker Peace and Legistation Committee (QPLC) have similar aims. QPLC releases regular white papers to broaden Quaker and public awareness of issues related to peace and justice. It also hosted the Anzac Conversations events and has published this book as a stimulus for further study and reflection.

One dimension of the struggle of pacifists is to find a productive way to live out their witness. British Quakers responded to the need for alternative service in WWI by establishing the Friends' Ambulance Unit (FAU) and the War Victims Relief Committee, which served the enormous need into the 1920s. Some Australian young people joined the Ambulance Unit, as well as non-Quaker pacifists, while others helped with the work of the Relief Committee. In the view of pacifists with particularly strong leadings, the Ambulance Unit was a way of helping the 'war effort' and it was felt that only complete resistance, and suffering a prison sentence where required, was a sufficient path and witness. Among those whose needs were attended to by the FAU were wives and families of internees in Britain. This formed another link with home, as a campaign for collecting garments resulted in sending many cases overseas to be distributed by Quakers serving on these committees.[217]

Far from cowardice, it takes great strength and creativity to be a peacebuilder, as we see with the work of QUNO and the suffering heaped upon whistle-blowers who have dared follow their conscience to reveal the darkest secrets of their own governments. Just as the veteran returns a different person, the peacebuilder is far from static within him or herself. The journey, the struggle, is often a trial by fire,

---

[215] http://christianporter.dss.gov.au/node/676, accessed 20/9/2016.
[216] http://www.quno.org/areas-of-work/peacebuilding-prevention-violent-conflict, accessed 20/9/2016.
[217] Australia Yearly Meeting, *op. cit.*

as Di Bretherton discovered in the making of *As the Mirror Burns*. David Halberstam reflected in a letter,

> I have thought long and hard about Vietnam over the last 20 years, for something like this does not lightly leave you, and I have decided that the true innocents are not those – as Washington would have it – who are afraid to use force and do not understand the real world, but those who still think in this day and age that we can impose our values and our will upon peasants by force.[218]

We are numb to the militarism, which escalates even in 'peace time'. This is probably as true or more so in Australia as it is in the United States. Yet the guerrilla warfare, dubbed 'terrorism', of groups like 'Islamic State' (IS) is having its effect. The tragedies that are resulting as Islamic extremist groups try to gain global attention are making people globally take a look above the parapet.

And it is not pretty. Nor are the clumsy answers we have found for the greatest wave of displaced people ever to hit the world: detention (again!), towing back the boats, putting up walls, turning our backs while people drown, admitting some but providing such meagre sustenance and inhumane conditions that they either return to a dangerous homeland, self-harm, suicide, or commit an infraction of the strict rules of their visa and are locked up or deported.

Our 'pulling up the drawbridge' tactics do nothing to build peace; indeed they are more likely to foment resentment and conflict. Those who are excluded from the 'safe' fortress are ripe for conversion to extremist movements, such are their losses and frustrations. This is the story of many 'home-grown' terrorists' from high-income countries. Spending their young lives at the have-not, marginalised end of societies with extreme inequality fuels great frustration. Some others are more middle class but still unemployed or disenfranchised. They may be even more frustrated by the disappointment that 'their' society has failed to accord them a sense of meaning or belonging. Becoming radicalised is a logical outcome and expression of their anger; they are enticed by the 'opportunity' that belonging or associating with a group like IS can seem to bring.

Our towers of wealth cannot by might alone withstand the assault of the needs of the millions or billions who are left out. Donald Trump's vision of building walls to secure America is no more medieval than the belief held by many in Australia. From a pacifist perspective, it is delusional to imagine that in an age of globalisation, a period in history when this doctrine has been imposed around the world at vast cost to religions and cultures, we can simply resist any blowback through heavy-handed weaponry.

In 2014, Christian Appy reported that US Special Operations forces conducted secret military missions in no less than 133 countries. They are busy 'protecting the freedoms' of Americans in 70 per cent of the world's countries, with the likelihood of expanding due to the 'home grown terrorist' phenomenon. Arguably, democracies may be at the top of checklists now, because of the innate rights and liberties that afford individuals more opportunity to plan and carry out atrocities. The US need not look past 9/11 and the phenomenon of school shootings or many other events within its borders to verify this, and the resulting loss of lives in Denmark, the UK, Canada, France, Spain, and Australia among democracies that have been hit. However, as suggested above, a more nuanced perspective might suggest that Western countries have behaved in antagonistic ways to Muslim societies in particular. The US's foreign policy, to which Australia as an ally is directly party, includes the American longtime siding with Israel and Saudi Arabia, interference and engagement with regional wars in ways that have enlarged and prolonged them, and has greatly added to the human, material and cultural losses. In addition, it is notable that American and other Western foreign policy has been heavily geared to

---

[218] David Halberstam, letter reprinted in Pratt, J. C. (1984), *Vietnam Voices*, New York: Penguin Books p. 665, as cited in Bretherton, *op. cit.*, p. 26.

oil and fossil fuel control, a motivating factor behind much violence.

World War I was a time when some vital efforts were made in the name of peace. In Melbourne, two Australian organisations that had been formed earlier, the Sisterhood of International Peace and the Women's Peace Army, affiliated with the international organisation, the Women's International League for Peace and Freedom (WILPF) as a result of the 1915 congress at The Hague. The new organisation's motto was 'Justice, Friendship and Arbitration'. At the core of their anti-war activism was a notion that had been made concrete in Australia. Conflict should and could be resolved through three measures, either separately or in combination: negotiation between parties, arbitration by a neutral and respected adjudicator, and conciliation over differences.

Australians had a particular familiarity with this mode of operating because it lay behind the distinctively Australian Commonwealth Court of Conciliation and Arbitration, established in 1904. The Attorney General of the time, Alfred Deakin, emphasised that 'war was destruction, whether it be waged on foreign battlefields or in local disputes between capital and labour'. The Court of Conciliation was established to secure social justice in relations between these groups in a spirit of fairness. 'The very creation of the Commonwealth of Australia – in a long process of debate and negotiation though the 1890s – was imbued with this spirit of idealism and optimism.'[219]

WILPF helped sketch out the foundations for the League of Nations and the United Nations that followed. The Congress resolutions included: resolving conflict by negotiation in a council of nations, universal disarmament, the establishment of permanent international courts, the removal of foreign bases from home countries, and centrally, for women and men to have equal rights and representation. It is not by accident that many western countries did give women the vote in the decade that followed. Vida Goldstein, an Australian founding member of WILPF, declared: 'We must oppose war because it is based on fear and hate and lies'.[220] WILPF has a long and admirable history of very significant peace activism. As a result of its work, a greater role has been achieved for women in decision-making about war and in diplomacy, and still more is sought.

After World War II WILPF members remained active on disarmament issues, particularly nuclear bans and limits. Australian members, together with other sympathetic organisations, opposed the establishment on Aboriginal land of the Woomera Rocket Range as well as injustices around citizenship and conditions for First Nations peoples. They challenged the plans to place any US bases on Australian soil. The organisation was also vocal in opposing the Vietnam War and conscription. At an international level, it worked at better informing the public and called for Peace Studies to be integrated into all levels of education. WILPF also focused on the effects of war, particularly on women, including the use of rape as a war strategy, and its terrible impacts on children.[221] A key agenda of peace movements in recent years continues to be disarmament and the reduction of stockpiles, as well as improved processes to cease armed conflict.

Australian Quaker Jo Vallentine (later Senator) describes a 'signpost' in the direction of political life when her friend Nancy Wilkinson (Sr.) encouraged her to attend the international conference of WILPF in 1983.

> When I protested that I had two small children and couldn't possibly go trekking off to an international peace conference, she replied that I had responsibilities to other people's children as well as to my own. But Peter Fry, my spouse, very obligingly took holidays

[219] Lake, *op. cit.*, p. 2
[220] Lake, *op. cit.*, p. 4.
[221] Lake, *op. cit.*, p. 3.

from work to care for the girls, Nancy Wilkinson paid my fare, and off I went. Of course, it broadened my perspective and made me more determined than ever to do whatever I could towards disarmament.[222]

Today WILPF works to end causes of war through local, national and international resolutions. In particular, it has played a significant role in the development, adoption and implementation of the UN Security Council Resolution 1325 on 'Women, Peace and Security', which recognises the crucial role women play in preventing and resolving conflict and peace building, and affirms women's equal right to participate in all peace processes.

Felicity Hill, Director of WILPF, in the United Nations (UN) office, played a significant role in facilitating the adoption in 2000 of the historic UN Security Council Resolution 1325 on 'Women, Peace and Security' that recognised the principles of:

- Women's full and equal participation in every aspect of the peace process;

- Protection of women and girls and their human rights in conflict zones;

- Provision of gender sensitive training in peace keeping operations;

- Gender mainstreaming in the reporting and implementation systems of the UN relating to conflict, peace and security.[223]

A new and revitalising dynamic in WILPF has opened up through the national formation of Young WILPF by Australia women, including Sharna da Lacy and Cara Gleeson. They attended the 2014 Commission for the Status of Women in New York.

In 2015 WILPF held a congress at The Hague to mark the centennial of its formation. Margaret Bearlin, a longstanding Australian member and a Quaker who contributed to the Anzac Conversations, attended this conference with 1000 women and men from 80 countries. The theme was 'Women's Power to Stop War.' During the 'Anzac Conversations', she shared some of the significant statements made by people from many different countries, and the affirmation of a strong commitment to the abolition of war. In particular at this time WILPF emphasised the importance of foreign policy as a women's issue; women must be enfranchised to have an equal role in peacemaking. To this end WILPF members and Quakers were involved in the peace convergence at Pine Gap in October 2016.[224]

WILPF states that to achieve peace and freedom, 'the causes of war must be eliminated, and economic and social systems based on profit and privilege must be transformed to societies based on political and economic equality, participation of women and men, and justice for all – regardless of race, sex or creed'. To this end, the organisation's intent is to challenge militarism, invest in peace, and to strengthen multilateralism.[225]

More specifically, WILPF aims to bring together women of different political beliefs and philosophies to study, make known, and help abolish the causes and the legitimisation of war. It also hopes to shift our global paradigm in favour of world peace, universal disarmament and the abolition of the use of violence to settle conflict. WILPF members hold that prevention, negotiation and reconciliation

---

[222] Jo Vallentine, 'A Quaker Senator's Story: Jo Vallentine' in Jo Vallentine and Peter D. Jones, 'Quakers in Politics: Pragmatism or Principle,' The Religious Society of Friends (Quakers) in Australia, 1990, p. 4.

[223] Lake, *op. cit.*, pp. 3, 4.

[224] Margaret Bearlin, Women's League for Peace and Freedom, 'Anzac Conversations: Citizen Voices for Peace', Canberra Quaker Meeting House, 8/11/2015; for more information on WILPF see www.wilpf.org.au.

[225] http://www.wilpf.org.au/what-we-believe/peace-and-freedom, accessed 21/9/2016.

are keys to this. By strengthening multilateralism and supporting civil society they hope to see the UN system democratised. WILPF wants to see the development and full implementation of international humanitarian law. Political and social equality and economic equity are conditions essential to such justice, which will pave the way toward cooperation among all people. Environmentally sustainable development is the only form that can assure human security into the future.[226]

Peace movements have had some success working for disarmament and improved processes to ease armed conflict. However, it is dismaying that even in this nuclear era the Australian Government still does not see the need to seek authority from parliament to become involved in wars. Not unlike the United States, backroom politics are having a profound impact on the prospect of peace and even the will for peace in the world. Most people do not want wars in their proximity: this is known as the 'NIMBY' or 'not in my back yard' philosophy and must not be mistaken for pacifism.

War appears to be the only way when facing groups who are angered to the point of violence. This reflects a collective failure of creativity and investment in alternative mechanisms for reconciliation and by no means the failure of pacifist options in themselves. No country has come close to using all possible options for peace. However, ignoring the need to work at peace until the eleventh hour is a means to ensure the failure of very potent nonviolent options. These are part of the relationship that is peace, and cannot be understood or practised as quick fix bandages on gaping wounds. Governments and military forces seem to have been remarkably slow in taking this perspective on board.

The suppression of peace movements, education in peacebuilding and conciliation initiatives has meant that the majority of citizens in democratic states are unaware of what pacifist approaches can achieve. We seem not to have progressed significantly from John Lennon's plea: 'All we are saying is give peace a chance'. We pity citizens of authoritarian countries for their lack of access to 'free speech', unrestricted access to the internet and such, and yet we are, most of us in 'free-speaking' countries, woefully ignorant about many aspects of war, from its market places to its psychologies, and equally of its very real alternatives. Furthermore, most seem to prefer discussing the weather than engaging in substantive consideration, one with another, about matters close to the heart and imperative to our futures and the wellbeing of coming generations.

Jonathan Curtis of the United Nations Association of Australia (UNAA) ACT branch was another who presented at the 'Anzac Conversations: Citizen Voices for Peace'. He described how, when countries are on a 'war footing', minorities frequently become enemies, as we see by the current treatment of asylum seekers by Australia. During such times, efforts are made to shut dissenters down, by legislation if possible, in other words by employing 'democratic' gagging techniques. Red herring legislation seems to be trumped up to distract public attention or at least absorb media energy and focus. Resources are dedicated to the preparation of war, and current very intensive defense spending by Australia is symptomatic of that. Another characteristic of the 'war footing' as outlined by Curtis is that civil rights tend to be jeopardised and propaganda is used to increase public support.[227]

It is one of the roles of the United Nations to manage this 'Jekyll and Hyde' character of the modern state and its relationship to war and peacemaking. The UN's work is based on international law and the Universal Declaration of Human Rights, the drafting of which was guided by the distilled wisdom of many faith traditions. The UN has a major role in helping us to set norms for behaviour and to respond to challenges such as climate change, pandemics, refugees, and famine – all of which can generate conflict if not wisely managed.

Unlike other international organisations, the UN has every state in the room, discussing the same topics, especially in the General Assembly. The role of the UNAA is to raise awareness of the UN's

---

[226] WILPF, *op. cit.*

[227] Jonathan Curtis, United Nations Association of Australia (ACT Branch), www.unaa.org.au

role and the relationship between it and the government. It is important that Australia be now fully engaging with the UN. Disappointingly, despite repeated reprimands by the UN on Australia's treatment of asylum seekers, international shaming has had no impact on government policy. The long-term results of this are very severe, and not only for the asylum seekers themselves. This signifies there is no real national memory about internment and its social effects. But far more seriously, there seems to be little recall of the downfall of the League of Nations that was one of the precipitating factors of World War II. The reason the League was unable to keep war from breaking out was that it did not receive adequate backing from its members when occasions required.

Similarly, Australia does not seem to be suffering any substantive sanctions from the other signatories to the Refugee Convention, who should be upholding it by confronting and shaming Australia, or by imposing sanctions for its infractions. If the Conventions of the UN hold no water, and there is no genuine commitment by the signatories, but they are only 'dressing', then the UN too will eventually fade into irrelevance. War will almost certainly be the outcome, or as Hobbes characterised such a condition long ago, 'a war of each against all'. This would be a sad and ugly scenario.

Sue Wareham, who contributed to the 'Anzac Conversations', represents the Medical Association for the Prevention of War, Australia (MAPW). She underscored the importance of more resources being put into mediation and diplomacy, rather than heavy defense investment. MAPW also advocates for creativity and the use of a greater range of non-military responses to crises and conflicts. The international campaign to abolish nuclear war is an important issue for MAPW, particularly because of its first-hand awareness of the immediate and long-term implications of nuclear weapons on human health. Medical practitioners remain on the front lines of wars and of the battle to heal and manage the horrific effects of nuclear, chemical and biological warfare in particular.

Another area of focus for the Medical Association for the Prevention of War is the need for war powers reform so that governments in general and Australia's parliament in particular have a say in whether Australia becomes involved in war. In Canberra the group has been very active in their attempt to remove arms trade advertising from Canberra Airport.[228] MAPW has also supported the High Court challenge to Australian Border Control by Doctors for Refugees.

Concern was raised at the 'Anzac Conversations' about the way the normalisation of war is being assisted by the military's access to schools. There was a strong feeling that this practice needs to be counterbalanced, if not eliminated, by more peace education in schools. Children are already exposed to enormous amounts of media violence, ranging from news programs that have become increasingly graphic to films and animated computer games. First-person shooter games give children the sense of power that comes with wielding a weapon or using violence, and become particularly destructive to the development of other social tools for conflict transformation.

The need to build bridges between groups and factions is central to a social fabric that is safe and inclusive. The unknown is always the greatest cause of fear. There was also reaction during the 'Anzac Conversations' against the 'double speak' of war, where terms like 'border security' become an ongoing feature of government policy, even in countries like Australia which have no borders, and 'collateral damage' has long been accepted in place of the much more confronting but truthful 'killing of civilians'.

Participants felt strongly about the importance of reclaiming the peace agenda by speaking out, raising the issue of loss of civil rights again. The Australian government's practice of monitoring phone and internet use without a warrant, whenever it suspects a 'security risk', puts the freedom of speech of all residents in jeopardy. Often such scanning is conducted by computers, so that even legitimate research, particularly about peacebuilding, can raise alarms for officials. The writing and publishing

---

228 Medical Association for the Prevention of War, www.mapw.org.au

of this book, and the vocabulary it uses, will raise red flags. The need to stand firm against hosting American military bases in Australia was seen to be particularly strong during the 'Conversations'. If Australia genuinely wants to safeguard its status as a safe and free country, it may negotiate but must reconsider alliances with countries like the US,which is perpetually at war.

It was agreed that finding those aspects of our own lives that are unpeaceful, and recognising the ways we contribute, however inadvertently, to violence, is a building block toward a widespread consensus to end war. Sharing with one another where we find the seeds of violence within our own activities and institutions becomes a central activity to building a peaceful future. Even naming the passive and occasionally active sense and language of violence within parliamentary bodies is worth highlighting.

The feeling shared by those who attended the final session of the 'Anzac Conversations' was that there are lots of hopeful signs and new organisations springing up to reclaim democracy. The sense that women are increasingly able to make a contribution was seen as a positive step toward a peaceful future. However, it was noted that women's role in warfare has not always been as peacemakers, going back to ancient times. Di Bretherton's film *As the Mirror Burns* also illustrates the significant role of women as Viet Cong soldiers; the 'troop of the long hair'. It has been a shock for Australian and American veterans to realise this, and their reactions are very telling. Bretherton cites the reaction of returned soldier David Donovan:

> I had never really thought about having to fight a woman myself... The knowledge that a woman had been trying to kill me made me very ill at ease. Threatening male ego there, I suppose, but psychology aside, the plain fact is I just didn't want to kill any women. I know that might sound silly. I didn't hesitate at killing men, did I, so what's the difference?[229]

Donovan's question is a penetrating one. Why be squeamish about killing women? Is a life not a life? Our government is certainly willing to drop bombs on women, for example in Syria. One might venture to suggest that the answer lies partly with the morality that is taught in most societies, that there is something sacred in the abstract or 'other' designation of women. This may suggest that a greater valuing of human lives may lie with leaving behind the social construction of gender. The reluctance to kill women is entangled in our construction of masculinity, and might say more about the role of the heroic male than about the identity of females. The growing gender-free movement offers exciting new ideas.

While women give life, they also have less brawn, overall, and have been constructed as frail. The ancient Greeks, like many traditions, regarded women as 'incomplete men' despite much evidence of their intellectual and military prowess at the time. However women also do the majority of the manual labour in many societies, which is self-fulfilling in making them 'less' in social stature. In *As the Mirror Burns,* Mrs Dinh says, 'Vietnamese women are very strong, they do all the fighting and all the housework'.[230] We hear that IS warriors in Syria avoid confrontation with female warriors. This of course does not protect women from the battleground in the privacy of the home, where women around the world are dying in astonishing numbers from domestic abuse. We have discussed the high rates of such violence in Australia. To say nothing of child soldiers: how do we feel about our own and allied sources targeting them in the Middle East? Historically Australia like America has not hesitated to train juvenile cadets.

Far from the heroic notion of warrior meeting warrior, it is dehumanising the enemy as simply an 'unknown' that makes killing easier. As Noam Chomsky pointed out, we can only kill people if we rob

[229] Donovan, D. (1985), *Once a Warrior King,* UK: Corgi Books, as cited in Bretherton, *op. cit.,* p. 28.

[230] Bretherton, *op. cit.,* p. 34, n. 43.

them of their human status. Today's parents often hear their children saying, if questioned about the killing they do with computer games, 'Oh, don't worry Mum, it's just a zombie'. Yet these zombies take human form. Their only difference is that they are entirely black and faceless. And they are eliminated with incredible speed by our kids. All in a bloodless massacre that leaves no guilt, no mess, and we are told, has no personal impact.

This is the aspect that should leave parents and others worried. Somehow our offspring have been desensitised to the extent that they can carry through with such games. Many readers will recall a deeply troubling American psychological study in which participants were asked to administer electric shocks to others. They did so obediently although there was no stated cause, and it was 'clear' (although a trick of the study) that the victims seemed to experience pain when they received these shocks. One generation on, and killing has become a game. There is apparently no collective memory that makes such behaviour taboo for those who play these games or those who buy them and allow them to be played.

In the famous My Lai massacre of Vietnam, the same kind of training was shown to have been so ingrained that the soldiers said 'they could not stop shooting' long after realising that no one in the village was armed. The simple psychology of 'Kill! kill! kill!' with which they were trained had taken hold. There had been a kind of seepage, so the blank identity of the elusive Viet Cong had spread to the whole society. The Viet Cong present a perfect example of this 'less (or more) than human quality of the unknown enemy', because time and time again it was described how they 'melted away' as if possessed of supernatural powers. Bretherton exposes the way women fighters went back to their villages and got on with the business of daily life, farming, feeding the family, hauling water. Unarmed civilians by day; warriors by night. Not mysterious when we think of the eternal double burden of women, but a great challenge to the fixed notions and unitary roles in warfare.

Central to Bretherton's film is the theme that the enemy lies within. She employs Jungian theory to suggest that the path to enlightenment lies in reconciling with those parts of ourselves that we suppress. Liberation is thus gained through understanding, not armed struggle. To welcome the encounter with the shadows is necessary to welcome the silence and eventually, peace. To take this step we must overcome our fear of encountering an inner void. However there is no such void but always a path that continues across the unknown. According to Bretherton,

> . . . sometimes the fear of loss of inner self seems greater than a fear of death. Death can have a sense of dignity and fullness, whereas the theft of another's sense of dignity can be more fearful. Jung sees facing the void as an inevitable stage of human growth. It will involve meeting the enemy within.[231]

Jung and Bretherton's model is not mortification by killing off the ego. But in learning to love ourselves and others fully, we learn a new kind of nurturing. Rather than avoidance of the dissonant inner voices we can take the opportunity to befriend them. 'To become less defensive, more open and able to listen to those who are different, to be able to see others as potential teachers rather than enemies, an inner change is needed.'[232]

Bretherton confronts what some call the 'soul-sickness' of rich societies, in which we are glutted with things but suffer from a meaning vacuum, and are infected by helplessness and despair. Restoring a sense of purpose, identity, and fulfilment in life is part of the process of recovering peace. We can be deceived by imagining that conquest over others will lead to such a place. But as the Anzac story itself demonstrates, war has led to more wars, and futile attempts at identification as a warrior society, which by its very destructive means cannot lead to such inner wholeness. The rate of suicide in Aus-

---

[231] Bretherton, *op. cit.*, p. 31.
[232] Bretherton, *op. cit.*, p. 34.

tralian as in other high-income societies is lamentable and indicative. In particular, rates of trauma and suicide among veterans, police and prison workers are worthy of note. Dehumanising work leads to being emptied and dehumanised oneself. Soul-sick play that involves killing is threatening for this reason.

Austrian psychoanalyst Viktor Frankl (1905-1997) who survived a Nazi concentration camp, a system in which the whole of his family perished, wrote extensively about this problem of meaning. Central components of this are our dignity, which is eroded in war whether we are combatants or not, and our individuality. Frankl sees boredom as the principle symptom of soul-sickness. However the second and more pervasive one is the crisis of individuality. Lack of belonging and sense of inclusion are dimensions of this. In the concentration camps people were worn down so that they could easily mistake themselves and others for interchangeable beasts, hovering between living and dead. They behaved like saints or animals, Frankl suggests, depending on whether they were able to hold fast to the meaningful core of their own and others' humanity.

> Under the influence of a world which no longer recognized the value of human life and human dignity, which had robbed man of his will and had made him an object to be exterminated (having planned, however, to make use of him first - to the last ounce of his physical resources) – under this influence the personal ego finally suffered a loss of values. If the man in the concentration camp did not struggle against this in a last effort to save his self-respect, he lost the feeling of being an individual, a being with a mind, with inner freedom and personal value.[233]

Refugees confronting possible lifetimes of boredom and meaninglessness sometimes tell of how they have restored hope. This can be achieved by access to the simplest of materials to make instruments, decorations, or simply by song. We know that music restores healthy brain chemistry and can help individuals and groups maintain a sense of purpose. But this cannot hold them indefinitely, if more lasting help is not soon forthcoming.

Sue Wareham of MAPW underscored some of the key tools for peacemaking that must be made available for the cause to progress. Among these, she emphasised the importance of investing human and material resources into mediation and diplomacy. Rather than using technology to stand between people and distract or shield us from the humanity of others, diplomacy and mediation prioritise relationships, bringing military technology in only as a secondary tool. Wareham's emphasis on skills means putting more investment into teaching as well as funding those in a position to use skills effectively on an international scale. It also implies supporting the bodies that undertake this kind of work. Citizens who are concerned to see Australia engage more meaningfully with alternatives to violence must commit to supporting these alternatives. Another area underscored by Wareham was the need for a greater range of non-military options as responses to crises and conflicts. While extremely large investments are being made into military hardware and training, only a tiny fraction is going toward exploring serious alternatives. Human creativity can be astonishing, as this book describes, but focusing it so intensively on military advances is to our ultimate detriment, not advantage.

A third issue Wareham reflected upon is the impact of cuts to foreign aid upon the capacity to build peace through meeting people's basic needs. Where needs go unmet, and scarcity is rampant, competition becomes intense over these key resources. Frankl described this as one of the factors that drove some people in the concentration camps to cruel and inhumane behaviour against other inmates. Those who have the might to threaten or injure others can ultimately succeed in capturing the essentials of life for themselves and controlling the price of access and distribution if they so choose. Basics

---

[233] Viktor Frankl, *Man's Search for Meaning*, p. 70 as cited in https://stuff.mit.edu/people/gkrasko/Frankl.html ,accessed 23/9/2016.

like food, water, shelter and medical care become pawns in such situations. There is in fact global abundance, but the very uneven and unjust distribution of assets is one of the causes of friction and ultimately violence. Those who provide medical care cannot intervene after certain levels of violence and inequality have been reached. As with other aspects of peacebuilding, investment at the eleventh or thirteenth hour can do little.

Karl-Eric Paasonen of 350.org spoke at the 'Anzac Conversations: Citizen Voices for Peace' event at Canberra Quaker Meeting House. 350.org is an international network of groups that seeks to reduce carbon emissions to below 350 parts per million (the 'safe' level). Military machines and operations are very large fuel consumers, and war is extremely high-impact and destructive to our environment. The analysis of 350.org shows that 'business as usual' will be calamitous for millions of people, and the organisation aims to remove the 'social license' or public support for energy companies seeking capital investment.[234]

Paasonen described the approach of 350.org to apply targeted popular pressure on those businesses, councils and organisations that invest in fossil fuel, educating them and urging them to divest. They have been led to use nonviolent civil disobedience where necessary. The recent decision by the ACT government to divest from fossil fuel investment is one successful outcome of a campaign by trade unions and community groups. Following pressure by 350.org, the Commonwealth Bank of Australia announced that it would not underwrite the Galilee Basin coal project in Queensland. Another goal for pacifists to pursue that will gradually lead Australia to research and invest in more is a prime export-resource in waiting; sustainable energy.

Paasonen indicated that there are moves by the authorities to restrict the capacity to protest, and this makes it important to develop new strategies. Nonviolent action includes negotiation, electoral work and direct action. A bigger difference is made, Paasonen underscored, when more groups join in coalitions, such as mass strikes. It will become more costly to protest for change over the next five years, he predicted, and it could cost Australians their jobs, if not their lives, as the government shows increasing signs of clamping down on such moves. This trend is tragic because it suggests the foreclosing of peaceful alternatives that are essential to democratic life, but also a greater prospect of violence and loss of life.

Robert Burrowes, another peace activist who is concerned about environmental impacts of war, made the news in 1986 when he arrived at the taxation office in Melbourne to pay his outstanding tax debt with 94 shovels. He had recently returned from doing relief work in the eastern Sudan. The protester explained that he wanted to be sure his tax payment would not be used for military purposes. The tax office refused the shovels on the grounds that they were not legal tender. For three years Burrowes had withheld about 10 per cent of his income which was estimated to be portion of the national used for defense at the time. 'Each military weapon is paid for with human lives, and it enrages me to see so many people die in the refugee camps of Africa.'[235] As discussed in the section on religion, tax resistance has become a growing area of conscientious objection.

In Burrowes' review of a recently published anthology, *The Secure and the Dispossessed: How the Military and Corporations are Shaping a Climate-Changed World*,[236] Burrowes summarises and assesses the engaging arguments made about connections between the military-industrial complex and the environmental crisis.[237] He underscores how war leaves many landscapes uninhabitable. It was only by an

[234] Karl-Erik Paasonen, 350.org, www.350.org, accessed 22/4/2016.
[235] 'Protester has a dig at the Taxation office', *Sydney Morning Herald*, 24/6/1986, p. 3.
[236] *The Secure and the Dispossessed*, Nick Buxton and Ben Hayes, eds., U. of Chicago Press, 2015.
[237] Robert J. Burrowes, 'Dispossessed in the name of "Security"', *Counterpunch*, 29/1/ 2016,

enormous and expensive reconstruction effort that Europe was put on its feet after the World Wars. A great amount of American money in particular was invested.

But this volume tells a different, more recent story that helps to describe the 'perpetual war' underlying of the comfortable peace in which most Australians live. Burrowes summarises the newfound interests of states and the security agenda in the environment, revealing their sinister side. Their engagement with renewable energy research and investment, for example, comes at a cost that is flying under the radar of most citizens.

> . . .'energy security' is used to justify the aggressive exploitation of 'unconventional' fossil fuels, the use of military violence to 'secure' energy transport routes, the suppression of protests against further fossil fuel extraction and 'the expansion of renewable energy in a way that ignores concerns about human rights, democratic governance, or energy access'.[238]

Burrowes goes on to suggest that, according to the book, 'land and water grabs' as well as the concentration of food production, distribution and access are protecting the interests of the global elite but starving 100,000 people a day and sending a billion more to bed undernourished. This trend is not even because of a genuine concern for a small sector of humanity, the book suggests, but because there is profit to be made in such 'security' businesses.

The problem that the capitalist social and economic model breeds aggression and greed has caused pacifists as individuals and organisations to look for alternatives that do not reduce people to competitors and do not promote the myth that shortage is dominant, particular in areas of greatest wealth. However, the socialist alternative has been discredited even without having been fully understood or attempted, with the advantage that such deeper comprehension would bring. There are few other models on the radar of Westerners.

It is probably clear to all Australians that 'security' plays an important role in government policy, and that outsourcing certain kinds of 'dirty' security is the most common means of allowing politicians to keep their hands clean. It is clear that the current global refugee crisis stems in no small part from the involvement of Western nations, including Australia, in the wars in the Middle East, among others. Burrowes argues

> . . . having created the 'refugee problem' by starving or bombing people out of their homes, elites now use a related set of corporations to erect border fences, provide 'border security' and maintain detention centres and prisons when these refugees seek a viable place to live away from the starvation/war zone they have been forced to flee. As always for the global elite, human beings are victims to be exploited or killed, not people to be supported and helped out of empathy and compassion.[239]

Some Australians will be responding with cautiously positive thoughts to indications that the US government, including its military, is changing to nuclear power and agro fuels and is shifting to making 'green bullets' out of copper rather than lead. The book, according to Burrowes, explores this 'greenwashing death' trend. 'Strangely, systematically reducing military capacities to reduce the devastating climate and other environmental impacts of the military is not an option being considered. Nor is the option of economic conversion to non-military (that is, socially valuable) production.'

http://www.counterpunch.org/2016/01/29/dispossessed-in-the- name-of-security/, accessed 12/2/2016.
[238] Burrowes, *Counterpunch*, op. cit.
[239] Burrowes, *Counterpunch*, op. cit.

In short, Burrowes claims, the military is looking to expand its role by emphasising what it portrays as 'security' threats arising from ecological disasters (although there has been no suggestion that military training and bases should be reoriented/converted to disaster training institutes).[240]

Burrowes, like a number of others, is interested in the root causes of violence as a behaviour. He like many others has come to the conclusion that fear is responsible both for making humans inflict violence and submit to violence. He confesses his own fear that ending violence is not possible, but also his greatest hope and vocation is commitment to that goal. For him, confronting his own fear has been the first step in working towards that goal. In his study of how fear operates, he has observed that it destroys the 'integrity of the mind'. This is perhaps a more contemporary way of speaking of shell-shock or PTSD. Burrowes believes that the disintegrated elements of the mind are highly vulnerable to being captured by outside forces. At a basic level, these can be approval, food, money, possessions or control. One's health can be very negatively impacted.[241] As Burrowes suggests, our society feeds on this primitive predisposition.

> It takes enormous and protracted violence to terrorise the individual into accepting paid work in a modern economy so that it can buy (rather than take) the resources that it needs to live. But the social interference of humans in the genetic programming of their offspring extends far beyond control over the method of resource acquisition and this is why the power of a hunter-gatherer is no greater than that of an industrial human. Terror is the most damaging form of violence … The violence inflicted by human adults on themselves, each other and the Earth is an outcome of the visible, invisible [emotional] and utterly invisible [subconscious] violence inflicted on them as children.[242]

Burrowes undertakes a detailed study of how the child's psyche is eroded and disarticulated in early life, creating a vulnerability that is prone to hijacking by violent forces. Having established a comprehensive list of all the ways a child can become emotionally damaged through its relationship with its parent(s), he goes on to examine the overall impacts.

> So what, exactly, does it mean when I say 'destroy the Self?' It means that invisible and utterly invisible violence destroys the components of Self-hood of the child, including its Self-awareness, Self-will, Self-power, Self-memory, Self-approval, Self-worth, Self-respect, Self-judgment, Self-authority, Self-governance, Self-defence, Self-reliance, Self-belief, Self-trust, Self-faith, Self-consciousness and, most importantly, Self-love, thus thwarting the realisation of its True Self. The individual that is left, having been stripped of its Self, is now (unconsciously) terrified, self-hating, powerless and violent (particularly towards itself but also towards others and the Earth) and is readily manipulated into becoming a passively obedient student, worker/soldier and consumer.[243]

The result of this early violence, in Bob Burrowes' view, is a ready-made actor socialised with the preconditions for violence during the vulnerable period of childhood.

A movement called Mothers and Others for Peace, initiated by English Quakers, provided the impetus for some Canberra women to mix mothering with their peace concerns during the 1980s. War toys were one of the main areas of focus. While the children maintained a fascination for war toys they did learn that in their mothers' eyes, violence and hurting each other was not acceptable. The Gulf War of 1991 was televised into homes and created anxiety for parents and children alike. Mothers and Others

---

[240] Burrowes, *Counterpunch*, op. cit.

[241] Robert Burrowes, 'Why Violence?' http://dkeenan.com/RJB-WhyViolence.pdf, accessed 12/2/2016.

[242] Burrowes, 'Why Violence?' op. cit.

[243] Burrowes, 'Why Violence?' op. cit.

continued with their message of peace. They realised that the victims of violence could be neighbours as well as people in distant lands.[244]

The Alternatives to Violence Project (AVP) is another peace movement that began in 1975 when American Quakers were asked to help end a pattern of recidivism among young prison inmates by older ones who did not want to see their life paths copied. Today it is an international movement that aspires for all people to live in peace and dignity, without regard for religious or other background, and is active in 53 countries.

> AVP is a network of volunteers running workshops for anyone who wants to find ways of resolving conflict without resorting to violence. We work in the community and in prisons. We understand that conflict is a natural and normal part of life, and that it is possible to learn new ways of handling it. By holding workshops in which the participants consider the underlying causes of friction and violence … Our workshops build on everyday experiences and try to help us move away from violent or abusive behaviour by developing other ways of dealing with conflict. They help us to increase the respect we have for ourselves and others.[245]

AVP has been widely used in settings of humanitarian disaster, and in high tension and war-torn locations, mixing groups that have been significantly at odds. Remarkable friendships and other beneficial outcomes have resulted. One region where they have been particularly brave and effective is in Central Africa, where there have been genocides and violent, traumatising civil wars. In this area they have worked through the African Great Lakes Initiative (AGLI) of Friends Peace Teams. AGLI has projects in Rwanda, Burundi, DR Congo, Kenya and Uganda. The inspiration for these comes primarily from AVP. They offer basic and advanced workshops as well as training all-important local facilitators. Among other effective initiatives inspired by AVP are:

> **HROC:** (pronounced HE-rock) HROC is a three day experiential workshop modeled on AVP that deals with the personal and community trauma from the violent conflicts in the region. There is a basic workshop with a follow-up day and then a community celebration. An advanced workshop and a special workshop for HIV positive women have also been developed.

> **Mediation:** Mediators in Rwanda, Burundi, and Congo (North and South Kivu) have been trained in transformative mediation. The program now has lead mediators in each region capable of training others. In Kenya mediators have been trained in the basic skills, but upgrading and mentoring is still needed.[246]

Particular strengths of AVP include peer training and the strong emphasis placed on finding commonalities even between people who have been socially constructed as having competing and diametrically opposed identities and interests. It is remarkable to see the expertise and nuanced approaches that facilitators acquire, and the enhanced self-esteem that is a yield for nearly every participant. Having trusted others and made oneself vulnerable has been shown time and time again by this model to have empowering results in the formation of leaders and peacemakers.

Many Australians have become involved in AVP beyond Australia through Friends Peace Teams Asia-West Pacific. In 2005, only a week after a peace accord was signed between Aceh and the Indonesian government, an AVP workshop was first introduced. It was decided that pursuing education about 'developmental play' for families and teachers would offer a good foundation for recovery from war and violence. It would enrich understanding of human development throughout the region. The

---

[244] Ronis Chapman, 1997, *this we can say, op. cit.,* S. 3.108.

[245] AVP, http://avp.international/the-avp-program/, accessed 23/9/2016.

[246] AGLI, http://aglifpt.org/program.htm, accessed 23/9/2016.

work of the area project is conducted on a people-to-people and community-to-community basis rather than being project focused. Using the AVP model, trauma healing workshops afford opportunities for grieving, mourning and offering of mutual support. Making peace with the land is a further focus.[247]

For all the efforts and successes of those working assiduously for peace, these are threatened with suffocation by people and dollars that stack up in favour of security, militarism and war. Does this mean that war, after all, and despite the ultimate hopes of the Anzac Diggers themselves, is the greater good?

---

[247] Friends Peace Teams, http://www.fpt-awp.org/index.php?q=content-activities, accessed 24/9/2016.

Chapter VIII
The Still Small Voice and the Great Wide World: Religion and War

> Either we sacrifice our pathetic rationality and get our spiritual and moral lives in order, or else irrationality will sweep over us in a reign of terror.[248]
> – David Tacey

David Tacey is a scholar in English and Australian literature and in Jungian psychology, and has written extensively on Aboriginal and men's issues. Carl Jung referred to 'soul sickness' to describe our modern condition. Sufferers give up defining their lives through meaning, and fall into states of deep emptiness and violence. They can regain meaning by living in mindful, intentional relationship to one another and to the great mysteries of the universe. As unfashionable as religion on the surface of today's secular Australia, it remains a formative foundation of all civilisations. Despite the high ideals that the warfare of the twentieth century claimed to realise, it fell very short in practice given the scale of violence and destruction of the human dignity of so many who survived as well as those who died. Although there were some notable achievements, these are overshadowed by unimagined and in some senses even now unimaginable barbarism. The evidence of many truths that confront us about these decades defy understanding, and yet we can see how they became the fallout of a 'disenchanted' and arrogant moment in history.

It is worth looking at the fate of religion, and in particular how people of faith in Australia responded to the challenges of the century. What approach did those who hung on to their sense of meaning take, and what difference did it have in outcomes and the contributions of these groups? We begin with a glance at how world religions position themselves and their members with respect to war and peacemaking.

'Islam' comes from selm and salam, the Arabic words for peace. Muslims greet one another 'As-Sala-mu-Alaykum', 'Peace be with you'. The first verse of the *Qur'an* (Muslim holy book) contains the wish for peace. One of Allah's names in the *Qur'an*, is 'As Salaam' which means peace. The *Qur'an* refers to Islam as 'the paths of peace' (5:16). It describes reconciliation as a basic stance (4:128) and states that Allah abhors disturbance of the peace (2:205). The mission of the Prophet Muhammad is one of peace

---

[248] David J. Tacey, *Edge of the Sacred Transformation in Australia*. Blackburn, Victoria: Harper Collins, 1995, p. 9.

and mercy to humankind (21:107). The ideal society is 'Dar al Salaam', the house of peace (10:25). The universe is characterised by harmony and peace (36:40).[249]

The Buddhist tradition is clearly associated with nonviolence and the principle of *ahimsa* (no harm). By eliminating their attachments to material things, Buddhists try to combat covetousness, a potential source of anger and violence. By tradition, the Buddha prevented a war between the Sakyas, his own clan, and the Koliyas. When he discovered the reason for the war was a dispute over water, he engaged the opposing rulers, asking whether water was more worthy than the blood of fellow human beings.[250]

Like Buddhism, Hinduism is a label embracing a range of more specific belief systems. These also adhere to *ahimsa*. One should avoid harming any living thing. *Ahimsa* is not just nonviolence – it means avoiding any harm, whether physical, mental or emotional. Its strongest modern proponent was the Indian leader Gandhi, for whom *ahimsa* was the highest duty. He taught that it 'comes from strength, and the strength is from God, not man. *Ahimsa* always comes from within'. However, he accepted killing for duty, in a detached way without anger or selfish motives, as compatible with *ahimsa*. *Ahimsa* is connected to *karma*, by which any violence or unkindness a person carries out will return to them at some time in the future by the natural law of the universe. When Hindus are violent, this signals they have yet to evolve to a level where they understand and seek peaceful conduct. Hinduism contains some of the earliest writings about peace, as this verse from the *Rig Veda* (10:191-2) shows.

> Come together, talk together,
> Let our minds be in harmony.
> Common be our prayer,
> Common be our end,
> Common be our purpose,
> Common be our deliberations,
> Common be our desires,
> United be our hearts,
> United be our intentions,
> Perfect be the union among us.[251]

The earliest Christian teachings describe a philosophy of love, which suggests that it is far better to 'turn the other cheek' than to seek retribution for wrongdoing. Killing is absolutely outlawed in the Ten Commandments. Church history, sometimes called 'churchianity', stands as a violent paradox to that moral dictum. Christians in the twentieth century did not find themselves of one accord about violent conflict. They were in some ways most confronted by their own members who took opposing views. Most Australians were practising Christians of one denomination or another well into the second half of the century, when secularism began to take hold as the dominant ethos. They were influenced not only by the framework of 'primitive Christianity' but also by the subsequent traditions and scholarship, in particular for many arguments, philosophies and long patterns of committed practice to a belief in 'just war'. Further to this was a great deal of violence that was not categorised as conventional war, such as the Frontier Wars. Modern Europeans had formulated their understanding of war as being between nation states. Since they had, and to a considerable extent even now have very little understanding of the political forms and practices of First Nations, they could only understand, or perhaps chose to brand, the actions of the Indigenous peoples as 'illegal'.

[249] http://portal.waverley.nsw.edu.au/library/SOR/11_religion_peace/ islam_summary.html, accessed 27/9/2016.

[250] https://berkleycenter.georgetown.edu/essays/buddhism-on-peace-and-violence, accessed 25/9/2016.

[251] http://www.bbc.co.uk/religion/religions/hinduism/hinduethics/war.shtml, accessed 9/6/2016

What does religion really have to do with the world of politics, diplomacy, conflict and war? Many see continuity between the inner and outer, and view the Divine or 'higher power' as a force that knows no limits. Sufis, originally a mystical branch of Islam, teach that the soul is a threshold with a current that flows in both directions: we are both the drop of water that is part of the great oceans, without which they would not be, but also each of us is like a gnat, a tiny creature containing all the mystery of life. In both respects, each life is sacred. All world religions teach the values of love, peace, forgiveness and community. They share a belief that the power of love must overcome the love of power, according to Dean Sahu Khan, President of the Canberra Interfaith Forum.[252]

Paradoxically, religion is often used by people as a reason for division and war. The fervent attachment to belief and passion for particular political outcomes means that few religions have escaped degrading themselves to this form of extremism at some point. This as Gandhi would have it is more a sign of our weakness than our strength, which lies with God. Leslie Jauncey wrote from personal experience that 'From the commencement of the [First World] war, pulpits became draped with the Union Jack and it was difficult at times to distinguish much difference between sermons and calls for recruits'.[253]

Quakers, although known for their pacifism perhaps more than other aspects of their witness, are in the main far from naive about violence. A 1991 statement by some Australian Friends makes this clearer:

> We know that violence is not a solution to anything yet we are all caught inextricably, it sometimes seems, in the mesh of a world where violence is a multi-billion dollar industry and the greatest spectator sport. In our attempts to 'live in the virtue of that life and power that takes away the occasion of all wars', we acknowledge how often we turn to the violence expedient. We recognise that we are part of the world's violence and must ask ourselves if we are prepared to pay the price of our convictions and to recognise 'the enemy within' as a priority to be dealt with.[254]

The centenary of World War I has provided an opportunity to share more publicly the Quaker peace witness, a testimony first declared to King Charles II 350 years ago. 'All bloody principles and practices we do utterly deny, with all outward wars, and strife, and fighting with outward weapons, for any end, or under any pretense whatsoever, and this is our testimony to the whole world.'[255] This public statement followed George Fox's own testimony. As a founder of the Quaker movement or 'Religious Society of Friends', he declined military service in favour of prison, saying that he 'lived in the virtue of that life and power that took away the occasion of war'.[256] Australian Friend David Purnell has expressed the logic behind this conviction.

> Quakers were heavily involved in the campaign to end slavery, in working for the right of conscientious objection, in pressing for religious and other freedoms, and in testifying to equality between men and women, and among races. In all these things Quakers saw a continuity between means and ends. They considered that peace could not be achieved by violence, but only by winning hearts and minds to a peaceful way, and by example.

---

[252] Dean Sahu Khan, speaking at the opening of the Quaker World War I Exhibition in Canberra, 12/04/2015.
[253] Leslie C. Jauncey, *The Story of Conscription in Australia* (London: Allen and Unwin, 1935) as cited in Catie Gilchrist, 'Religious Opposition to World War I' in the *Dictionary of Sydney* (2014), dictionaryofsydney.org/entry/religious_opposition_to_world_war_i, accessed 29/1/2015.
[254] *this we can say, op. cit.,* S. 3.101.
[255] *Quaker Faith and Practice of Britain Yearly Meeting, op. cit.* 24.04.
[256] *Quaker Faith and Practice of Britain Yearly Meeting, op. cit.* 1.02.

Hence in their corporate life they made decisions not by voting but after considering all views and seeking Divine guidance. Nonviolence has the capacity to achieve long-term change, whereas violence may have temporary success but breeds enormous resistance and resentment.[257]

By the mid-18th century the early American colonies, New York, Virginia, Massachusetts, North Carolina and Rhode Island, allowed Friends exemption from military service because of their well-known refusal to fight. In Pennsylvania there was no conscription until 1775 when Quakers lost control of Friend William Penn's 'holy experiment'.

The 20th century opened with British Quaker opposition to the Boer or South African War (1899-1902). During the following decade the Quaker Peace Committee (1902) and Northern Friends Peace Board (1913) campaigned vigorously against militarism and compulsory training for all young men. The cost of the ongoing naval arms race with Germany was also highlighted, and Quakers were in the vanguard of efforts to improve Anglo-German relations through meetings, exchange visits and condemnation of xenophobic propaganda.[258]

Quakers express their experience, guidance and discernment processes through a series of 'Advices and Queries' that are used among many Quakers around the world. One of these suggests 'Respect the laws of the state but let your first loyalty be to God's purposes. If you feel impelled by strong conviction to break the law, search your conscience deeply. Ask your meeting for the prayerful support which will give you strength as a right way becomes clear.'

World War I brought challenges for Friends. In Britain out of a membership of 19,000 about 1000 volunteered for military service. In 1915 the Society reaffirmed that 'there is a better way and ... Love alone can avail to find and follow it ... It has been an encouragement to us ... to know that the bulk of our young men are prepared to refuse military service of any kind.' In 1917 they objected to regulations that all pamphlets (a common vehicle for reflection, study and discussion among Quakers) be submitted to the censor during the war.[259]

In Australia, Friends were all too aware of the compromised context in which they were immersed. How to position themselves, in practical terms, became a very real question. With the prospect of so much suffering, and more than they could have imagined in 1914, they concluded:

> Our meeting has been held under a solemn sense of the war cloud now hanging over the civilised world ... war involves the suspension of so many moral restraints that we cannot regard it with anything but abhorrence ... At the same time we encourage our members to bear their full share of the national burden by helping to relieve the misery and distress certain to be caused by the present conflict ... We earnestly pray, and believe that when the war clouds have passed away a rational system of international arbitration will be universally adopted.[260]

They turned creatively to alternative actions that individuals could take, according to how they felt led. Among these were non-combatant service with the armed forces; serving in the Friends Ambulance Unit; relieving the suffering of war victims; doing alternative civilian service of national importance at home; or going to prison for refusing to perform any service which might assist the war. For some

---

[257] David Purnell, *this we can say, op. cit.,* S. 3.87.

[258] 'QPLC: Conscientious Objection', p. 1.

[259] *Quaker Faith and Practice of Britain Yearly Meeting,* 1995.

[260] Society of Friends, Queensland, 16/8/1914. http://c.ymcdn.com/sites/ www.quakers. org.au/resource/resmgr/WW1_poster/WW1_Exhibition_banners_ Part5.pdf, accessed 27/10/2016.

people, much as relieving suffering might be seen as a desirable objective, it might also prolong the war by making it tolerable to the population.

In his letter of application for membership to the Religious Society of Friends (Quakers), Bill Oats expressed the longings that many Friends feel today. What has been revealed to one is true for them but each person must follow their own conscience without dictates from a religious hierarchy. The desire for community service that demonstrates the many reasons why a nonviolent life is compelling, spiritually rewarding and effective is widely felt. Oats wrote from Europe back to his home Meeting in Adelaide:

> Since [1934] my ideas have been tempered by experience of what has been happening in Europe during the last six years. I have had continually to search the grounds for my pacifism and to rethink my position. I have come to the conclusion that all I have the right to claim is that for me, it is the only way, but that for others there may be the equally sincere feelings that the cause of peace can best be served by some other means ... There seems to be a great need for some form of community service which would provide group witness to the truth of pacifism as a way of life.[261]

The Friends Ambulance Unit (FAU) had been formed in 1914 in Britain. It eventually recruited over 1800 members, not all of them Quakers, and many from the Dominions, to work closely with the Red Cross and the army. Its focus was primarily on soldiers in World War I, and so was open to the accusation of patching combatants up so they could return to the front. Some Quaker members of the FAU eventually joined the forces, while others left to desist from any supportive role after the introduction of conscription. By the end of the war, 1500 'COs' (as conscientious objectors became known) were in prison in Britain, and some were not released until August 1919.[262]

In Australia, many Friends felt led to made common cause with others struggling for nonviolence. In part, this was a way to surmount the problem of having small numbers and what they worried might be too quiet a voice to make themselves heard. Among the newly established groups that they supported or assisted in founding were the Australian Peace Alliance, the Fellowship of Reconciliation, the Sisterhood of International Peace, the Women's Peace Army, the No-Conscription Fellowship, and the Australian Union of Democratic Control for the Avoidance of War.[263]

Friends Committee on National Legislation (USA) issued a statement in 2004 quoting John F. Kennedy as saying that 'war will exist until the conscientious objector enjoys the same reputation and prestige as the warrior'. The UN Human Rights Committee, which oversees implementation of the International Covenant on Civil and Political Rights, has made it clear that it covers conscientious objection ' ... the Committee believes that such a right can be derived from article 18, inasmuch as the obligation to use lethal force may seriously conflict with the freedom of conscience and the right to manifest one's religion or belief'.[264]

The Committee made two further important advances in 1995 in the direction of protecting the right to conscientious objection. The first was that 'persons performing military service should not be excluded from the right to have conscientious objections to military service'.[265] So for example, when American soldiers appealed to Canadian Quakers for asylum from persecution by the US Armed

[261] Oats, *op. cit.*, p. 89.
[262] 'QPLC: Conscientious Objection', p. 2.
[263] http://c.ymcdn.com/sites/www.quakers.org.au/resource/resmgr/ WW1_poster/WW1_Exhibition_banners_Part5.pdf, accessed 27/10/2016.
[264] Rachel Brett, 'Quaker United Nations Office paper 2011', as cited in 'FCNL: Conscientious Objection', p. 3.
[265] *Wikipedia,* as cited in 'QPCL: Conscientious Objection', p. 3.

Forces who wished to court-martial them, because the soldiers felt they could no longer serve in what they regarded as an inhumane and illegal war, they should have received protection in Canada under the conditions of the Covenant. However, they had to seek refuge from Quakers and others to hide from Canadian authorities while they lodged their claims and appeals.

The second important statement of the Commission was that alternative service must be of a civilian character and not punitive, and should not exceed the time expected for military service. To keep conscientious objectors in detention for almost a year after the armistice of World War I would certainly not in any respect conform with this interpretation, but of course the United Nations did not yet exist.[266]

There are still many countries where the imprisonment of COs is a reality. Some soldiers, for example in Israel, have taken a stand against military action targeting unarmed civilians, such as Palestinians. The world is far from being a safe place for those with a strong conscience. Interestingly, there remains little appreciation even today among many or perhaps most people about the courage required to take such a stand, and the costs involved to oneself and family, costs which ripple on to future generations. The stigma on families, sometimes Post Traumatic Stress Disorder suffered by COs who have been abused or even tortured because of their moral stance, and loss of employment and social position are significant factors.

Australian Friends experienced a boost to their peace witness with the 1888-9 visit of English Quaker William Jones. This helped to reinforce their objection to the compulsory training of boys that was so very effective later when recruitment began for World War I. During and after this war, Quakers worked steadily to assist its victims.

Quaker Di Bretherton acknowledges that she was inwardly enriched by the making of the film *As the Mirror Burns* about Vietnam, including acquiring new meaning about her own womanhood and personhood.

> In retrospect I feel that the greatest gain is in courage and the experience of being encouraged. Speaking truth to power means not just challenging the power in others; it also means confronting the power of fear in oneself. To speak well of the enemy is to be seen as a traitor; to risk rejection, to stand alone. But my fears were ghosts, spectres, to be confronted not by weapons but by faith. By following as truthfully as I could in the footsteps of my leading ... seeing that which is of God in those who we represent as the enemy, so I learned to walk where it is lighter and there are fewer ghosts. What was uppermost in my relationship to the Vietnamese women was not so much the importance of loving the enemy, but of not being afraid to learn from them. For war can only be based on ignorance, not on knowing the other as a human being, on not greeting that which is of God within.[267]

While most churches supported the preparations for World War I, a few Independents and Methodists were the only protestants to join Quakers in taking a consistent view that military training and participation in the war were unjustified.[268]

The extent to which protestant churches fell in with the government position on the war was for some people completely mystifying. They were not innocent actors, in the view of some, but active players that used the full scope of their influence to swing the public opinion. Reverend WH Beale penned in 1915 his outrage that the church was not upholding its teachings.

[266] Rachel Brett, *op. cit.*
[267] Bretherton, *op. cit.*, p. 40.
[268] Gilchrist, *op. cit.*

That conception and ideal of peace which has been clothed and garlanded in the Christian thought with every fantasy of attractiveness and beauty has been so completely thrust in the background that, by almost common consent, it is now held to be untimely, if not unpatriotic and disloyal, for even Christian teachers to sound its praises, bemoan its absence or insist upon efforts for its restoration. The pulpit has become as belligerent as the press, with the added blemish that the war is being justified and apologised for in terms of religion and morals, at the peril of including the most fatal condition of moral obliquity when men call evil good and good evil.[269]

Some Australian pacifist Christians suffered for their faith, and a few were prosecuted under the Wartime Precautions Act, proving that there was little distinction between the line of most churches and that of the government. One such was the Reverend Thomas Bede Roseby, a Congregational minister at Orange, New South Wales, who was deemed responsible for a riot at his own church. This underscores the internal divisions that Christians felt but which had become so powerfully squelched by the institutions of church and state.

Roseby was already well known as an anti-conscription activist and pacifist, and during the referendum debates had called for an immediate armistice. He took every opportunity to support this witness, both in church and in the street. On 5 June 1918 he refused to stand, take off his hat and sing the national anthem. He was attacked by families who had members at the front as well as some returned soldiers, and there was substantial damage to the church. Such physical conflicts between the 'pros' and the 'antis' had become commonplace in Australia. Curiously Roseby was fined for being 'liable to disloyal utterances'. He resigned from the church soon after. Shortly after being attacked in his church, a Labour meeting was held on freedom of speech, but the Oddfellows Hall was only secured for the event on the condition that Roseby not address the audience.[270]

A fellow Congregationalist pacifist and well-known activist and champion of the poor, Albert Rivett, edited a monthly journal, *The Federal Independent*, which was Christian, pacifist and anti-conscriptionist. Obviously there were interested readers or no such paper could have existed. When the Lord Mayor of Sydney offered prizes of six guineas to school children for the best essays on war, Rivett countered with the offer of 10 guinea prizes to children for the strongest essays on peace. He did so with the full support of the Peace Society of New South Wales. His differences with the church also increased to the point that he resigned from the Whitefield Congregational Church in 1915. For the duration of the war and until his death in 1934 he remained active in the Peace Society and in the Australian Peace Alliance.[271]

Bernard Linden Webb was the Methodist minister at Hay in southern New South Wales. His three pacifist sermons of 1915, which he later published in a pamphlet entitled 'The Religious Significance of War', drew the adverse attention of the church committee. At first they simply labelled him 'impractical' and 'idealistic'. Eventually in October 1916 he felt that his moral opposition to the position of the Methodist Church was so deep that he could not remain as its paid agent and resigned.[272]

It can be considered nothing less than tragic that institutions whose core teaching is that of 'gospel love' were so unable to find compassion, if not understanding, for their servant-leaders. These men were simply standing up for the age-old teachings of the church, for which they were excoriated and shunned, not by all but by many. How can this phenomenon be understood? It certainly anticipates

---

[269] William Henry Beale, 'Foreword' in Brendan L. Webb, *The Religious Significance of War*, Sydney: Christian World, 1915, p. 3 as cited in Gilchrist, *op. cit.*

[270] Gilchrist, *op. cit.*

[271] Gilchrist, *op. cit.*

[272] Gilchrist, *op. cit.*

the eventual downfall of the mainstream churches in the 20th century, because they simply did not practice what they preached. This traditional relationship to warfare was of long standing in most churches. Some of the oldest churches in Britain are decorated with the regimental flags of wars from centuries past, and tattered as many are, some still bear blood stains. It is obvious that Christians have been, in the main, vulnerable to political brainwashing that informs them that God is on their side. Even as they heap criticism upon Islamists today, there remains a strong tendency to fall in line when the bugle calls in 'Christian' countries. Yet pacifists remain in all Christian and Muslim communities, and there are a few 'peace churches' that stand strong for conscientious objection.

Sectarianism between Protestants and Catholics in Ireland was brewing as the 'Home Rule Struggle' before the war and heightened during wartime.[273] Australians of Irish Catholic descent were outraged by the 1916 event that came to be known as the 'Easter Uprising' against British rule in Dublin, Ireland. The English feared civil war, and their response to the political action of the Catholics was one of brutal repression. They clearly had no patience for internal troubles during wartime.

This alienated many Catholic Australians for whom this exposed 'the ugly side of British Imperialism'.[274] For Protestants, by contrast, these events confirmed their worst suspicions that Australian Catholics, who represented nearly a quarter of the population, could not be counted on for loyalty and patriotism. Little surprise that there was a political price to pay when Catholic Archbishop Daniel Mannix spoke out against conscription in the 1916 and 1917 pre-referenda periods.[275] He was wrongly considered to be echoing the vast majority of Australian Catholics. Other Catholic leaders either remained silent or continued to support the war (such as Archbishop Kelly in Sydney).[276]

The dedication of Quakers to providing aid took on particular urgency when in the 1930s boatloads of refugees began arriving from Europe. Some were placed in detention, but in or out, many received assistance from Quakers. The 'Dunera boys' as they became known, arrived as mentioned earlier on a ship largely carrying Jewish refugees fleeing the Nazi regime. They were assisted quite considerably during their time in internment camps in Victoria and New South Wales.[277]

When conscription was imposed in Australia during the Vietnam War, Friends issued a public statement in 1965 that emphasised not only the importance of conscientious objection to war but also the commitment to take positive action toward becoming a society where war would be unthinkable. They authorised older Friends to support younger ones in considering their options in relation to the law and the difficult decision of whether to register as a conscientious objector on religious grounds, which was the only basis for exemption. The other alternative was to refuse to register at all. One Australian Quaker who was a conscientious non-complier was David Martin, who wrote that he refused to register as a CO because this would 'acknowledge the authorities' right to use this law to conscript other men for military training'.[278]

Many people felt that Australia should not have been active in Vietnam. Partly there was a sense that 'it wasn't our war', and that it was being fought on false ideological grounds, the thin argument that communism would infect Australia unless Vietnam was won. A second reason was that Australia was fighting simply to uphold its alliance with America, but that this too was an insufficient reason. Although World War II produced extensive film coverage that was eventually widely viewed by Aus-

---

[273] National Library of Australia, *On the Idle Hill of Summer*, BBC film, *op. cit.*

[274] 'The Impact of the Irish Crisis' in *Historical Studies* 14, no. 53, 10/1969 pp. 54-72 as cited in Gilchrist, *op. cit.*

[275] Salmon, *op. cit.*

[276] Gilchrist, *op. cit.*

[277] QPLC: Conscientious Objection', p. 3.

[278] QPLC: Conscientious Objection', p. 3.

tralians, Vietnam was in many cases instantaneously shot on camera and atrocities were captured as they happened and were aired soon after on television. This left Australia suffering a kind of trauma on a national scale. As well, the rotation of tours of duty, and the return of body bags were new aspects of war (since during the World Wars those who died abroad were buried there), leaving Australians much more confronted. Not only the media but first-hand accounts from frequently returning veterans played into negative, indeed horrified responses from many people.

One outcome of the Vietnam War was the Defence Legislation Amendment Act 1992 that changed the conscientious objection provisions, so that objection to a particular war became an acceptable ground for seeking exemption, with decisions being made by a special tribunal of lawyers. This kind of legislation might have opened the door for the American soldiers who sought protection and assistance from Quakers in Canada, not because they were pacifists but because they objected *in particular* to the Iraq war, once they got to the front.[279]

Quakers have taken a lead in another area of conscientious objection, through their refusal to pay for war. Bob Burrowes, though not a Quaker, demonstrated this with his truckload of shovels. John Woolman, an American Quaker, in 1755 expressed great concern about the payment of taxes for war. Japanese Quaker Susumu Ishitani become convinced of the importance of conscientious objection in this matter and made a statement to a Tokyo court in the 1980s to express his opposition to tax payment for military expenditures. He said that 'with military power we cannot protect our life nor keep our human dignity'.[280]

In Britain, the United States and Canada, this became an issue because income tax was deducted at source, putting Quaker organisations with employees in the impossible position of having to deduct the tax, doing the government's bidding, or take the consequences as organisations, schools and other services disobeying tax laws. In Britain, Friends attempted to divert the portion of taxes owed by employees to non-military use, but after losing a court case they were forced to pay the arrears. The European Commission of Human Rights also offered them no satisfaction. In the United States, some individuals and Quaker organisations refused to pay the telephone tax that had been imposed to finance the Vietnam war. A group of Quakers initiated a bill that proposed a Religious Freedom Peace Tax Fund Act in 1972. It remains on the agenda for Congress today. Its aim is 'to affirm the religious freedom of taxpayers who are conscientiously opposed to participating in war, to provide that the income, estate, or gift tax payments of such taxpayers be used for nonmilitary purposes, to improve revenue collection, and for other purposes'.[281]

Canadian Quaker organisations have found themselves in a similar dilemma. They support an independent organisation, Conscience Canada, which promotes the right of conscientious objection to military taxation. It has a website that compares military and civil expenditures and offers a form that allows people to register with a peace fund.[282]

In Australia a Peace Tax Campaign began in 1983 with support from Quakers. In 1988, Jo Vallentine, a Quaker and Senator at the time, redirected 10 per cent of her taxes to Melbourne's Peace & Development Foundation. She also introduced a Peace Trust Fund Bill to Parliament. Under this, conscientious objectors could have that portion (roughly 10 per cent) of their tax diverted into a fund to promote peace research and education, conflict resolution and improving international relations. It did not pass into law.

---

[279] QPLC: Conscientious Objection', p. 4.

[280] *Quaker Faith and Practice of Britain Yearly Meeting*, 1995, s. 24.16 as cited in QPLC: Conscientious Objection', p. 4.

[281] QPLC: Conscientious Objection', p. 5.

[282] www.consciencecanada.ca/, as cited in 'QPLC: Conscientious Objection', p. 5.

Recently Jan de Voogd of New South Wales Regional Meeting of Quakers has raised the possibility of putting the right not to pay taxes on the same level as CO status for serving in the military, reflecting a conscious decision or leading to oppose war as unjust and illegitimate. He sees it as possible to campaign for a provision that would allow conscientious objectors to choose to use their tax money to support any of several 'peaceful' purposes (peacekeeping, the UN High Commissioner for Refugees, the Red Cross, the International Criminal Court, or overseas aid) to which that portion of tax could be diverted.[283] The objection consistently raised by authorities illustrates their lack of comprehension for this moral position. 'But what if everyone did this?' they moan. Indeed, there might be no Defence Force and no wars. It would be a democratic decision.

In times of war, many Quakers and others of different or no persuasion have at crucial moments made considerable difference by being bold, creative, and faithful to their convictions. Bill Oats wrote to his mother on 28 September 1939:

> This morning I met an American Quaker who is leaving on Tuesday for Vienna to assist in getting Jewish refugees out of Germany. If she were British, such a mission would be impossible, but America is still neutral. She is going all alone – and that, I think, is courageous.[284]

Given their small numbers (in 2016 less than 1000 members across Australia), Friends have shown a disproportionate leadership with respect to conscience. In the 19th century, three members of the Allen family in Sydney held office in the New South Wales Legislative Assembly. William Bell Allen, who served from 1860-69, set up soap and candle works after emigrating from Ireland in 1842, and was the founder of the Protective League of Australian Industry. Interestingly, his two sons, William and Alfred, sat facing one another across the Assembly. Alfred had been associated with the early closing and eight-hour day movements, but while his father and brother were protectionists, he was a free-trader, and represented Paddington (1887-1894). He was an active philanthropist, supporting the Sydney Night Refuge and Kitchen and the Temperance Movement. Each followed his conscience, it would seem.[285]

From 1964 to 1982 Robert Mather, a Tasmanian Quaker, served in the state parliament as a Liberal MLA. This was a challenging time for a person of strong conscience to be a Liberal, especially when his party voted against the abolition of the death penalty while they were in opposition. He voted in favour, of course. Mather chose not to enter federal politics in no small part because he did not want to deal with defense issues.[286] For a time Mather was Education Minister, a fitting position for a person who had had a keen involvement with the Friends School in Hobart. As Minister, Mather guided through policy to formalise inter-denominational religious education in schools, however because of a change of government this was not implemented. The Friends School is the largest Quaker school in the world, with an annual enrolment of some 1300 children, welcome from any or no religious background. It offers education based on Friends' values and cultivates interfaith knowledge and understanding. It was important too at Mather's time, when the choices in Hobart were Catholic, Anglican or state/secular, which did include protestant religious instruction.

Across Australia many families were impacted by the Vietnam conscription scheme. It did not increase the popularity of this war. Voices were raised and religious groups, families, trade unionists, academics, and young men began to organise against the policy. The Youth Campaign Against Conscription (YCAC) had formed in late 1964 and was closely aligned to the ALP, and Save Our Sons

---

[283] 'QPLC: Conscientious Objection', p. 5.
[284] Oats, *op. cit.* p. 91.
[285] Vallentine, *op. cit.* pp. 11-12.
[286] Vallentine, *op. cit.,* p. 14.

(SOS) was founded in Sydney in 1965.[287] Laurie Wilkinson, who had personally applied for Conscientious Objector status during World War II, was an ALP Senator for Western Australia (1966-74) and the first Quaker to enter federal politics. He was a keen supporter and member of the Western Australia executive of the Moratorium Movement, in which many Quakers were active. When in May 1966, the government increased its commitment to using conscripts by sending them overseas, there was considerable and more intensively organised public opposition. The Movement quite ob-

---

[287] Australia and the Vietnam War', http://vietnam-war.commemoration.gov.au

viously supported draft resisters, to the point that the Parliamentary Labour Party could no longer ignore the fact. Members were told to campaign for changes to the conscription provisions of the National Service Act, but to desist from civil disobedience. Wilkinson was forced to resign from the Moratorium executive.[288]

Jean Hearn was another Labour Senator of Friendly persuasion who represented Tasmania from 1980-85. She was a cooperator rather than an adversarial thinker, according to Vallentine, and an advocate of Rudolph Steiner's philosophy as well as Quakerism. For her, Canberra was a learning experience, and she used the opportunity to share the resources of her office with the community. Hearn was known as a listener as much as a speaker. She wore her pacifism and Quakerism on her sleeve. Her commitment to peace was so central to her understanding of her political mandate that she called her newsletter 'Ploughshares', referring to the lesson from the Bible which appears in several verses. In Isaiah 2:4 and Micah 4:3, it is argued that God will cause people to lay down their weapons, 'they shall beat their swords into ploughshares and their spears into pruning hooks; nation shall not lift up sword against nation, neither shall they learn war any more'.[289]

Jean Hearn focused on giving people information that might otherwise not be accessible. She was involved in the formation of the 'Parliamentary Disarmament Group' in 1984, which included, importantly, members from all parties. Some might have found her emphases curious, for example she advocated for plant rights, because she was worried about the loss of biodiversity and the monopolisation of species. 'It was after she left the Senate that legislation was passed that gave large companies undue control over the world's seed banks', as Vallentine regretfully noted.[290]

Lynn Arnold was a South Australian Quaker politician who struggled with the duties of his role and the rigours of his faith. He served from 1982 in the Labour Government, and when in power was given the role of Minister for State Development and Technology. This required him to preside over a huge increase in defense industries in the state, such as the much-sought-after $4 billion submarine contract. He had his own misgivings, not least because the state economy was so heavily dependent on a single industry. He also understood the weapons as defensive, not offensive. The situation was not easy for Arnold, nor for local Quakers, who did not share his perspective on a number of key issues. Yet this was a man of conscience, who had exercised such a vote many times: voting against the Adelaide casino, 24 hour liquor trading including Sunday trading in alcohol, and the decriminalisation of marijuana. Respected and valued within the party, when the South Australian Bank collapsed to the tune of $3.1 billion and considerable public outrage, Arnold became Premier. He held the reins from 1992-3, when the party was defeated in a landslide. Eventually Arnold spent ten years working for World Vision and was ordained as an Anglican priest.[291]

Many individuals of courage do make a difference. Jo Vallentine, a Western Australian Quaker, has always seemed to have 'the courage of her convictions'. Yet she admits that getting into electoral politics

> ... was by no means an automatic yes from me ... It was a huge dilemma. How did Peter Fry [her spouse] feel about it? There was no doubt that our lives would change dramatically. We thought and prayed about it, and eventually I felt calm about saying yes, I felt led into the decision. But, of course, doubts constantly recur, particularly when the going is

/conscription/moratoriums-and-opposition.php, accessed 13/2/2016.
[288] Vallentine, *op. cit.,* p. 12.
[289] *Jubilee Bible,* 2000, adjusted for Australian spelling. https://www.biblegateway.com/quicksearch/?quicksearch=swords+plowshare s+&qs_version=JUB&limit=25, accessed 09/20/2016.
[290] Vallentine, *op. cit.* p. 13.
[291] Vallentine, *op. cit.,* pps. 14-16.

tough at home, for whatever reason. In subsequent decisions regarding re-election in 1987 and 1989-90, dilemmas remain, and the same degree of clarity of purpose is missing – a sure sense that the parliamentary role needs constant evaluation. It is a danger to one's search for wholeness, to one's integrity, not to constantly re-consider whether one is in the right place, whether one is doing the right thing.[292]

Before Vallentine stood for election, she was involved with a group called 'Project Iceberg', which boldly went aboard nuclear warships to hang banners over the side announcing that the arms race was 'bad news'. On the occasion of Bob Hawke's delivery of the Curtin Memorial Lecture, in 1983, Project Iceberg draped a banner inside Winthrop Hall saying 'What we need is a Labor Government'. After the lecture she approached Hawke and said to him how disappointed many ALP supporters were at the prospect of further uranium mining in Australia. I warned that Labor would lose votes over it. He turned to me and said: 'Who else are you going to vote for?' Thought-provoking and challenging words that stayed with me.[293]

However, working at the cause of nuclear disarmament, she knew of the American bases in Australia, heard Reagan calling the Soviet Union the 'Evil Empire', and was well aware of Australia's complicity in the arms race. While there were many of her co-citizens worrying for their lives, the majority of the public seemed dangerously ignorant of the threat. So it was primarily as an educator, and to satisfy her own unanswered questions that she entered politics. 'It is the never-ending and often frustrating search for truth which is a constant motivation in my work for peace.'[294]

Indeed, the layers of deception that seem so often designed to misguide, to entice, to reflect, to transfer responsibility make the pacifist's calling a most challenging and often solitary one. What does lie behind the smoke and mirrors? Of course there is no one answer. Different dynamics in different times and places, but not without trends and patterns. What Quakers as a general witness keep at the forefront of their minds is that nothing that is social, cultural, or historical happens without human actors. And as humans we share a great deal across our cultural, racial and religious diversity. While they may act out of fear or even despite themselves, as Bob Burrowes suggests, all live and breathe, or have done so. Making them into cardboard cut-outs is not a helpful means to get at the truth. Jo Vallentine suggested in 1990, in a statement that is perhaps more true than ever 26 years later,

> It seems to be considered dangerous in Australia to allow the public free access to information. The increasing monopolisation of the media . . . is a very real threat to alternative viewpoints getting an airing . . . business people with vested interests to protect . . . wield power in the less-and-less investigative journalistic circles. Truth is constantly sacrificed on the altars of politics, power and profit. Not that a trend to lack of information, or misinformation, is new on the Australian political scene, but media monopolisation highlights it to a painful degree . . . to people who like to know what's going on, to people who (perish the thought) cherish the notion that ordinary people have a right to information which affects their lives and their children's collective future. The 'mushroom treatment' has been the norm ever since convict days when decisions were made by 'superior beings' . . . Successive governments have kept generations of Australians in the dark on a whole range of topics.[295]

Hector Kinloch was an American-born and Cambridge-educated Fulbright professor, and Quaker. He taught US History in Kuala Lumpur and from 1968-88 at the Australian National University (ANU). He was elected to the ACT Legislative Assembly in its first year, 1988, as a member of the 'Residents Rally' and worked assiduously as a spokesperson opposing the prospect of a local casino.

---

[292] Vallentine, *op. cit.* pp. 4-5.

[293] Vallentine, *op. cit.,* p. 4.

[294] Vallentine, *op. cit.,* p. 5.

[295] Vallentine, *op. cit.,* p. 6.

He was a longtime opponent of gambling and helped establish the National Association of Gambling Studies.

Kinloch like other Friends carried a centuries-old concern about gambling. They opposed the barter system and introduced fixed pricing. Their argument was that there is a fair price for everything, and that the deception of 'getting lucky' played unjustly on the poor and downhearted, who were susceptible to gambling addictions. Indeed, it is striking how widespread the various forms of gambling are in Australia compared to other Western countries, from two-up (a coin-toss game from 18th century Britain), horse, dog, and car racing to pokies, bingo and lotteries.

Kinloch's work in this area earned him much respect and he was given responsibility for the Arts, Ethnic Affairs, Tertiary Education and Municipal Services portfolios. He was perhaps happy with the system in Canberra compared to the state and federal levels, but saw public life as an opportunity for peacebuilding, and was dismayed at the way the political system polarised people and cultivated 'institutional aggression'. He noted that not only professional difference but personal abuse was heaped on those who take a position different from their peers. One of his first amendments in the Assembly was to overturn a limitation preventing those over 65 from serving on advisory boards for vocational training. He was pleased at being able to achieve unanimous consent.[296] Kinloch's public contribution was cut short by illness in 1992, when he resigned his seat, and his death in 1993.

It has been challenging for women to be peacebuilders because of the commitments that so many have to children, aging parents and spouses, the lack of support for their calling, and the social opprobrium that acts as a further burden. As late as 1990, Jo Vallentine noted that there were only two women in the Australian parliament with children below teen age, in sharp contrast with Norway, where eight of seventeen members of cabinet were women. She was touched when she heard her six year old dismiss 'yet another meeting' with the explanation, 'You've got to understand, Sam, Mummy *is* trying to save the world'. Critics might say that children should not even be aware of such threats, but it has not been the way of Quakers to shield their children from the big questions of the day. Later, the same daughter sent her a card, 'Dear Mummy, I am so proud of you for going to jail'.

Being an example to her children has always been a guiding principle for Vallentine, but just as serving the public well, it begins by staying centred within herself. 'The start of my daily routine is fresh air and exercise, coupled with meditation, supplication and affirmation all combined. That 30-40 minutes is invaluable as a reminder of the wholeness I seek – the connection between the physical, mental and spiritual aspects of life.' This affirmation of herself as a living being, as a woman, as part of a larger web, reflects into her decision-making and the light she sheds for others, from a Friends' perspective.

An example of acting as a witness for peace occurred in response to the unprecedented action of the Minister of Defense, when on the 30 September 1989, he sent Australian troops to defend the US military base at Nurrungar, on Australian soil. Vallentine asked that the action be debated as a 'Matter of Public Importance' or 'MPI'. Nearly 500 people had been arrested, opposing the base that directly tied Australia into the US nuclear war strategies. However Vallentine was told she had already had her quota of 'MPIs'.

Senator Jean Jenkins, who had been at the demonstrations, then put the motion forward. Vallentine's name was omitted from the speakers' list, ensuring that there could be no quorum. The second time it came up, the Government discouraged Senators from being present, to the point of shooing them out of the Chamber. Vallentine later argued 'This was an outrageous denial of democracy. Obviously the Government and the Liberal-National Party Coalition want to continue keeping Australians in the dark about the functions of Nurrungar. The 37 per cent of Australians who oppose the Nurrungar

---

[296] Vallentine, *op. cit.,* p. 16.

base have been denied a voice in Parliament ...'[297]

Families are the primary institution where most people learn to relate, either through peaceful and loving interactions, or through violence and bullying. The pattern modeled by parents is generally replicated by children. Over the course of the 20th century, while wars were waging, home lives were changing. We have seen earlier how some families were drastically damaged or broken apart by the fallout from war. But it is not war alone that causes such situations. Friend Topsy Evans has documented her concern, widely felt among Quakers, about domestic violence.

> I believe that violence is used at many levels to control other people. For many years Quakers have held that international violence is to be avoided at all costs. I believe that violence in relationships is the ground in which other violence grows and that, if we are to develop a just and peaceful society, we must look to reducing the violence within our families. Thus, for me, working towards a reduction in domestic violence is very much part of my belief that peace is an essential component of life as it should be.[298]

When Jo Vallentine was arrested in the US in May 1987 at the Nevada test site during the Mothers' Day Action, a Liberal Party Senator told the media that 'my behaviour was disgraceful and I should have been at home with my children'. Vallentine had struggled inwardly but came to peace with her leading for public service, knowing that this would have an effect on her family. She began a movement to return Mother's Day to its original intention, not chocolate but a day of peace, as the Mother's Day Declaration of 1870 by Julia Ward Howe suggests. Howe called for a peace council for women after the double carnage of the American Civil War and the Franco-Prussian War. Although nowhere did women yet have the vote, yet they had power in the family, the institution that was perhaps at the root of peace or war. Vallentine had this lesson brought home to her by her daughter Sam, early one morning when the family was curled up in bed together. 'Sam reminded me of the sticker on our front door which says "Peace is a Group Effort", saying that peace in families was a group effort too, and that meant all being together.'[299] In 1870 Howe wrote:

> Arise then ... women of this day!
> Arise, all women who have hearts!
> Whether your baptism be of water or of tears!
> Say firmly:
> "We will not have questions answered by irrelevant agencies,
> Our husbands will not come to us, reeking with carnage,
> For caresses and applause.
> Our sons shall not be taken from us to unlearn
> All that we have been able to teach them of charity, mercy and patience.
> We, the women of one country,
> Will be too tender of those of another country
> To allow our sons to be trained to injure theirs."
>
> From the voice of a devastated Earth a voice goes up with
> Our own. It says: "Disarm! Disarm!
> The sword of murder is not the balance of justice."
> Blood does not wipe our dishonor,
> Nor violence indicate possession.
> As men have often forsaken the plough and the anvil
> At the summons of war,

---

[297] Vallentine, *op. cit.* pp. 33-4.
[298] Topsy Evans, 1990, *this we can say, op. cit.,* S. 3.107.
[299] Vallentine, *op. cit.,* pp. 17-19.

Let women now leave all that may be left of home
For a great and earnest day of counsel.
Let them meet first, as women, to bewail and commemorate the dead.
Let them solemnly take counsel with each other as to the means
Whereby the great human family can live in peace . . .
Each bearing after his own time the sacred impress, not of Caesar,
But of God -
In the name of womanhood and humanity, I earnestly ask
That a general congress of women without limit of nationality,
May be appointed and held at someplace deemed most convenient
And the earliest period consistent with its objects,
To promote the alliance of the different nationalities,
The amicable settlement of international questions,
The great and general interests of peace.[300]

In 2014, Quakers made a submission to the Australian Department of Defence, drafted by the Quaker Peace and Legislation Committee. It concluded:

The Australian Defence Force (ADF) should operate within an integrated and independent foreign policy set by the civil power. The following are features we would like to see applied:

• Parliament's approval for the engagement of the ADF in war-fighting overseas

• Priority given to involvements that are authorised by the United Nations and involve peacekeeping, peacemaking and peacebuilding

• No conscription to the armed forces, and no recruitment of people under 18

• Greater participation of women in decision-making roles within the ADF

• Phased withdrawal of the ADF from border protection, and replacement by a coastguard

• Increased emphasis on the skills of mediation and negotiation in ADF training

• More resources to assist those returning from war zones, and their families.[301]

During the 'Anzac Conversations: Citizen Voices for Peace', Friend Ronis Chapman spoke about the national day of action by *Love Makes a Way* (LMAW) groups across Australia. *Love Makes a Way* is not an organisation but a collection of individuals from Christian groups who join together to speak out about the government's current policies regarding the detention of asylum seekers.[302] Groups staged peaceful sit-ins in the offices of federal parliamentarians on Human Rights Day, 10 December 2014, protesting the detention of children under current asylum policies. Chapman was arrested in the event in Canberra, but charges were not laid.

All who participate in LMAW actions are required to participate in nonviolent direct action training. Inspiration and lessons come from other activists around the world – both current and past. Chapman said that it is not only the action itself that is important. Telling others about the event is a way to give voice to the refugees who are silenced, many by being held in detention and offshore.

Jean Zaru, the Christian Palestinian from Palestine and active Quaker mentioned above, is an active peacemaker.[303] She has served on the Central Committee of the World Council of Churches, among

[300] http://www.poemhunter.com/poem/mother-s-day-proclamation, accessed 13/2/2016.
[301] As cited in 'QPLC: Conscientious Objection', pp. 5-6.
[302] Anzac Conversations: Citizen Voices for Peace' Canberra Quaker Meeting House, 8/11/2016. See also http://lovemakesaway.org.au/
[303] Rosemary Radford Ruether, 'Foreword' to Zaru, *op. cit.*, pp. xi-xvii.

many roles. Her involvement with this body brought her to Australia in 1991, and she continues to have rapport with like-minded Australians. She plays a leading role in the YWCA. She has sought for many years to deconstruct the misrepresentations of the Palestinian reality in the West. These, she feels, cover up the structures of violence and oppression that lie at the roots of Palestinian resistance. 'Peace and respect for Palestinian human rights is not only for the sake of Palestinians. It is essential for the sake of Israelis as well, and for the wider region. It is essential for the future peace and stability of the Middle East and the world', Zaru argues.[304]

A common factor in military violence is the deception of symmetry between two sides of a conflict. Sometimes this is caused by misunderstanding, as we have seen, and at others such confusion is promoted for political ends. Zaru reflects,

> . . . Israel is systematically violating human rights in order to make its occupation permanent. And yet the occupation – and the massive US aid that funds it – is slowly killing us all. In the two years of crisis at the start of the second intifada in 2000 and 2001, more than 646 Israelis were killed and 4,706 injured. In the same period, over 1,846 Palestinians were killed and 20,900 injured. The refusal of the international community to intervene made it complicit in the violations of human rights and war crimes. Of course it is important to recognise that the victims of oppression are not blameless. Too often, they themselves become the oppressors of others. I admit that some Palestinians, in their anger and despair, have resorted to violence. I, personally, do not think that violence can lead us anywhere, neither morally nor strategically. Luckily, this has become the position not only of faith-based organisations, but many Palestinians have adopted it as well. Violence feeds upon itself. While the means of violence are not symmetrical, its results are. Violence creates a symmetry of emotion, pain, fear, mistrust. Violence creates mutual suspicion and mutual accusation.[305]

In her daily life and witness, Zaru offers another way, one in which people are good neighbours, recognising the humanity of each side and their interdependence. Education and friendship, deconstructing injustice, whether it is against Jews, Palestinians or others, are the primary ways forward in her view. Inspired by a Japanese poet who once wrote that 'The world grows stronger as each story is told', Jean Zaru tells stories from her own life to help illustrate the conditions in Palestine and the need for a peaceful solution.

> In the war of 1948, I was only eight years old. Yet I can remember the fear very clearly. I remember hiding in the basement in our home. I remember the refugees coming to Ramallah from the coastal plain of Palestine. I remember how my father and my older brother took a truck with water and bread and drove west to deliver supplies and pick up women and children who were running away from the dangers of war but could not go on walking. Fifty of these people shared our house for a period of six weeks. Another one hundred camped under our pine trees. Our Friends Meeting House in Ramallah sheltered many more families until they found a way of settling somewhere else. I have lived most of my life next to a refugee camp. The war ended, but the plight of those refugees continues. A fourth generation of refugees has now been born.[306]

In describing her daily life, Jean Zaru provides texture to the repressive constraints under which Palestinians are living. She can no longer travel to Jerusalem, dear to the heart and spirit of every Palestinian and a mere ten miles away, for life's basic material and cultural necessities without the greatest of difficulty.

---

[304] Zaru, *op. cit.,* p. 37.
[305] Zaru, *op. cit.,* p. 60.
[306] Zaru, *op. cit.,* p. 4.

I was born and have lived all my life in Ramallah . . . one of the beautiful summer resorts in the Jerusalem mountain range . . . From the roof of my home, I can look south and see Jerusalem glittering like a ball of crystal in the night. I agonize that I am not allowed to go there. Jerusalem has always been for us the centre, the heart that pumped life into all of Palestine . . . All my children and seven grandchildren were born in Jerusalem. Over the years, we have been treated in its hospitals. We have gone there for worship, cultural activities, visits to our family members, for work, and for getting visas to travel . . . You see it in pictures, carvings, paintings and posters in our homes, schools, public buildings, taxis and buses. You hear the beautiful songs about it. Jerusalem is called the flower of all cities . . . You hear the bells of the churches joined by the muezzins, the call to prayer, from minarets within the city. For me, Jerusalem stands for freedom of mind, diversity, and universality.[307]

In 1980, Israel formally annexed all of Jerusalem. Before 1967, more than 85 per cent of East Jerusalem had been Palestinian territory. The wall now incorporates all of Jerusalem and a significant additional tranche of the West Bank, excluding Palestinian direct access without permits. Normally only students, medical personnel and workers are granted these, with rare exceptions. Even those who get permits usually cannot bring their cars into the city. Transport within the city becomes a further challenge for the elderly, poor and disabled. This has also meant that it is difficult to travel between the north and south of the West Bank, because of the blockage created by the wall, and Palestinians are divided from one another.[308]

Jean Zaru is also cut off from meeting with other Palestinians in places like Nablus or Bethlehem, never mind Gaza, which has been severed for many years. The two hour trip to Amman, Jordan for a back operation stretched into an agonising two days for Zaru because of checkpoints and the restriction which allows only Israelis to use the modern road system. Life is so disrupted that nothing can be taken for granted, nothing planned, even simple hopes must be kept in check. This is the nature of war, that it shakes the life of citizens at the most basic levels. Yet most people in the West do not think of Palestine as being 'at war'.

> When my daughter got engaged during the invasion of Lebanon in 1982, we had to cancel the reception and any festive celebrations in solidarity with our people. When I learned with great joy that I was going to be a grandmother, I kept my fears to myself. Many women aborted from tear-gas bombs, and my children and I were worried.[309]

The West, Jean Zaru feels, has accepted all too easily the argument that the new wall that stands not only between Palestine and Israel, but cuts many parts of Palestine into tiny territories, as well as all the other militarisation is necessary for 'security'. Why can't the provocation, the injustice of it, also be sensed? Zaru's feeling is that these measures are playing another, more sinister role, of gradually 'ethnically cleansing' Palestine of Palestinians. Certainly the Israeli 'settlements' that continue to mushroom inside Palestine encroach on the remaining fragments of the territory. Life becomes so very constrained that everyone who can possibly leave seems to be doing so or has already fled.

The wall and the bypass roads that slice the land into impassable fragments result in the dissolution of any possibility of a basis for territorial integrity. Far from settling anything or anyone, they conflict as both Jewish settlers and Palestinians resent the 'need' to share a tiny patch of land. Someone has painted in large graffiti, 'To exist is to Resist' on the Palestinian side of the wall.

The wall is to be 450 miles long and defies any current peace plan. The International Court of Justice ruled in 2004 that the wall was contrary to international law and required Israel to dismantle it and to

---

[307] Zaru, *op. cit.,* pp. 39-40.
[308] Zaru, *op. cit.,* p. 44.
[309] Zaru, *op. cit.,* p. 6.

make reparations for the damage it has caused. 'When it is completed, thousands of Palestinians will be trapped in the no-man's land between the wall and the State of Israel, cutting them off from the rest of Palestinian society and from their agricultural land.'[310] Sadly, for many, this isolation is already a reality in their region. Palestinians have no reason to believe that it is sharing rather than confiscation of land that is the order of the day. In 2016, about one fifth of the wall remains to be built.

Now all the members of Zaru's large family have left Ramallah, and most are gone from Palestine, for education, health care, and work. Her brother, Hanna (John) Mikhail, poet, writer, and political scientist, moved to the United States where he obtained a PhD from Harvard and became a lecturer at Princeton. Eventually he became a member of the Russell Tribunal on Palestine at The Hague. However, when he sought to return home to Palestine in 1967 he was refused entry. He moved to Jordan and finally Lebanon, before mysteriously and tragically disappearing in 1976.[311] Jean Zaru's reflection on the vulnerability and fate of the displaced should offer a reality check to Australia and its policies on asylum seekers and refugees. Very few people from any part of the world leave their homes, their families, the land they love by choice. The 'push factors' are far more compelling than many Australians seem to understand.

> More than half of the Palestinian population of Ramallah had to leave for many reasons – economic, educational, health and general well-being. Those who left are called by different names: refugees, internally displaced, asylum seekers, deportees, and economic migrants. We should remember, however, that all who are compelled by severe political, economic and social conditions to leave their land and culture, regardless of the labels given to them by others, are uprooted people. They have been forced to leave their land because of persecution, war, violation of human and community rights. The deliberate displacement of the Palestinians by Israel as a matter of policy continues today through the confiscation and expropriation of our land, natural resources, and water; through the demolition of villages and houses; through the imposition of closures and embargoes on food and medicine; through restrictions on our movement; and through making it almost impossible to run a business or earn a living. Direct and structural violence directed at persons, communities, and the entire Palestinian population, are gradually destroying our social fabric, economic infrastructure, and natural environment. We experience permanent unemployment, increased marginalisation, and exclusion.[312]

Jean Zaru sees one of the lost narratives globally as that of the Palestinian peace movement. Lack of recognition of the strenuous efforts of this movement contributes to the notion that Palestinians, Arabs and Muslims are universally violent and only understand lessons taught at the end of a gun (or worse). Founded in the early 1980s, the Palestinian Human Rights Campaign brought together Palestinian Christians, Muslims, and Israeli and Western Jews to challenge the occupation. Zaru traces the constant nonviolent protests of Palestinians, seeking to find alternatives to occupation. The first 'intifada' or uprising in 1987-92 was almost entirely nonviolent. It was staged through boycotts rather than arms. Her own founding of a peace centre at Ramallah was a contribution but by no means the beginning of this peacebuilding movement.

Although she is a pacifist, Zaru understands why Palestinians have grown disillusioned with the 'peace process' and in considerable numbers have entrusted their future to the militant Hamas party. However, far from making this choice because they wanted a Muslim state, she understands most Palestinians as simply wanting what Israelis want: peace and land enough.

---

[310] Zaru, *op. cit.,* p. 34.

[311] Zaru, *op. cit.,* p. 17.

[312] Zaru, *op. cit.,* pp. 13-14.

Far from the myth that Muslims have driven Christians out of Palestine, she reports that her Muslim neighbours accept her and other Christians as one Palestinian people with themselves. Furthermore, Jean Zaru has great appreciation for the ways that Islam is in harmony with Christianity. Their common roots are an important place to start to discover this. But the Jewish religion also shares this. The one thing that prevents her from being heard within her own community is being female. But gender segregation also lies at the root of much violence, as we have seen previously. Zaru is more than prepared to be a peacebuilder to overcome such prejudice, and all prejudice, wherever she finds it.

Jean Zaru is not an Australian, but she has made her mark here. Her friendships with Australians and her example as peacemaker are salutary to conversations about many related aspects of the problems of violence and militarism for Australians. While religious extremism has historically been a significant source of violence, it must be remembered that in many instances religion is used as a way to claim the moral high ground or foil when other issues are in fact at stake. It is also used to cast blame, willy-nilly. Australians risk being drawn into conflicts such as Afghanistan that are understood only too little or too late by allies such as the US. The Australian public, at least, is placated apparently quite easily about the importance of yet another conflict in a distant land for which Diggers must die. As the (now) old folk song goes, 'How many deaths does it take, my friend, 'til too many people have died?'

These conflicts often include land, natural resources, and power of various kinds. The ongoing military interventions of the 'Great Powers' into the Middle East, to take the example of one region, have a good deal to do with control of highly valued oil reserves in a carbon fuel and capital driven world. Such engagements and invasions are often couched in that vague 'security' claim and funded by individuals and corporations who have as much to gain as states. Their ultimate aims may diverge, but there can be a complementarity in 'strategic' goals along the way.

As Zaru underscores so well, religious explanations for warfare are suspect at best. By contrast, it is faith that often does undergird the most staunch and profound witnesses to peace. As we have seen, individual witnesses often provide the leadership that generates broader, highly effective movements. Little if anything is likely to deter the conscience of those deeply committed to nonviolence. Whether financial penalties, prison terms or alternative service, these seem to goad the pacifist through their very coercion into increased conviction.

Perhaps most scarce today is liberal public dialogue, in large part because of the almost complete erosion of independent media outlets. Changes that have been wrought by the electronic media have also impacted on public discourse. Individuals publish what is normally private; personal events, feelings about things, relationship status, or even when it comes to political issues, responses are on the level of like/dislike emoticons rather than grounded critical engagement, potentially supporting religious convictions. Results include our loss of linguistic eloquence and greater difficulty tolerating or risking difference, such as the distinctions between immigrants and Australian-born, and religious adherence. To some extent this may also be to conceal class diversity in a 'classless' society. The overall affluence of Australians may cause us to take too much for granted, including our rights and freedoms. However, the cost appears to be that Australia's civil society itself is being eroded. As we know from many other states that are reaching for more robust interactions, these qualities are not gained or restored easily.

Chapter IX
'Lest We Forget': Honest Memories, Just Futures

There is a saying that 'To remember is to work for peace'. Certainly to forget death and violence is to deny dignity to those who have suffered and to shut away possibilities for peace. However, remembrance is not idle and innocent but loaded. It is necessarily imbued with meanings and values that are weighted, attributed to particular individuals, groups, and events. To remember is to sort through the known totality at a given time and to construct a narrative. In doing so, there is always the risk of sidelining other narratives, and congealing preferred or more widely disseminated accounts as 'the truth'.

Memories can only be incomplete fragments. No person, nor group of people, can know everything, all points of the compass and the full spectrum of an event from the microscopic and subconscious, the neurological up to the grand pageant of circumstances. Over time, new lenses are offered as more people reflect upon the assemblage of what is known with the perspective of time. More and more artifacts and accounts can come into play as the years elapse and across contexts. Technological changes and the release of previously closed documents also shed new light.

Memorialising is necessarily interpreting history. It may or may not lead to further enduring artifacts, banners, books, monuments, or to conversations and commemorative events that themselves add to the narratives. Some have considered commemoration as a form of pilgrimage, in which those who participate retrace the path of those who went before. Often the intention is to create such a path, like the stations of the cross. Not surprisingly, over time, the forerunners become legendary, larger than life, mythological.

Critical perspectives are required to provide balance. They are not intended to wipe out all that is precious, including the cherished memories of people, places and culture lost. Rather, by taking more perspectives into account and digging deeper, a greater justice can arise. By creating such openings we contribute to peacemaking. Becoming and remaining prepared to be surprised, to welcome alternative accounts and understandings is foundational to peace. Recognising that history is always unfinished, and always political, in that it is loaded in its writing with the commitments and world views of its narrators, is also essential to nonviolence. If we hold too strongly to one lens, we risk closing our eyes and ears to other truths.

Historian Henry Reynolds has done extensive research into the fraught relationship between First Nations Australians and the country's more recent arrivals. He reflects that

The Department of Veterans Affairs and the Australian War Memorial commemorate the service of Aboriginal and Torres Strait Islander servicemen and women and are currently involved in a large research project with the Australian National University to fully document their military careers. But they are both silent about the frontier war. It is as though it didn't exist. We have the extraordinary situation that Aborigines who died fighting on the other side of the world are recognised while those who were cut down defending their homelands are studiously ignored. It is no longer possible to feign ignorance of conditions on the frontier to explain the oversight. It is a deliberate choice to perpetuate the 'great Australian silence' and the underlying hint of racial contempt.[313]

As Christian Appy has also pointed out, this 'forgetting' is institutional as well as personal. There are vast machines chipping away at our memories, especially those of subsequent generations who are dependent upon the records, narratives, legends and myths of their forebears. Foreign students from China, Vietnam and even countries such as Thailand and Japan are not sure what to believe when they read the Australian press and Australian literature on the politics and history of the region. They find the new perspectives introduced bewildering and confronting to the 'realities' upon which they have built their accounts of themselves and their citizenship.

For some, the rug is pulled roughly and alarmingly out from under them as they lose any sure compass. For others, their eyes are opened to the politics of lies and ideology at work within their own countries. But they often fail to appreciate that what they hear in Australia may also be loaded with political agendas. The capacity to reflect critically on what is dished up as truth by figures in authority can be eliminated as antisocial. Recognising what is 'fact' and what is opinion does not necessarily come easily. A Japanese foreign student in Australia in 2016 said,

> I don't understand. My professor [in Australia] told me that we are so lucky to have the American military base in Okinawa. But in Japan we don't think so. Most of the population there is old. They are very frightened and disturbed by the noise of the fighter jets flying low and so often over the city. It makes them sick.[314]

If modern warfare and 'security' are confusing, then how much more so is the staunch refusal of the Australian nation to come to terms with the frontier wars. Prime Minister John Howard thought the issue could be whisked away by the sleight of hand he called 'shared nationhood'. This was a very different concept from sovereignty for Indigenous people. He offered only 'passing references to past unspecified wrongs and regrettable blemishes', according to Reynolds. Meanwhile the commemoration machine continued to work in full gear for the Australian Defense Force. One of the many ways we need to restore right relationships with our First Nations is by according them the respect we have accorded others in our memorialising. Reynolds notes the paradox of the contrast,

> . . . When the remains of servicemen are found beneath European farmland or in enveloping jungle no expense is spared to retrieve them and provide a military funeral, often in the presence of surviving family members. We react to the Aboriginal dead in a totally different way. No attempt is made to find, record or mark sites of multiple deaths. Australia has between 4000 and 5000 war memorials for those who did not return from overseas engagements. There are less than a handful of monuments relating to frontier conflict. Attempts to enumerate deaths in that conflict are met with everything from mild embarrassment to open hostility. Conservative historians who deride the necessarily rudimentary attempts to count the dead have been applauded and rewarded as defenders of the national honour.[315]

[313] Reynolds, *op. cit.*, p. 234.
[314] Pamela Leach, personal communication, March 2016.
[315] Reynolds, *op. cit.*, pp. 237-8.

There is a saying that 'it is the victors who write the history' and it may be so, but in Australia as elsewhere, this 'right of rebuttal' comes at a great price. Of course monuments are significant, but they, or their absence, point to a much deeper and more fractured and painful truth in the national psyche. Intentional forgetting of suffering, death and what has amounted to a genocide for Australia's First Peoples is the most toxic, indeed violent, kind of memorialising. It will continue to leave deep scars on the whole social fabric of the country, wounds that will fester until all of us are ready for a new day of inclusion, recognition and respect. It requires that the Commonwealth of Australia not only say 'Sorry' (meaning mainly that 'we are sorry you are still upset after all this time but after all we can't be held responsible for the actions of our ancestors and don't you need to grow up about that too?') but accord the right of self-determination that is unquestioned for other citizens to First Nations people, freeing them of patronising colonial policies and governance.

It becomes evident that remembering has not been easy for Australians from our earliest history. Only through a very gradual process have Australians identified and become easy with their convict roots or with our eclipsed Aboriginal, Chinese, or Afghan backgrounds. It may be that Federation was seen to bring a release from much of that history which, at the turn of the 20th century, still carried a measure of embarrassment or 'taint'. Everyone wanted to be British and a free settler. From this came a complex process of attempting, against all odds, to rewrite personal and Australian history to make it uniquely white. This meant denying or destroying evidence to the contrary. Soon the tracing and history became a cherry-picking process, rather than one of engagement with evidence where it could be found. One result was a general vagueness about many aspects of the past. Another was a deceitful sense that World War I was Australia's first war. It was most evidently not.

Thus it came to be that even Australian Quakers, with all their freedoms, in considering memorialising World War I from the vantage point of the 21st century, had first to admit that they knew too little. Peacemaking, whatever else, must certainly be a very active process in which we keep ourselves apprised and reminded, with courage, in order to teach each new generation all we know about the complex dynamics of violence and our part in it.

David Stephens has spoken of how the real nature of war is too often not reported in the popular media. This is one of the reasons that 'keepsakes' and cultural expressions, from the visual to music and literature, have a special importance. Stephens depicted commemorative ceremonies as having been hijacked by images of heroism and memories of warriors battling and laying down their lives for our freedoms. Yet as we have seen, a number of the wars in which Australia has fought did not come close to threatening its freedoms. Of course there is always a catastrophising logic which suggests that if a conflict takes on proportions one hundred times larger than where it starts, it *might* impinge on Australia. The case is made that adversaries need to be 'nipped in the bud'. As yet we have not heard the excuse that this is for environmental reasons, but conflicts such as Iraq and the Gulf War can hardly be seen as successes in this regard any more than Australia's involvement in earlier conflicts. Whatever we feel about the benefits or hazards of engaging in theatres of war such as Afghanistan or Syria, we must acknowledge that becoming yet another player enlarges each front. More civilian lives are at stake, more fighters are likely to be recruited on opposing sides.

In the course of preparing the commemorative banners for World War I, Chloe Mason described how Sydney Quakers found unity in their anxiety about the increasing militarisation of our society, and its implications. This trend may impact present and future Australians and others, and seems already to be affecting the most vulnerable, such as asylum seekers. Yet many citizens find that it is easier to turn away from the uglier periods of the past and the facts of history even as it is being shaped. Mutual support is required for us to face the truths that are still being exposed about our history, and to engage the many lenses upon events, without rancour or defensiveness. It must be understood that one of the reasons we turn away from war narratives, keepsakes and issues is that we know, either from direct experience, media exposure or simply gut reaction that the trauma of war touches everyone in its path, however indirectly.

To fail to disturb the 'skeletons in the closet' is not to bury them forever but rather to add impact to their inevitable resurrection. This is apparent, for example, in the case of First Nations Australians. The very damaged relationships between them and other Australians past and present, as well as the corrosive impact this has on the social fabric for the future and the credibility of institutions cannot be underestimated. Postponing the work of building right relationships does not seem to have benefited anyone. Yet for most people words such as 'recognition', 'reconciliation' and 'representation', much less 'decolonisation' and 'sovereignty' remain a herd of elephants in the room that will only trumpet louder and louder in the conscience of the nation until they are stampeding round. When they are finally heard, confronted and a peace process has been seriously worked through, Australia will find itself on happier footing both within the Commonwealth and internationally. The world is certainly watching and waiting for our country's conscience to mature.

The Australian War Memorial remains, as the most significant public institution representing issues of war and peace, highly contentious. Stephens revealed that the War Memorial gives naming rights of some of its areas and programs to arms suppliers, and uses elements of a 'fun park' to engage children. The more previous wars are sanitised or sentimentalised, the easier it is to promote and sanctify current or potential conflicts, as Stephens pointed out. Sentimentalising war makes it harder to objectively ask questions about why we go to war or might involve ourselves in any specific conflict. While some shift in policy has occurred within the War Memorial, it has yet to embrace peacemaking as the ultimate goal towards which it ought to be pointing its activities.

Perhaps this is little wonder since it is a body of the Australian government, which engages in a variety of peace-oriented initiatives even while heightening its militarism, engagement in conflicts, and the use of the ADF in activities that could be conducted by civilian bodies. The government seems to speak out of both sides of its mouth in a manner that obfuscates the truth. It is far from achieving a status of 'net peacemaker' nationally, regionally, or globally.

There have been numerous cases where 'for security reasons' war becomes policy in Australia rather than a matter of national debate. It is taken out of the public arena and becomes merely an administrative question: how will we fight this war and how will we finance it. Furthermore, the 'deployment' of all forms of militarised language means that we do find ourselves in a condition of perpetual war: the war on drugs and the war on terror have replaced the Cold War in a smooth dovetailing which no longer leaves any space for public input. We might now long for the vehement debates over conscription that characterised so much public and media exchange in the First World War. At least there was a space on the streets, in the pubs, in the churches and public halls, and yes, finally, at the ballot box for popular input.

Stephens also raised another worrisome issue. He drew connections between the focus on 'heroes' and blood sacrifice, as taught both at school and learned through the form of memorialising that has become common, in computer games, and the grooming of children by pedophiles. Certainly what we now know about the developing brains of children indicates they are particularly susceptible to damage, even by the raised voices of adults, and that they are very vulnerable to suggestion. The training of boys in World War I can now for certain be related to the readiness of many to go to war, such that a large number lied about their age successfully. This fact also indicates that the government was not nearly as motivated to protect children until they reached the age of majority and could make mature decisions as it was to find recruits for its front lines indiscriminately.

Furthermore, we now know that the human brain is not mature until a young person is well into his or her 20s, information which better helps us to understand that the majority of those who enlisted would not have fully developed cognitive networks. This would have made them particularly vulnerable to recruiting propaganda, to taking training very literally and without fully engaging their own judgment, and finally and most sadly, to the impacts of traumas they would have witnessed or experienced first-hand. Little wonder that there has been so very much suffering from PTSD.

Memorialising is a process which can promote militarism or challenge it. Bill Oats reflected on this as war was breaking out in Europe from his school in Geneva.

12 November, 1939 – Armistice Day

Armistice Day observance again at the School – and no two minutes' silence. We had a shadow of a ceremony, three readings as usual . . . The second and third readings both reflected the realities of modern warfare in terms of memories of the trench warfare of the first World War – dull, deathly dull, corpses, mud, dirt and rain. People seem to be blank these days, believing that to think is to despair. That's why in the capitals of the world, I guess, the two minutes' observance was cancelled, for what would you think of but the mockery of men's sayings? In other years we stood there and thought that "they did not die in vain." Now I seem to remember seeing on the cenotaph in London the call to recruit – "See to it that we did not die in vain". And so men are to go on dying in vain to prove that those before did not die in vain. Armistice Day has been a memory of war rather than a vision of peace, an enshrining of war memories, and not a dedication to the building of peace . . .[316]

In a concern expressed by Mason regarding more recent efforts in America and England to commemorate the Vietnam war, historians have observed that it is ever more possible for memorial planners to persuade us that it was and is possible to 'separate the warrior from the war'. Commemoration then can have the effect of washing away, forgetting the political decisions and dissent in favour of 'a more unifying emphasis on honouring veterans and promoting national "healing".' Anzac Day itself provides a good example of this. Indeed, the emphasis on ramping up patriotism during all national days plays a deeper and more sinister role in providing a facade of unanimity and erodes the voices of those who see such policies as thinly-veiled propaganda for militarism. All sectors of society are carried off in the feel-good festival atmosphere. Fortunately, there are now a few more occasions to round out public perspectives, such as a Turkish film that exposes their experience of Gallipoli.

Chris Sheedy and Steve Offner have reported on the distinctive Australian pattern of commemoration in 'Busting the Myth of Anzac', which considers Great War I commemoration in the course of an American scholarly conference held in 2015.[317] University of New South Wales professor Jeffrey Grey was confronted by the truth of the assessment that 'Australia is without doubt the most aggressive of the centenary commemorators'. The half-billion dollar price tag was calculated by author James Brown in his book *Anzac's Long Shadow*. Brown is a fellow at the Lowy Institute for International Policy. He contrasts the words of the war memorial in Sydney's Hyde Park, 'Let silent contemplation be your offering', with the actual tenor of the Anzac and World War I commemorations.

'Instead, Australians are embarking on a discordant, lengthy and exorbitant four-year festival for the dead,' Brown argues. $325 million is coming from the taxpayer via the government, and this is being complemented by more than $300 million in private donations. His primary concern is that the result will be 'an Anzac centenary that risks fetishising war'.

Grey looks at the perplexing nature of this enthusiasm. While tragic, he suggests that Britain's losses in terms of deaths were ten times larger, while the French lost 1.4 million. Yet Australia is spending more than twice what Britain has budgeted and is outstripping the French in its budget for memorialising, indeed celebrating these events. It is a phenomenon that should give us pause.

[316] Oats, *op. cit.,* p. 95.
[317] Chris Sheedy and Steve Offner, 'Busting the Anzac Myth' in *Uniken,* University of New South Wales, 19/2/2016.

Scholars Peter Stanley and Craig Stockings agree with Grey that Australians are nothing short of obsessed with the Anzac story and the 'Great War', and they find convincing though very unsatisfactory reasons for it, according to Sheedy and Offner. Anzac Day has trumped Australia Day as the 'national day' ('The One Day of the Year') and Gallipoli has become 'the' national story. Perhaps the previous national iconic myth of the pioneering bushmen has become too stale for a largely urban population more fearful of bushfires than any other aspect of conquering the bush. The idealised virtue of bravery, which was present in the bushmen and pioneers, is modernised by the Anzac story in a way that can be taken into the heart of national and individual self-identity in the 21st century. The Digger idealised is larger than life, bronzed without being brown, ready to fight or die for his mates. He is the model Australian. Offner and Sheedy quote Stockings on the dangers of this trend,

> The driving need to celebrate the deeds of past servicemen and promote conceptions of national identity wrapped in the imagery of war have come to dominate our national discourse. These misunderstandings shape our picture of ourselves in obscuring and inaccurate ways … they situate our attitudes to the past falsely, distort our reading of the present and our expectations of the future. They are monsters of the mind. With the centenary celebrations it stands to get a lot worse.[318]

However, Australia's first military engagement was not Gallipoli, the British actually landed at the best place they could have – given what they knew, Australia's was not the only volunteer army in World War I, there is questionable evidence of inherently superior skills, and a patchy record when it comes to morality. Alcoholism was rife. Venereal disease was widespread, and many Diggers languished in hospitals with this affliction while their womenfolk naively knitted them more warm socks and baked cookies for their wounded heroes. Stockings underscores that Australia was not forced to fight. 'Australia's wars have been her own. For better or worse, successive Australian governments have chosen to fight. They have done so in the main for cold, calculating, *realpolitik* reasons.'

As we have seen, Peter Stanley is another scholar who has critically explored the enticements of military myth. His book *Bad Characters: Sex, Crime, Mutiny, Murder and the Australian Imperial Force*, was jointly awarded the Prime Minister's Prize for Australian History in 2011. In it he feels he fills a gap by exposing the ordinary nature of the Diggers. For example, they had a higher desertion rate than any other soldiers on the Western Front. This is not a record to build national identity upon. Stanley emphasises that it has never been his intent to cast aspersions on the Australians, but to humanise them. 'To know all is to forgive all' is the conclusion of his book. For example, he also highlights that all credible authorities seem to agree that the Aussies were the best fighting force.

Challenging history that has 'jelled' or calcified and is no longer open to interpretation will always bring out naysayers. However the best historians realise that history is never definitively written, but must always remain open to new discoveries, like any science. One example of a critic of the views of those such as Stanley, Grey, Stockings and Brown is scholar Mervyn Bendle, who accuses them in *Quadrant*, in an argument picked up by *The Australian*, of having declared 'war on the Anzac legend'. These words alone speak volumes about the protective shroud so many Australians wish to lay over Gallipoli, even as boats, bodies, accounts and artifacts from the campaign are still surfacing.

Bendle attributes the critical insights of his peers to something of a conspiracy, originating largely in Canberra, which exhibits 'a distain for ordinary Australians and their beliefs'. It is no less than an ' … elitist project explicitly dedicated to destroying the popular views of these traditions …[Australians] should be allowed to honour the centenary without constant sniping from an anti-Anzac elite of obsessive academic leftists and disgruntled ex-officers'.[319]

Stockings clarifies that every country is entitled to and perhaps needs its foundation stories. And these often are grounded in historical events. However, the trouble arises when we cannot distinguish

---

[318] Sheedy and Offner, *op. cit.*
[319] Sheedy and Offner, *op. cit.*

the ways that the stories have become more tied to mythologies than to truth. For example, the founding story of Rome tells how twin babies, Romulus and Remus, the sons of gods, were abandoned and swept down a river but rescued and suckled by a wolf before being raised by shepherds and founding Rome, all without knowing their divine origins. This story gave them both noble, heroic status and a common touch at once. Myths can be foundational legends, providing footings and identity that are common. They often reflect characteristics we want to hold true about ourselves collectively rather than having much relevance to history. Stockings argues there is greater strength and authenticity of Australian identity in the stories of 'normal people in harrowing circumstances who still achieved amazing things' than in the larger than life gods we can be inclined to construct, such as the over-inflated myths about Diggers.

It is important to recall that we may do ourselves more harm than good in getting carried away with commemorations that lead us further and further from the truth. Stockings reflects, 'I have friends who were wounded in places like Afghanistan. I have no problem with commemorating loss, but I have no interest in carnival-like, almost joyful celebrations. A very large proportion of the first Australian Imperial Force was not interested in marches or the like – they just wanted to get on with their lives.' [320]

However it is too late for us simply to get on with ours. We not only have a responsibility to those who have died, but more importantly to the living, both Australians and people of other nations whose lives, now or in the future, depend on our actions.

Just as Australia has rewritten Gallipoli as a national celebration, it has with the passage of time become possible, as Christian Appy points out, to celebrate the incredible fiasco of the Vietnam war. This is despite the fact that more than 58,000 Americans were killed, and more significantly, four million Vietnamese, Laotians and Cambodians. The rewriting begins with what has now become routine, the honouring of all military veterans for their service and sacrifice. There remains curiosity about Vietnam, but little substantive knowledge. Students have the sense of a skeleton in the closet. The antiwar movement has disappeared and so has the popular culture that accompanied it, films like 'Apocalypse Now' and 'Platoon', never mind documentaries of what actually went on. As a teacher, Appy finds an advantage in presenting the realities of the Vietnam fiasco to students who have formed no opinion about the subject, because even their parents were too young for it to be a significant event in their formation. They are therefore shocked by what they hear.[321]

Why would the United States, champion of democracy, have blocked Vietnam's internationally sanctioned reunification election in 1956, simply because of the American aversion to Ho Chi Min who was very likely to win? Even more stunning is the 'free-fire zone' of bloodshed that the US swept through South Vietnam. Most shocking however, to students, is the My Lai massacre, in which American troops killed more than 500 unarmed and unresisting civilians, mostly children, women and old men.[322]

The killing was so extreme and uncontrolled that one of their commanding officers warned the Americans that he would open fire on them if they did not cease their carnage. 16 March 1968 should be a dark day for Americans and the world. Indeed many of the American soldiers did suffer post-traumatic stress from that event, because it made apparent the extent to which they had become barbaric puppets. Many are still not getting the treatment they need. Others have suicided to end their ongoing nightmarish cycle of self-loathing, flashbacks, medication, alcohol and drug dependence. They too are victims.

---

[320] Sheedy and Offner, *op. cit.*

[321] Appy, *op. cit.*

[322] Appy, *op. cit.*

According to Appy, the rewriting of Vietnamese history began even before the war was over. Americans were encouraged to 'put aside the war as far as America is concerned'. In 1971, 58 per cent of the public told the pollsters that they thought the Vietnam war had been nothing less than immoral. A kind of willful amnesia, Ford suggested, was necessary to 'regain the sense of pride that existed before Vietnam'. This was wise from the perspective that there was no positive way to remember the carnage. If there had to be a happy ending, it would be fictitious.[323] However, the US showed no moral fibre in making peace in that region, where to this day the clean-up is incomplete and dire impacts on health, even of newborns, continues.

White-washing has been achieved, primarily, by making it an American tragedy. The disaster became not the incalculable loss of lives in Southeast Asia but the fact that American patriotism had been shaken. So 'Vietnam' could become, not a 'dirty word' but a clarion call for a revived nationalism and militarism, through which nobility would be restored to the American name. US veterans themselves became the greatest victims of the war, wounded by the lack of warmth of antiwar protestors (many of whom themselves were returned Vietnam vets) when the 'heroes' returned home. This was the greatest of shames, and could never be allowed to happen again.[324]

When the new Vietnam War Memorial was opened in Washington in 1982, Americans were ready to embrace the new account of heroism and warfare. This too was strategic. The black marble memorial afforded the possibility of honouring the veterans without commenting on the war. In a poignant and classic statement, this intention was expressed by defense contractor United Technologies on the 10th anniversary of the end of the war, 'Let others use this occasion to explain why we were there, what we accomplished, what went wrong, and who was right. We seek here only to draw attention to those who served . . .' In short, Vietnam is not our problem. Only the loss of these soldiers is ours to mourn.

The Pentagon has a new addendum to its Vietnam propaganda. It is to be a partnership with more than 10,000 corporations and local groups, which are to sponsor hometown events to honour veterans and to pay tribute to contributions made on the home front. This vast festival is being organised to endure from Memorial Day 2015 for a decade. This has drawn heated criticism from groups such as Veterans for Peace and Vietnam Peace Commemoration Committee. It was planned as a super-sized occasion to also feature new technology, science and medicine related to military research: a golden money-making proposition.

Nothing has been said about whether veterans will receive pay-outs for their often ongoing health and survival needs, much less whether Vietnam might receive compensation. In 2014 the media leaked the news that the Veterans Administration had left some 100,000 ex-soldiers waiting for medical attention. Government costs alone are budgeted at $65 million for the commemoration events.[325]

Above all veterans were victims of their own democratic government. It lied about the causes and nature of the war, then sent them off to fight for an unpopular, dictatorial regime in a land where they were regarded as invaders. It exposed them, often without the troops' knowledge, to chemical as well as conventional weapons. On their return, they were failed again: this time by being deprived of adequate support and benefits, according to Christian Appy.

Even the American Legion and Veterans of Foreign Wars cold-shouldered the returning soldiers. In fact, the new version of history describes how the veterans were spat upon by protesters. If there is a drop of truth to this, it was nowhere documented as a common event. But such a legend cements the sense of disgust *against* the peace movement, which in fact was a phenomenon that should have been

[323] Appy, *op. cit.*
[324] Appy, *op. cit.*
[325] Appy, *op. cit.*

a credit to ordinary Americans. It remains the largest antiwar movement in history.[326]

The release of American personnel from the hostage-taking in Iran in early 1981 provided a golden opportunity for the government to model how a hero's welcome should appear. There was a party at the White House, ticker tape parades, and other awards such as seasons' tickets to sporting events. They had survived a horrible ordeal, but they had chosen the risks they endured. They simply served America; this was all it took.[327] The good news was then that every man or woman might become a hero, just as any can (theoretically) be president.

Democracy had landed on its feet again, with new propaganda that sat very well with most of the population. Since 9/11, supporting troops has taken on grand and ritualistic proportions: yellow ribbons, airport greetings, ceremonies, memorial highways and other infrastructure, benefit concerts, and again, sporting connections with stadium flyovers.[328] These highly publicised events and monuments are designed to point to the veteran, not their actions, nor links to government policy. According to Rory Fanning, they may assuage veterans but gag them from having a voice. Heroes are bought into silence from dissent.[329]

These examples illustrate how memorialising and commemoration can build myths that spin further and further from fact, with calculated political motives. These are not invested in an accurate historical record, nor in providing solace to those who have experienced pain and loss. The members of the forces and their families become pawns in machines that more often contribute to certain policy agendas and strategic interests, to considerable effect.

A significant but largely unpopular approach from within peace movements has been to pick apart the calcified 'truths' that sit heavily over the possible revelation of any other insight. But this impulse has often caused them to suffer severe criticism and ostracism from their communities. In making *As the Mirror Burns*, Di Bretherton was challenged sharply by Australians. Critics included Vietnamese Australians, her family, scientists, many women who argued among other points that to talk of deformities in foetuses is insensitive to the disabled. In her workplace too Bretherton was pressured and her message dismissed.

'With the wisdom of hindsight things look different. This brings me on to think about what we mean by truth. The film is, after all, about the idea that what is seen depends on where you are looking from; that truth is not singular and unitary.' Despite her challenges and the personal costs of making the film she describes a powerful energy that drove her on and buoyed her up throughout.

> There was within me a voice that argued that we in the West were deluding ourselves, and in our films of Vietnam were not clearing the air but rather giving expression to and reinforcing our own myths. This voice did not seem to be my own, though I spoke from my personal experience. It was as if the voice was there and my task was to find the way of conveying its words to an audience that didn't actually want to hear it. The voice did not give direction and say 'Go and build an Ark' though my actions seemed as odd. It did not say 'This is the real story, the truth about Vietnam.' What it did say is that the 'real' story is unreal, that what was needed was to begin to peel away layers of illusion, to question the myths, to look at things from different perspectives.[330]

---

[326] Appy, *op. cit.*
[327] Appy, *op. cit.*
[328] Appy, *op. cit.*
[329] Appy, *op. cit.*
[330] Bretherton, *op. cit.*, p. 37.

Australian members marked the Women's International League for Peace and Freedom's centenary by mounting a display drawing significant public exposure. Margaret Bearlin, a longtime member of WILPF and Quaker, had a significant role in the creation of a collection of essays celebrating the centenary of WILPF. The women wanted to demonstrate the lasting value of their witness and the way it has retained currency over the decades. Today the continuous and energetic contribution of Australian women stands as a proud witness to the global tradition of peacemaking, and their display recognises this. Further, the very meaningful contribution that can be made by women is celebrated through the recognition of this centenary.

Some of the other most significant contributing members of WILPF and Australian peacebuilders have been women whose names and lives should be, but rarely are, known to most Australians: Eleanor Moore, Vida Goldstein, Edith Waterworth, Mabel Drummond, Doris Blackburn, Anna Vroland, Nancy Wilkinson, Margaret Holmes, Oodgeroo Noonuccal, Mildred Thynne, Margaret Thorp, Margaret Forte, Maud McBriar, Lorraine Mosely, Jean Richards, Fran Boyd, Shirley Abraham, Irene Greenwood, Evelyn Rothfield, Freda Brown, Betty King, Stella Cornelius, Nancy Shelley, Kay Mundine, Cathy Picone, Lyn Lane, Ruth Russell, Chris Henderson, Helen Cooke, Eve Masterman, and Barbara O'Dwyer.[331]

Sydney Quaker Chloe Mason has reflected that memorialising can add to the multiple meanings that commemorative events take on over time. She emphasises the complexity that accompanies memorialising, but this fragmentation and pluralisation of lenses lends a richness and deeper understanding to our history. For example, Australia Day is marked by many as the occasion of the arrival of the First Fleet, but for First Nations people it has come to be known informally as 'Invasion Day' and is for them, and others in solidarity, a sober occasion. It marks the founding of a Western nation but the beginning of a genocide. Ultimately the latter smears the former with an indelible mark of shame.

Today, one might argue that no one still living was responsible for the deaths of these people and their many cultures, so we can get on with our lives. However, there are many Indigenous people alive today who continue to experience the effects of policies that separated individuals from their families, culture and country, that abused their ancestors and has left a legacy that still shatters their lives. Policies such as the 'Intervention', whatever good they have done, have also been experienced as very destructive for those who lost jobs, who saw the disappearance of teaching of their language in local schools, saw the evaporation of small measures of independence and self-determination. The destruction and pollution of Country and waterways in the name of industries such as mining, shipping, military uses and agribusiness is not, in the main, being compensated. Nor can such impacts ever be, when individual and group identities are thereby lost for all time.

Even now, new policies such as the closing of remote communities, where people live closer to tradition and their own country, are being proposed and implemented on the basis that isolation or community self-governance is a 'lifestyle choice' rather than a core feature of identity preservation. Thus to be a First Nations person is likened to being a member of a football club or enjoying smoking. In other words, these are personal choices. Except that while the government is happy to pick up the cost of many lifestyle choices, such as smoking or owning and driving cars, which with millions of 'participants' have enormous costs to the taxpayer, the Commonwealth is not willing to sustain the essential customary practice of living on the land for small numbers of Indigenous people.

So, one might argue, the guerrilla war against the First Nations peoples continues quietly, by stealth. It is not so much that we are unaware of these policies, but apparently indifferent enough that we do not react against them. Like the destructive wake of the Vietnam War, the suffering and suffocating

---

[331] Lake, *op. cit.,* p. 1.

of Aboriginality is not our problem. This is a choice, as much as the Australian War Memorial is a choice, except that we are selecting the option of non-reaction, which has a far greater direct impact on lives than does the War Memorial.

Mason shared the perspective of Quakers that because each day is sacred, there are no special holy days set apart. For this reason, Friends are regularly challenged by the memorialising of events such as Gallipoli. For example, much discernment by British Friends' preceded the installation of the Quaker Service Memorial at the National Memorial Arboretum, which was a project of the Royal British Legion (RBL).[332] It is supported by a permanent exhibition, located offsite.

Within the New South Wales Quaker community, after considerable discernment about the meaning of commemoration, the occasion generated a number of actions. First, sharing family stories and recognition of significant gaps within these, in part caused by wars themselves, was revealing. Many felt there was also insufficient knowledge of how Friends responded to World War I. It was decided that further research, study and collaboration with other groups was desirable. There was a sense of leading to commemorate ancestors and Quakers during World War I, wherever they were and whatever their roles, whether as soldiers, peacemakers or other. Also, there was a wish to know and show, as seed for inspiration, the work of Friends with others in support of peace, opposition to war and conscription, helping victims of war and post-war reconstruction.[333]

One of the forms memorialising of World War I by Quakers has been the production of a series of banners, intended both for Friends themselves to delve deeper into their own history, and for the public. As Chloe Mason explained, this Quaker exhibition endeavours not to separate the peacebuilder from making the peace. In today's world, making peace is being helped by those doing the difficult work of staffing the Quaker United Nations Office, and through national committees such as Quaker Peace and Legislation Committee and Quaker Service Australia. Friends take heart from the faith and commitment of people who voiced their dissent to war, to compulsory military training and combat. They are also encouraged by those who spoke truth to power, many of whom were imprisoned or worse. And today, inspiration can be derived from those who work at various ways to discontinue and prevent war and structural violence as well as interpersonal abuses.

There can be no ultimate conclusion to this work. It is an offering, perhaps an enticement for some, to encourage readers to draw their own conclusions and not to be reliant on 'party lines' about the history of Australia, of their families, their friends, neighbours and communities. It is hoped by those who have contributed to this project that we will all be more aware, more questioning, more reflective, of what has been and what is yet to come. The notion is supported, through this work, that collaboration in study and action for social justice within our country and around the world is the way of peace. Marilyn Lake offers this conclusion:

> Let's applaud the historical significance of the endeavours of all our fellow citizens, who have been active in WILPF and associated bodies . . . This is surely the minimum recognition required in the interests of achieving historical balance and to recognise the distinctive contribution made by women to the achievement of freedom and democracy

---

[332] Also at the Arboretum, following the posthumous pardon by the British Army, the Shot-at-Dawn memorial was erected in 2001 for 306 soldiers from Britain and its dominions who were executed for refusing to fight. According to Chloe Mason there are no Australians on this list.

[333] The Committee obtained a grant from the History Council of NSW, who had adopted the theme of The Great War for History Week, which assisted in the production of the ten commemorative panels.

in our country and across the world ... so many others of us seek recognition of the fact that the outbreak of war generated a vigorous anti-war movement in Australia and elsewhere. And just as the official commemorations of the Gallipoli landings attribute unique national significance to those events – claiming that the ANZACs' military actions gave birth to the nation – so the commemoration of WILPF's long history of peace activism reminds us of an international movement initiated by the women of the world, in which Australians played an important role from the beginning.[334]

The alternative narratives that have been too often left in the shadows, erased or forgotten, do not speak with one voice. The actions against which we failed to cry foul are not all forgotten. But they demonstrate that if we do not seek to know the whole story, we make ourselves vulnerable to becoming puppets. We lose the fine texture of individual experience and witness in a cloud of rhetoric and hyperbole. In doing so, we lose parts of ourselves. Sadly, we are not whole so long as we participate, through the mechanisms of Australian democracy and society, in the implementations of any policies that cause pain and death. We are even more maimed if we let ourselves remain ignorant of the instruments of government that act in our names and with our hard-earned money. If there is a lesson here, it is simply that remaining passive is not an act of innocence but a crime. Blessed *are* the peacemakers. To remember, to become informed about all that we have never known, is to move, however incrementally, towards a just, respectful and healthy future. Lest we forget, indeed.

---

[334] Marilyn Lake, *op. cit.,* p. 1.

Appendix A
Abbreviations

ADF: Australian Defence Force AIF: Australian Infantry Forces AIF: Australian Imperial Forces ALP: Australian Labour Party

ANZUS: Australia, New Zealand and United States Pacific Security Treaty AVP: Alternatives to Violence Project

BCOF: British Commonwealth's Occupation Force CMAG: Canberra Museum and Arts Centre

CMF: Citizen Military Force CO: Conscientious Objector

CSL: Commonwealth Serum Laboratories FAU: Friends Ambulance Unit

GHQ: General Headquarters

HMAS: Her Majesty's Australian Ship

IS: Islamic State (sometimes known as ISIS)

IWW: Industrial Workers of the World ('Wobblies') LMAW: Love Makes a Way

MAPW: Medical Association for the Prevention of War MJA: *The Medical Journal of Australia*

NCO: Non-commissioned officer OC: Officer Commanding

POW: Prisoner of War

PTSD: Post Traumatic Stress Disorder

QPLC: Quaker Peace and Legislation Committee QUNO: Quaker United Nations Office

RAAF: Royal Australian Air Force RAN: Royal Australian Navy

RSL: Returned & Services League of Australia UN: United Nations

UNAA: United Nations Association of Australia UNCEF: United Nations Children's Emergency Fund

UNHCR: United Nations High Commissioner for Refugees UNTCOK: United Nations Temporary Commission on Korea VSP: Victoria Socialist Party

WILPF: Women's International League for Peace and Freedom YWCA: Young Women's Christian Association

Appendix B
Contributors to the 2015 Anzac Conversations

Diana Abdel-Rahman is a peace activist and member of the Canberra Multicultural Community Forum

Margaret Bearlin is a Canberra-based Quaker, academic emerita and longtime and active member of WILPF.

Tessa Bremner is a theatre and opera director and Canberra-based Quaker Ryan Johnston is Head of Art at the Australian War Memorial

Ronis Chapman is a seasoned peace activist involved with Love Makes a Way, a Quaker,andtheSecretaryoftheAsia-WestPacificSectionoftheFriends World Council for Consultation(FWCC)

Glenda Cloughley is a Jungian analyst and poet-composer

Jonathan Curtis is a representative of the United Nations Association of Australia (ACT Branch).

Anthea Gunn is Art Curator at the Australian War Memorial

Guy Hansen is Director of Exhibitions at the National Library of Australia Dean Sahu Khan is Chair of the Canberra Interfaith Coalition

Chloe Mason is a Sydney-based Quaker who was responsible for encouraging the development of the WWI Quaker Exhibition.

Karl-Erik Paasonen is a member of Climate Network 350.org

Peter Stanley is a military historian at the University of New South Wales, Canberra

David Stephens is the Secretary of the Honest History Coalition and editor of their website

Graham Walker is a veteran of the Vietnam War and a strong advocate for disabled veterans and their families

Sue Wareham is a member of the Medical Association for the Prevention of War

Pamela Leach
Biographical Note

Pamela Leach was born and raised in Canada. She has lived in the United States, Europe and Africa. She earned a doctorate from York University in Toronto in the area of Political Studies before enjoying a career in academe. She had previously been a Visiting Scholar at Australian National University, and moved to Australia in 2010. Pamela has been active in the Religious Society of Friends (Quakers) since 1981. She cherishes her adult son and large Australian step-family. Pamela lives with her partner in Hobart, Tasmania. She is an emerging poet and keen chook keeper.

Selected Bibliography

Australian War Memorial. 'Out in the Cold'. www.awm.gov.au/exhibitions/korea/ausinkorea

Australian War Memorial. *Too Dark for the Light Horse: Aboriginal and Torres Strait Islander People in the Defence Forces* (2013).

Australia Yearly Meeting of the Religious Society of Friends (Quakers). *this we can say: Australian Quaker Life, Faith and Thought* (2003).

Bean, C. E. W. *Anzac to Amiens* (1961).

Beros, H. E. Bert. *The Fuzzy Wuzzy Angels, and Other Verses*. Sydney: F. H. Johnston Publishing (1943).

Bollard, Robert. *In the Shadow of Gallipoli: The Hidden History of Australia in WWI*. New South Publishing (2013).

Bretherton, Di. *As the Mirror Burns: Making a Film about Vietnam*. The Thirtieth Backhouse Lecture. The Religious Society of Friends (Quakers) in Australia (1994).

Buxton, Nick and Ben Hayes, eds. *The Secure and the Dispossessed*. U. of Chicago Press (2015).

Dennis, C. J. *Selected Verse of C. J. Dennis*. Angus & Robertson (1950).

Flinders Council. www.flinders.tas.gov.au/aboriginal-history

Government of Australia. 'Australians at War'. www.australiansatwar.gov.au/throughmyeyes

Kent, Jacqueline. *A Certain Style: Beatrice Davis, A Literary Life,* Camberwell, Victoria: Penguin (2001).

Malouf, David. *Fly Away Peter*. Penguin (1983).

McCormack, Gavan. *Cold War Hot War*. Sydney: Hale & Ironmonger (1983).

National Archives of Australia. 'Wartime internment camps in Australia'. www.naa.gov.au/collection/snapshots/internment-camps/introduction.aspx

National Library of Australia. 'Keepsakes: Australia and the Great War'. www.nla.gov.au/exhibitions/keepsakes

Oats, William Nicolle. *Choose your Dilemma: an Australian Pacifist in Hitler's Europe*. Hobart: Montpellier Press (1999).

Pascoe, Bruce. *Dark Emu: Black Seeds*. Broome: Magabala Books (2016).

Reynolds, Henry. *Forgotten War*. Sydney: NewSouth Publishing. (2013)

Reynolds, Henry. *The Other Side of the Frontier*. Townsville: James Cook University (1981).

Reynolds, Henry. *Why Weren't We Told? A Personal Search for the Truth about our History*. Ringwood Victoria: Viking (1999).

Seymour, Alan. *The One Day of the Year*. Angus & Robertson (1962).

Stoessinger, John G. *Why Nations Go to War*, 3rd ed. New York: St. Martin's Press (1982).

Tacey, David J. *Edge of the Sacred: Transformation in Australia*. Blackburn, Victoria: Harper Collins (1995).

Tasmanian Museum and Art Gallery. *The Suspense is Awful: Tasmania and the Great War*. <u>ww1exhibition.tmag.tas.gov.au/the-islanders.net</u> (Roar Film, 2015).

Vallentine, Jo and Peter D. Jones. *Quakers in Politics: Pragmatism or Principle, The Religious Society of Friends* (Quakers) in Australia (1990).

Zaru, Jean. *Occupied with Violence: A Palestinian Woman Speaks*. Minneapolis: Fortress Press (2008).